Jesus the Wicked Priest

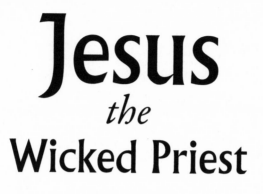

Jesus
the
Wicked Priest

How Christianity
Was Born of an Essene Schism

MARVIN VINING

Bear & Company
Rochester, Vermont

Bear & Company
One Park Street
Rochester, Vermont 05767
www.BearandCompanyBooks.com

Bear & Company is a division of Inner Traditions International

The author and publisher gratefully acknowledge permission to use excerpts from the
following copyrighted material:
Unless otherwise indicated, all Dead Sea Scrolls translations are from *The Complete
Dead Sea Scrolls in English* by Geza Vermes. Copyright © 2004 by Geza Vermes.
Reprinted by permission of Penguin Press.
Unless otherwise indicated, all Bible quotations are from the Revised Standard
Version of the Bible, Apocrypha, copyright © 1957; the Third and Fourth Books
of the Maccabees and Psalm 151, copyright © 1977 by the National Council of the
Churches of Christ in the United States of America. Used by permission.

Library of Congress Cataloging-in-Publication Data
Vining, Marvin, 1963–
  Jesus the wicked priest : how Christianity was born of an Essene schism / Marvin
Vining.
    p. cm.
  Includes bibliographical references and index.
  ISBN: 978-1-59143-081-0 (pbk.)
  1. Jesus Christ—Person and offices—Miscellanea. 2. Essenes—Miscellanea. 3. Dead
Sea scrolls—Relation to the New Testament—Miscellanea. I. Title.

BT205.V47 2008
232.9—dc22

                                                                        2007046006

Printed and bound in the United States by Lake Book Manufacturing

10 9 8 7 6 5 4 3 2 1

Text design by Virginia Scott Bowman and layout by Rachel Goldenberg
This book is typeset in Garamond with Albertus used as the display typeface.

To send correspondence to the author of this book, mail a first-class letter to the author
c/o Inner Traditions • Bear & Company, One Park Street, Rochester, VT 05767, and we
will forward the communication.

For Joshua . . .

Contents

———•———

3 Understanding the Essene Pesher Method 57

4 The Lost Christian Doctrine of Reincarnation 77

5 The Teacher of Righteousness Revealed 111

6 The Secret Role of Gabriel in the Virgin Birth 149

7 The Teacher of Righteousness and the Passion of Christ   167

Acknowledgments

---•---

It took fourteen years to complete this book, and during that time so many friends and colleagues have helped me that I am unable to name you all here. Know that you have my thanks. Special thanks go to my literary agent, Stephany Evans; her partner, Gary Heidt; and my dear friend Cassia Herman for developmental editing and encouragement. I am also grateful for the many Dead Sea Scrolls scholars who preceded me. Although this book calls for a realignment of the present consensus, I could not possibly have formulated my arguments without the collective effort of practically the entire community of Dead Sea Scrolls scholars. I am especially indebted to the late Otto Betz, because his identification of the Essenes in the New Testament was the cornerstone for my entire restoration. Last but not least, I thank Inner Traditions • Bear & Company for their willingness to publish a first-time author of such a controversial book.

1

A New Day Dawns in Dead Sea Scrolls Research

The Dead Sea Scrolls are the most important archaeological treasures of all time. Though most scholars do not yet realize it, the Dead Sea Scrolls provide direct historical information concerning Jesus, the early Church and its break from early Judaism.

Most serious New Testament scholars believe the modern search for the Jesus of history, as opposed to faith in Jesus as the Christ, began in the 1800s. Probably the most famous attempt was Ernst Renan's well-researched biography called *The Life of Jesus* (*La Vie de Jésus*), published in 1863.[1] Numerous nineteenth-century scholars offered their attempts. Albert Schweitzer collected and published what he thought were the most important of these in his 1906 book *The Quest for the Historical Jesus*.[2] Then in 1914, Rudolf Bultmann came upon the scene and introduced what became known as *form criticism,* bringing the search for the historical Jesus to a crashing halt. Bultmann questioned the authenticity of the New Testament as a reliable historical source having anything to say of the life and times of Jesus: as Bultmann put it, "The early Christian sources show no interest in either."[3] According to Bultmann, the New Testament letters were primarily concerned with spiritual rather than historical matters, and were thus untrustworthy for the latter purpose. Because scant historical resources outside the New Testament were known at the time, Bultmann's criticisms were then insurmountable. In fact, Bultmann has dominated serious scholarly New Testament study to this day.

Subsequent to Bultmann, scholars attempting to recover the Jesus of history took alternate routes. One example is the 1945 book *Two Types of Faith* by Martin Buber.[4] Buber explored the historical, religious context of Jesus by using *reverse extrapolation*. That is, Buber suggested that Jesus taught doctrines similar to those found in later rabbinical writings, primarily the Mishnah and Midrashim. Buber's book makes for good reading, especially since it explores the fact that Judaism is a living, growing religion and has been since the days of early Judaism and the early Christian Church. In many instances, Judaism has grown into the reforms Jesus taught two thousand years ago. The Dead Sea Scrolls were discovered just two years after Buber published *Two Types of Faith*. Buber died in 1965 and unfortunately never had the chance to revise his work in light of the Scrolls, because their recovery and publication were so slow. This was because in the early days of Scrolls research, scholarship was closed to all except the official editorial team. The monopoly was thankfully broken in 1991 when, largely due to the efforts of Robert Eisenman, Martin Abegg and Ben Zion Wacholder, and the founder of the Biblical Archaeological Society, Hershel Shanks, the Israel Antiquities Authority under the direction of new chief editor Emanuel Tov who finally allowed open access to the Scrolls.[5] This delay is particularly unfortunate because Buber made great study of Hasidism, and it is my belief that the Essenes—who scholars generally agree wrote the Scrolls—were the ancient forerunners of the Hasidim.

A book similar to Buber's was written in 1993 by Geza Vermes called *The Religion of Jesus the Jew*,[6] which likewise viewed Jesus through the lens of Judaism found in later rabbinical sources. What is surprising about the book is that Vermes is best known for his work on the Dead Sea Scrolls, but the book makes comparatively little use of Essene Judaism. This should not be surprising to anyone who is up on current Scrolls research. When the Scrolls were first discovered and their publication and translation slowly commenced, it was obvious that the Scrolls bore similar language and ideology to the New Testament. Many were confident that Jesus's religious background had been discovered. But then reaction set in. Most of the Scrolls were dated safely before the dawn of Christianity, at least a generation earlier than Jesus was supposed to have lived.

1 IS THIS WORK "FRINGE" SCHOLARSHIP?

Not all scholars agree with the consensus view. James H. Charlesworth's book *Jesus and the Dead Sea Scrolls,*[7] a collection of chapters by the most renowned scholars in the field, is marketed with the banner "The Controversy Resolved." The main controversy has divided Scrolls scholars into two camps. Mainstream scholars still shy away from dating the Scrolls in the Christian era. But dissident scholars such as Robert Eisenman and Barbara Thiering contend the Scrolls speak directly of Christian origins. They say the Scrolls have been misinterpreted and misdated, typically by those who let their faith obscure the scholarship. The present work falls squarely in the camp of the dissident scholars who use the Scrolls to explore Christianity's break from early Judaism.

2 A QUESTION OF SCIENCE

The mainstream scholars appear to be winning the debate, primarily because they claim to have empirical science on their side, which "proves" the Scrolls speak of a historical period at least a generation earlier than the dawn of Christianity. For example, in 1994, the Accelerator Mass Spectrometry (AMS) Laboratory team of the

University of Arizona was called on to radiocarbon date numerous scroll and linen fragments from Qumran.[8] The new AMS method allowed radiocarbon dating to be safely performed on actual Dead Sea Scrolls parchment for the very first time, because it did not destroy a significant amount of parchment in the process. One of the scrolls the Arizona AMS team tested was the Habakkuk Commentary (1QpHab), a scroll that scholars of the dissident camp have interpreted as describing events in the New Testament. This is a key text for those of us of the dissident camp. Not only have Eisenman and Thiering relied heavily upon it, but it is also a key text in this book, particularly in chapter 7. Vermes cited the Arizona study in his work: "Arizona has scored on one significant point: the Habakkuk Commentary, chief source of the history of the Qumran sect, is definitely put in the pre-Christian era between 120 and 3 BCE. In consequence, 'fringe' scholars who see in the writing allusions to events described in the New Testament will find they have a problem on their hands."[9] What a careful choice of words. By deliberately calling scholars who believe the Habakkuk Commentary speaks of New Testament events as "fringe," Vermes has marginalized our work, made it unworthy of serious attention. Vermes is such an authority in the community of Scrolls scholars; this one comment alone would normally be enough to dissuade entrance scholars, such as myself, from pursuing the point further. The problem is that while Vermes is deservedly an authority in the fields of ancient Hebrew texts and history, he is *not* an expert in the field of radiocarbon dating. Since, as Vermes said, I would have a problem on my hands with my Scrolls restoration, I ceased all work on this manuscript until I could solve this problem to my satisfaction.

Time passed, and I contacted William Meacham, an archaeologist who has been very active in debates over radiocarbon dating the Shroud of Turin.[10] Meacham is a research fellow at the University of Hong Kong and has conducted more than 150 radiocarbon dating tests over the last thirty years. I forwarded him the journal article written by the Arizona team and asked if my proposed date of ca. 23 CE* of the Habakkuk Commentary could be ruled out. He wrote me that in his view radiocarbon dating "could not possibly settle so tight a chronological issue." Meacham cited three archaeological discoveries where the dates of the objects were known in advance, but multiple tests produced wildly inconsistent results: the Lindow Man, Akrotiri in Greece, and a bronze drum site in Malaysia.[11] Evidently radiocarbon dating is not always an exact science. The Arizona AMS team's dates of 120–3 BCE were determined within a statistical likelihood of two standard deviations. Similar ancient parchments, whose dates were known in advance, have produced radiocarbon dates supposedly within two standard deviations off by as much as one hundred years.[12] My proposed date of ca. 23 CE is therefore certainly within reason. In addition, there are numerous practical reasons the dates may be off. For example, it is quite possible that the parchment upon which the Habakkuk Commentary was drafted may have been harvested and stored long before its use. For such reasons, Meacham felt that the radiocarbon dating estimates posed no difficulty to me whatsoever.

3 PALEOGRAPHY

Meacham did feel I might have difficulty explaining the discrepancy with the paleographic estimates. Paleography has been the most relied-upon method of dating the Scrolls thus far. It depends on the shifts in the handwriting styles of scribes in different eras of history to sequentially date the texts they wrote. I have observed the same phenomena personally throughout my legal career. The handwriting found in courthouse records dating to the late 1800s looks very different from

---

*I believe the Habakkuk Commentary regards Gospel events. Jesus was about thirty years of age at the time of his ministry (Lk 3:23). The Julian calendar started in the year 1, not 0, thus it is at least a year off from the actual birth of Jesus. And according to some historians the Gregorian calendar now in use is also off by six years or so. See Werner Keller, *The Bible as History* (New York: Bantam, 1981), chs. 35, 36.

handwriting today. Likewise, the handwriting found in legal documents dating to the late 1700s—like the U.S. Constitution and the Declaration of Independence—looks even older. In 1961, Harvard professor F. M. Cross used paleography and internal references to date the Qumran Scrolls to three different periods:

archaic	250 to 150 BCE
Hasmonean	150 to 30 BCE
Herodian	30 BCE to 70 CE

Subsequent scholars typically placed greater faith in these paleographic estimates than radiocarbon science. For example, the Arizona AMS team wrote of the strong correlation between their tests and the paleographic dating (certainly suspect, since they had reference to the paleographic dates before their tests were run). They cited Cross's work, which places the Habakkuk Commentary in the Early Herodian era: "The manuscript is written in an Early Herodian hand (ca. 30–1 BCE), affecting the Paleo-Hebrew script in a degenerate form when writing the Tetragrammaton."[13] Numerous and complex criticisms have been written of the paleographic method by other scholars. My criticism is simple and straightforward. Aside from the possibility that early scholars may have pegged events in the Scrolls to the wrong historical periods to begin with,* the paleographic divisions between the periods cannot possibly be smooth and continuous. If a scribe learned to write within a particular period, it would be logical that he would keep that handwriting style all his life, while the handwriting

---

*Keep in mind 1QpHab was one of the first manuscripts discovered and published and scholars have always viewed it as the chief source of the history of the Qumran sect. Many consensus paleographical dates were based on Vermes's Maccabean theory. However, careful review of Cross's major work on this subject shows that he, himself, recognized there are no absolute dates in the paleographic dating of manuscripts, only relative ones. The absolutes are always subject to change if new evidence comes forward. See Cross's chapter, "The Development of the Jewish Scripts," in G. Ernest Wright, ed., *The Bible and the Ancient Near East* (London: Routledge & Kegan Paul, 1961), especially 136, 192 note 28.

style changed around him due to adaptation by the younger generation. I saw this exact same phenomenon when my father showed me
old courthouse records as a child; I personally witnessed how elderly
men who wrote out deeds fifty years earlier used the same archaic
handwriting style until the day they died.* The professional life of an
Essene scribe ran from thirty years of age (1Q28a I, 15) to one hundred
years of age (*War* 2.151), which makes for a span of seventy years. I need
only twenty-one years beyond Cross's estimate of 1QpHab for my restoration to be viable, so I am well within reasonable variance (especially
since 1QpHab is likely to have been written by a high-ranking elder due
to its content).

4 LET THE READER DECIDE

We must not fall into the fallacy of thinking that a consensus view
is correct for that reason alone. As James H. Charlesworth worded it,
"It is not a consensus of leading scholars that makes a historical judgment valid. It is the knowledge, relevant data amassed, wise insight,
precise methodology, careful exegesis of all relevant passages, and
solid argumentation that makes a position sound."[14] True enough, but
Charlesworth still failed to present an *epistemological standard* for eval-
uating whether truth claims about Dead Sea Scrolls interpretations are
justified. Namely, if radiocarbon science cannot conclusively prove or
disprove the dates needed for my historical restoration, then I contend
its correctness should be judged by whether it is coherent, and internally and externally consistent. That is, my restoration should make
overall sense to the reader; it should explain more data than previous
attempts; and it should be able to withstand close and rigorous scrutiny
without yielding contradiction, either with itself or with the historical
sources upon which I rely.

---

*Cross himself recognized "allowance must be made always for the extension of the pro-
fessional life of a conservative scribe beyond his generation." *The Bible and the Ancient
Near East,* 192 note 29.

As an entrance scholar into this field, I will naturally face opposition, some of it deserved and some of it not. I readily confess I am not as yet a particularly learned Hebrew and Aramaic scholar, so I will have to rely upon the translations of others. But this in no way invalidates my restoration. First, were I to spend a lifetime studying ancient languages, I still could not escape relying on the accuracy of other scholars in transmitting what they have learned. At least critics cannot question my translations, because I have used those of mainstream Scrolls scholars. Second, it is rarely the translations of the Scrolls I have a problem with; rather, it is that their historical and theological context has been misconstrued. Thus, in addition to exploring the Dead Sea Scrolls, I will also be exploring the reports of ancient historians, such as Josephus's *The Antiquities of the Jews* (*Ant* 18.63) and *The War of the Jews* (*War* 2.119ff.), as well as conducting an in-depth study of the New Testament. Let the reader make up his or her own mind whether my restoration is correct, despite what current mainstream scholars may say.

5 UNASHAMEDLY APOLOGETIC

Apologetics is a justification or defense of the Christian faith. The primary differences between our two types of faith have been that Christianity is an evangelical religion, whereas Jews are primarily born into Judaism; that Christians have relaxed the Mosaic law more so than Jews; and, last but not least, that Christians believe Jesus was the Messiah and Jews do not. As a Christian, I believe that biblical prophecy points toward the historical Jesus as the Messiah. Much of my restoration will only be cognizable in that context. In other words, I often start with the working hypothesis that Jesus fulfilled biblical messianic prophecies, then I explore that hypothesis to make greater sense of the Dead Sea Scrolls. Moreover, as the Essenes who wrote the Scrolls believed fervently that they were living in messianic times, I believe the Scrolls also point to Jesus as the Messiah and are more naturally interpreted that way (although the messianic expectations of the Essenes and Jesus surely differed, a fact which I will be exploring in great detail). Thus, I believe the Dead Sea Scrolls serve a legitimate apologetic purpose and will make no attempt to hide that in my work. I recognize this is a highly controversial approach, but at least it is honest and straightforward. Christianity is inescapably an evangelical religion. Unfortunately, out of evangelical zeal, Christians have often been guilty of anti-Semitism. John Strugnell, former chief of the Scrolls editorial team, made numerous anti-Semitic remarks. Add to that the fact that the first Scrolls editorial team had not a single Jew on it, and it is easy to see why Scrolls research has often had to labor to rid itself of the specter of anti-Semitism.[15]

There are some who will ask how can I write in an apologetic tone and even dare to speak of anti-Semitism. The criticism is that if we Christians truly respect Jews, then we should leave them alone and allow them to exist as Jews. Actually, I agree. Paul wrote that our Jewish brothers and sisters should be seen as a special exception to the evangelical march of Christianity (Rom 11:25–32)* until, as the old Methodist hymn says, "Every age and race and clime shall blend their creeds in one, and Earth shall form one great family by whom God's will is done."[16] So while this work is intended as an apologetic for the day in which our religious differences will pass away, and is more naturally written that way, I have no desire for Jewish readers to convert to mainstream Christian orthodoxy in its present form; my goal is to reform Christian orthodoxy in order to make it *worthy* of conversion. I wish to explore and celebrate Jesus's Jewishness because it leads to a fuller and deeper understanding of the gospel, and there is absolutely nothing anti-Semitic about that. Jesus said, "Salvation is from the Jews" (Jn 4:22b).

---

*This passage has been interpreted numerous ways, some of them very anti-Semitic. For an orthodox Christian exclusivist who believes that people go to hell unless they are formally professed Christians, and that there is no reincarnation, Paul's verse implies God has deliberately hardened the heart of the Jews for two thousand years and irrevocably sent them to hell for the sake of Gentiles; ergo, God is anti-Semitic. I reject this interpretation on all fronts. Paul was simply recognizing that all things happen in God's good time.

While I am on this difficult subject, there is another area of concern. In chapter 7, I explore the Essene participation in Jesus's trial and crucifixion, otherwise known as *the Passion*. Some Jewish readers will have difficulty with my Passion story. Just before this manuscript was completed, the Mel Gibson film *The Passion of the Christ* appeared in theaters. Jewish leaders were horrified by this film, and understandably so. In his book *Constantine's Sword: The Church and the Jews,* author James Carroll pointed out that Passion plays have historically ignited anti-Semitism. In the first half of the sixteenth century, Pope Paul III banned performances of a popular Passion play in the Roman Coliseum because it incited attacks on Jews. And in prewar Germany, Passion plays took root as nowhere else, foreshadowing the Holocaust.[17] Due to its graphic violence, *The Passion of the Christ* was bound to cause controversy. Personally, I found the movie spiritually lacking. Two hours of watching Jesus sadistically tortured with very little emphasis on his teachings did not present a balanced picture of his life. In particular, I feel that had Gibson driven home the nonviolent heart of the gospel more effectively, the movie might have been better received by the Jewish audience. Like authors John H. Yoder and Stanley Hauerwas, I identify with a radical Protestant school of thought known as Anabaptist. We Anabaptists interpret Christian history in terms of the Constantinian Fall of the Church. The title of Carroll's book, *Constantine's Sword,* is well chosen. When Constantine made Christianity the official faith of the Holy Roman Empire, when he assembled bishops to tell his soldiers what and how to pray, Jesus's message of nonviolence was corrupted. But for the Constantinian Fall, the horrors of the Inquisition and Holocaust would never have occurred. The true gospel is nothing to be ashamed of. Recovering it is why I study the Dead Sea Scrolls.

It is always difficult for a Christian to write for a Jewish audience. For example, I will rightly criticize the Essenes, for they were Jesus's greatest enemies. But Jewish readers should not take offense at this, for the ancient Essenes were rigid and fanatical, bearing little resemblance to any Jewish sect living today. Whenever I address Jews or Jewish concerns, I must always remember I am a guest in that house. I see no harm in requesting a genuine dialogue between our two types of faith, provided I do so respectfully and my scholarship is thorough and in good faith.

Let us not overlook that a genuine dialogue is interactive. Because I am Christian, in criticizing Christians I can be as heavy-handed as I want. I believe the Scrolls, because they revitalize Jesus in his historical context, challenge much thought that has come to be known as Christian. Christians who are legalistic and ascetic will find great discomfort in the fact that it is precisely Jesus's abhorrence of this flight-from-life ideology that led to his break with the Essenes and eventually to his crucifixion. Likewise, Christians who reject nonviolence will find that Essene militancy is why Jesus would have no part of them. I also believe the Scrolls reopen numerous doctrinal questions supposedly long settled. For example, in chapter 4, I draw upon the Scrolls to show that the Essenes and the early Christians believed in reincarnation. The Essenes and early Christians were opposed to other Jewish sects in this belief, just as the Hasidim are opposed in this belief to Orthodox Judaism and Christianity today. And in chapter 6, I draw upon the Scrolls to dispute the sacred Christian belief in the virgin birth.

I invite the reader on a rich historical journey. Readers of all faiths should be fascinated to learn more of Christianity's emergence from within early Judaism. To Christians, you will likely rediscover the faith you thought you once knew. And to Jews and Christians alike, I pray this work will open doors of mutual understanding long closed.

2

Identifying the Essenes in the New Testament

By now, most informed readers should be familiar with the scholarly consensus that a Jewish sect known as the Essenes wrote the famous Dead Sea Scrolls discovered between 1947 and 1956 near a small Judean village known as Qumran.[1] But who were the Essenes? We know that the Essenes existed from at least the second century BCE to the fall of Israel to the Romans in 74 CE, though in all likelihood they were around much earlier. In other words, we know the Essenes existed before and well through gospel times.* But this fact

---

*The most reliable extra-Scrolls accounts of the Essenes are found in the classical works of: Hippolytus, *Refutation of All Heresies* IX, 14–23; Josephus, *War* 2.119–161, *Ant* 18.18–22; Philo, *Every Good Man Is Free* 75–91; and Pliny, *Natural History* 5.15. The accounts of Josephus and other classical historians speak of the Essenes in the present tense, which suggests they were in existence at the time of writing. Josephus wrote from about 75 to 94 CE, and claims to have dabbled with the Essenes and the other Jewish sects from the ages of sixteen to nineteen. According to his account, that would be approximately the years 53–56 CE (*Life* 4–15). Whether or not Josephus actually made trial of the Essenes, we can confidently posit the existence of the Essenes through the life of Jesus of Nazareth, a fact that every major Scrolls scholar has agreed upon. What is surprising in light of this overwhelming consensus is how few have attempted to explain the absence of the Essenes in the New Testament.

makes no sense. Why is it that the Essenes never once appear by name in the New Testament? Reason says we should find them there, right alongside the Pharisees, Sadducees, and Zealots. Yet we find no mention of them whatsoever. It has been suggested that the New Testament is silent about the Essenes because the Essenes themselves *were* the early Christians. In 1863, long before the Scrolls were discovered, Ernest Renan published a biography called *The Life of Jesus* (*La Vie de Jésus*), one of the first scholarly attempts at recovering the historical Jesus of Nazareth. Renan, a controversial biblical scholar even in his time, made the claim that Christianity was a branch of Essenism that survived. While I, too, believe this to have been the case, Renan's claim was somewhat premature and needs qualification. In this chapter, I will explore Renan's claim more fully. I will identify the Essenes in the New Testament, shedding new light on Jesus and the origins of Christianity.

6   THE HISTORICAL PARADOX

Renan published his views before he could possibly have understood how complex the relationship was between the Essenes and the early Christians, a relationship that might have remained hidden forever except for the discovery of the Dead Sea Scrolls. A curious fact emerged once scholars began to translate and understand the Scrolls. The Essenes seemed to influence the early Christians more than any other Jewish sect, yet the Essenes were the very sect whose ideology the early Christians most despised. The late Yigael Yadin, an Israeli archaeologist who published numerous books and articles on the Dead Sea Scrolls, called this finding a "historical paradox." He knew the Scrolls presented us with a great many mysteries that would not easily be resolved.

[The Essenes] clung tenaciously to the most rigorous interpretation of the Law of Moses in general, and in particular to the ordinances on the Temple and its rituals, festivals and sacrifices alike. Yet it was this very sect, of all the Jewish sects, that had the most profound influence on the beliefs, practices, organization and even the phraseology of early Christianity. Christianity eventually strove to detach itself from the Law of Moses. How was it, then, that this most extreme and Orthodox Jewish sect had this impact on Jewish Christianity which was subsequently to fight against the legalist and rigid interpretation of the Law of Moses, and finally to reject that Law?[2]

How can this paradox be resolved? It is resolvable only by recognizing the revelation, the life and teachings, of a former Essene known as Jesus of Nazareth.[3]

The formative years of Jesus, perhaps many of the mysterious missing years between the ages of twelve and thirty,* were undoubtedly spent with the Essenes. More than likely, the majority of Jesus's Jewish followers were Essenes also. The point at which the Christian movement became the "Church" has produced a great deal of speculation through the years. I prefer to think that the Church was born the moment of Peter's confession (Mt 16:13–20), the moment Jesus's messianic secret was first fully realized among his disciples. If we take this as the point of departure, the relationship between the early Church and the Essenes was very complex indeed. Peter was a former disciple of John the Baptist, as was likely Andrew, Peter's brother (Jn 1:35–42). If John the Baptist was an Essene, as I argue in chapter 5 (sections 43–47), then it is possible that at least these two disciples, Peter and Andrew, were either Essenes or Essene proselytes. I think it likely that most of the disciples were Essenes. Yet there came a time when Jesus broke from the Essenes, when his theology was no longer theirs. What is so remarkable about the Dead Sea Scrolls, and so challenging to scholars—which explains why so few have been able to make sense of them—is that they give us a reverse perspective of the four Gospels. The

---

*These are called the "missing" years of Jesus, because the four Gospels in the orthodox canon are completely silent about them.

Scrolls record in great detail much of Jesus's life: important dates, references to persons, places, and events; but we see these details through the eyes of his enemies. It was the strong negative correlation to gospel events that convinced me my restoration was accurate. I am sure the reader will see it likewise.

7 RECOVERING JESUS'S FORMATIVE BACKGROUND

Because the relationship between the Essenes and Jesus was so complex, it is best understood if we start from the beginning. From what I can gather, neither the Gospels nor the Scrolls, nor any other reliable historical source likely to be recovered, mention anything directly of Jesus's formative years. Yet we can reasonably conclude that Jesus was raised an Essene because, like any real person, his thoughts and actions reflect his upbringing. The Gospels show that Jesus taught distinctively Essene doctrines, such as a strict prohibition of divorce (Mk 10:2–9; cf. 11Q19 LVII, 18). He was apparently not married and honored celibacy in service of God (Mt 19:12), a fact that is quite striking considering the Essenes were the only Jewish sect who practiced celibacy at the time (*War* 2.120). Both he and his followers used the same phraseology or concepts as the Essenes, like the term "Holy Spirit," which appears nowhere in the Old Testament but was found abundantly in the Scrolls, or "sons of light," "sons of darkness," reflecting the Scrolls' Zoroastrian influence (Lk 16:8; cf. 1QS III–IV). He was a cousin of John the Baptist, whom many scholars, including myself, have held to be an Essene, as was also James, Jesus's half-brother.

Why do I believe James was an Essene? The church father Jerome quoted from the now lost *Commentaries* of the second-century historian Hegesippus:

After the apostles, James the brother of the Lord surnamed the Just was made head of the Church at Jerusalem. Many indeed are called James. This one was holy from his mother's womb. *He drank neither wine nor strong drink, ate no flesh, never shaved or anointed himself with ointment or bathed.* He alone had the privilege of entering the Holy of Holies, since indeed he did not use woolen vestments but linen and went alone into the Temple and prayed in behalf of the people, insomuch that his knees were reputed to have acquired the hardness of camels' knees. (*On Illustrious Men* 2; my emphasis)

The characteristic Essene traits of asceticism and vegetarianism are well known from the classical sources. The fact that James never bathed seems to pose a problem, for the Essenes were known to have practiced frequent ritual baptism. However, Josephus reports that the Essenes "think that oil is a defilement; and if any one of them be anointed without his own approbation, it is wiped off his body; for *they think to be sweaty is a good thing,* as do they also to be clothed in white garments" (*War* 2.123; my emphasis). The Essenes never used cleansing oil, thus the connection is established. These familial relationships imply that Jesus, too, was an Essene, for, as it does today, one's religious orientation generally mirrored family lines.*

The above and many other telltale traces of Essene doctrine are why the Scrolls gathered so much attention when they were first discovered, and why they have been called the greatest archaeological treasures of all time. Gone forever are our simplistic notions of Jesus as a dusty, barefoot preacher with no rational preparation whatsoever for his world-changing ministry. Jesus showed distinctive signs of an Essene upbringing.[4]

---

*Some historical accounts of the Essenes show them to be celibate. If the Essenes were all celibate males, it would make no sense to speak of Essene families. But this was not the case. Female skeletons were found by the archaeologists at Qumran; and, upon closer examination, Josephus speaks of divisions within the Essenes that differed on the question of celibacy (*War* 2.160).

8 THE CHRISTOLOGY QUESTION

No man can be entirely reduced to a product of his raising, especially one held to be the walking incarnation of God. I hesitate to mention that Jesus is believed by Christians to be God incarnate, but I must, for the greatest obstacle in the quest for the historical Jesus is the Christology question. *Christology* is the attempt to rationalize the divine and human nature of Jesus."[5] Note that I have said "nature," not "natures." Christological errors are usually committed whenever one attempts to lessen the humanity of Jesus to make room for his divinity, rather than recognizing that the perfected human nature and the divine nature are one and the same. Through the years, many have thought that Jesus had no normal human growth, either intellectually or spiritually. We must reject the remnant heresies of Christology once and for all. Jesus was as *fully* human as you or me. And if he was fully human, there must have been what I would call a "rational development" of his messianic awareness.[6]

The Gospel narratives show glimpses of messianic awareness even at the tender age of twelve, when Jesus deserted his parents in Jerusalem (Lk 2:41–51). When Jesus's parents found him in the Temple, they scolded him because they had been desperately searching for him for three days. Jesus replied to his distraught parents, "How is it that you sought me? Did you not know that I must be in my Father's house?" (Lk 2:49). Some speculate that in the Temple Jesus might have actually encountered the Rabbi Hillel, who was known to have flourished about this time. Hillel was known for formulating a *restrictive* golden rule: "Do *not* do unto others what you would *not* have them do unto you; this is the summary of the Torah." In contrast, Jesus taught a *proactive* golden rule: "*Do* unto others as you would have them *do* unto you." This ethical difference arguably separates Judaism and Christianity to this day. I can easily see the twelve-year-old Jesus engaging the great Hillel in such an important debate. But whether it actually happened is a matter of speculation.

The point is, despite this glimpse into Jesus's evolving messianic awareness,* the Temple incident clearly shows a developing Jesus, a *learning* and *growing* Jesus. Jesus was hungrily engaged in a dialogue with the elite teachers of his day.

This relentless quest for truth was to characterize all of Jesus's life. And when one considers that this life was lived when religious pluralism in Israel had reached its greatest height, his acumen and capacity for spiritual discernment must have been incredible, even from his infancy (cf. Is 7:14–15). In support of an educated Jesus, I suggest that he read and spoke Greek, a topic that has been hotly debated among Bible scholars. The reason I believe this is so is not only that Jesus reportedly spent his infant years in Egypt and grew up in Nazareth— both then Greek-speaking regions—but because I accept the historical accuracy of a particular Gospel passage. Luke has Jesus recite the commandments in the order that they appear in the Greek Septuagint, not the Hebrew Masoretic (18:18–20). Francis Potter, one of the earliest American commentators on the Scrolls, noted that we have finally been presented with a much more sophisticated picture of the founder of Christianity:

> [Jesus was] not only well-versed in the knowledge and culture of Rome, Persia, Athens and Alexandria, a wide traveler and a great teacher, but also an existential empiricist in the midst of absolutists, ever deliberately seeking new truth by observation and experiment, even unto death.[7]

This was the historical Jesus. The teacher of the ages was also the student of the ages. Jesus began with the Essenes, yes, but he could not be contained by a systematic theology, Essene or otherwise. Jesus was, as Buber so aptly put it, "a teacher, whose teaching depend[ed] entirely upon the effect produced by his person and therefore by his nature."[8]

---

*Note that Jesus's parents were surprised at his answer (Lk 2:50). This indicates unusual behavior on the part of Jesus, a break from his everyday awareness.

9 A DYNAMIC RELATIONSHIP

Jesus's developing messianic awareness best explains why, as Scrolls scholarship progressed, it became evident that there were fundamental differences between Essenism and Christianity; differences so great there must surely have been a schism. Before we can investigate or even speculate as to the particular reason or reasons that drove Jesus away from the Essenes, it is best that we get an overview of each side's doctrines. That way, we will learn the fundamental differences between them.

James H. Charlesworth has done a fine job articulating these many differences,[9] and I could do little more than rehash his work here. But the greatest difference between Jesus and the Essenes, a difference that cannot be stressed enough, is without a doubt the former's teachings of universal love. Jesus opened his heart to everyone: Samaritans, tax collectors, even the Roman occupiers. His intent was to fully open Judaism to the Gentiles. We find no such doctrine in the Essenes. The Essenes were a closed and hate-filled sect who cursed Gentiles as well as other Jews, whom they perceived to be wicked. The Dead Sea Scrolls exhibit a dualistic worldview that is appalling by true Christian standards, an ugly "in-group" versus "out-group" mentality. In the Community Rule, we find that the Essenes set up a practice whereby their Levite priests regularly cursed the "lot of Belial," meaning essentially anyone outside their sect:

> Be cursed because of all your guilty wickedness! May He deliver you up for torture at the hands of the vengeful Avengers! May He visit you with destruction by the hand of all the Wreakers of Vengeance! Be cursed without mercy according to the darkness of your deeds! Be damned in the shadowy place of everlasting fire! (1QS II, 5–8)

No genuine Christian love and mercy are to be found here. If we can trust the Gospels at all in giving us an account of the historical Jesus, this cursing of one's enemies would have been utterly antithetical to him:

> You have heard that it was said, "You shall love your neighbor and hate your enemies." But I say to you, Love your enemies and pray for those who persecute you so that you may be sons of your Father who is in heaven; for he makes his sun rise on the evil and on the good, and sends rain on the just and on the unjust. (Mt 5:43–45)

Note the opening of Jesus's address above, where he quotes the dictum, "You shall love your neighbor and hate your enemies." The first part of the quotation can easily be derived from Leviticus 19:18, but the second part of the quotation has often perplexed biblical scholars. Nowhere in the Old Testament or later Jewish writings is there ever found the concept of hating one's enemies. From what or from *whom,* then, was Jesus quoting? The answer is that Jesus was preaching against the Essenes. According to the Scrolls, the Essenes were to "love all that [God] has chosen, and hate all that he has rejected" (1QS I, 4).[10]

The Essenes also believed in strict predestination and that only they were the true Israel, the "elect" of God (*Ant* 13.171–72; 1QS III, 15–16). They loved only those of their immediate sect while condemning and despising the rest of the world. Evil was eternally identified as "otherness," otherness from one's group, even otherness from one's physical self. Jesus taught an exactly opposite, life-affirming way of resolving evil. You cannot hate your brother if you are praying for him. Love, and not hate, was the way of Jesus, even to the point of suffering oppression without resistance: "Do not resist one who is evil. But if any strikes you on the right cheek, turn to him the other also" (Mt 5:39). Yadin comments on the "love your enemies" passage:

> There seems to be no doubt that Jesus was referring to the Essenes when he spoke scathingly of those who urged it as a duty to hate one's enemies, and it is my opinion that the people he was addressing were familiar with this Essene injunction, having been close to the

Essene sect and believed in its doctrines, but who had now converted or were about to convert to the views of Jesus and follow him.[11]

Thus Yadin would surely have agreed that Renan's original claims about Christian origins are accurate, insofar as some Essenes became early converts to Christianity. But their ideology had to change in the process. Essenes who followed Jesus had to leave their former teaching of hatred behind.

10 DID JESUS HIMSELF LEAD AN ESSENE SCHISM?

If we understand that Jesus was brought up an Essene, which is clearly shown by the telltale similarities in his and their doctrines, then we must draw an additional inference from the previous section. Before Jesus could convert his followers from Essenism, either he converted himself or another had to convert him. What other explanation is there? *Someone* had to cause the schism. And when we review the historical figures of the period, who else do we find saying the wonderful things Jesus said, acting as Jesus acted, but *Jesus himself*?

Once we know what we are looking for, the Scrolls themselves speak of the schism with great specificity. They speak of Jesus as the leader of that schism: "a Wicked Priest who was called by the name of Truth when he first arose" (1QpHab VIII, 8–9). The question then arises: At what point did the Essenes no longer call this Priest by the name of Truth? I do not believe, given presently available sources, that we can know with a certainty to satisfy modern criticism exactly when the break took place,*

---

*Some speculative answers present themselves, however. If Jesus's baptism was intended as an Essene initiation ritual, then the temptation in the wilderness that occurs immediately afterward could very well have been Jesus's point of departure from the Essenes (Mk 1:12–13 // Mt 4:1–11 // Lk 4:1–13). The "Satan" of the temptation story might have been an Essene leader—perhaps even the Righteous Teacher. Obviously something big happened to Jesus around this time. Archeologist and Holy Land scholar Charles Page writes that Jesus's subsequent move from Nazareth to Capernaum (Mt 4:13–16) was the result of a "major theological shift." In Page's view, the small village of Nazareth was Hasidic, whereas cosmopolitan Capernaum would have embraced a more liberal Hillelian form of Judaism. See Charles Page II, *Jesus & the Land* (Nashville: Abingdon, 1995), 34, 62–66.

or if it was instead a gradual process. We must realize that we can never fully reconstruct another person's thoughts and emotions no matter how detailed the textual evidence. Unfortunately, we cannot find a direct statement in the Gospels in which Jesus affirmed his Essene upbringing, or, for that matter, where he said anything concerning his upbringing at all.

We can know this much with certainty: Jesus did not go to, in today's parlance, a "seminary" of any kind, with the Essenes or otherwise. As Geza Vermes rightly concluded, "[Jesus] was not a member of any recognized teaching group."[12] John's Gospel reports that the Jews were amazed at Jesus's scriptural knowledge because he lacked formal training (Jn 7:15). This is confirmed in the first three Gospels, where we find the chief priests, scribes, and elders questioning Jesus's teaching authority (Mk 11:27–33 // Mt 21:23–27 // Lk 20:1–8). Clearly Jesus's authority did not derive from the Essenes, a point that this and later chapters establish all too clearly. Jesus's authority, his rabbinical "platform," if you will, seems to have derived solely from his charismatic presence. Here was a man filled with God who, like other great religious teachers, simply spoke his heart. Jesus spoke out with the sort of conviction one would expect of a rebel rejecting his religious upbringing. He spoke like Guatama Siddhartha who rejected the Hindu caste system; like Mohandas Gandhi, who rejected British imperialism; or like Martin Luther King Jr., who rejected American racism. What each of these men had in common, the source of their charisma, was the life experience that inspired their preaching. Jesus's message was refreshingly informal, direct, and powerful. Unlike the Essenes, who would have quoted the prophets and the Torah rigidly, Jesus spoke with a personal authority to which his listeners were unaccustomed (Jn 7:15; Mk 11:27; Mt 21:23; Lk 20:1). Jesus preached, "I say—." To first-century Jewish ears, Jesus spoke with reckless abandon against the establishment. This is why he was able to gather five thousand people to hear the Sermon on the Mount.

One scholar notes, "Certain aspects of Jesus's preaching seem to betray a deliberate preoccupation with defining himself over against Essenism."[13] For example, in the famous Sermon on the Mount, it seems that Jesus took the literary form and content of the Beatitudes from the Dead Sea Scrolls (Mt 5:3–12; cf. 4Q525).[14] Yet Jesus carefully edited away every portion that disagreed with him. He replaced Essene Beatitudes that taught meditation on the letter of the law with simple life-teaching Beatitudes that point one toward the Kingdom of God. These and many Gospel passages like them, though they clearly show parallels of Jesus to the Essenes, also show the dynamics of that relationship. They show how the gospel emerged within the Nazarene himself, within the breakaway Essene who was to become the founder of Christianity. Says Yadin, "I am convinced that Jesus was anti-Essene. . . . Indeed, his whole approach was anathema to the Essenes, with their rigid legalism and their insistence that their rigorously interpreted laws of purity be carried out to the letter."[15]

Without the Essenes opposing him, I doubt Jesus would have been the powerful figure we know from the Gospels. The Essenes were to Jesus as the Sophists were to Socrates, as the Manichaeans were to Augustine, as the medieval Catholics were to Luther. They were his dialectical baptism by fire. The Dead Sea Scrolls frame Jesus within his historical context, within the religious matrix of his day. But they do so much more. The Scrolls give us a crystal-clear picture of who Jesus was *not*, freeing the man from years of doctrinal baggage and historical distortion.

11 THE REAL JESUS

Unlike the Essenes, Jesus was not an ascetic. Far from it; as Charlesworth puts it, "Jesus loved a good party" (cf. Jn 2: 1–11).[16] Jesus drank hard wine. He was even called "a glutton and a drunkard" (Mt 11:19a). Jesus associated with the "laughing people," with prostitutes and lepers, and with every other religious outcast, including Gentiles (Mk 14:3).

Jesus taught a middle path of moderation and an inner purity. He did not teach the outer purity associated with fasting or dietary laws, in part because such practices could not be followed by the poor. Jesus cared nothing about clean hands or kosher foods, for in his view these things had nothing whatsoever to do with the source of the true *ethos,* the inner person (Mk 7:15).

As if his behavior were not shocking enough, Jesus's introduction of what is now known as *liberation theology* would have been utterly unthinkable for first-century hierarchical Judaism. Jesus was a radical subversive. He called for a sweeping social, economic, and political reform of society from the bottom up: "But many that are first shall be last, and the last first" (Mk 10:31). The most dramatic example was Jesus's revolutionary treatment of and attitudes toward women. As Dead Sea Scrolls scholar Magen Broshi notes, the Essenes treated women with scorn, believing them to be spiritually inferior to men and a source of temptation:

> Certain metaphors recur frequently in the Dead Sea Scrolls, indicating Essene abhorrence of sexuality. Sometimes the full impact is lost in translation. For example, in one translation of the Thanksgiving Scroll, man is described as "a creature of clay, kneaded in water, a fundament of shame and a source of pollution" (I, 21–22). Actually, the word *ervah* translated as "shame," is really "pudenda," and *nidah* translated as "pollution," is really "menstruation." These terms occur dozens of times in the Scrolls.[17]

In contrast, Jesus was a feminist.[18] In a patriarchal age when most Jewish women were shut-ins and not even allowed to read the Torah, Jesus took on female disciples and treated them as equals. The presence of female disciples is constantly confirmed in the Gospels (Mk 15:40–41; Mt 14:21, 15:38, 27:55; Lk 8:1–3). So common was their presence that the apostles referred to them as "some women of our company" (Lk 24:22a).

Most importantly, Jesus taught that reform would come about only by nonviolence. But for God's pardon of Cain for slaying Abel, Jesus taught nonviolence in a religious tradition that had very little historical basis for it. It is important to understand that some basis for nonviolence was to be found in Judaism all along. The law as handed down by Moses called for limitations on blood vengeance, but it was still blood vengeance: "life for life, eye for eye, tooth for tooth" (Ex 21:23–24). It was not this way in the beginning. God spared Cain despite Abel's posthumous cry for blood vengeance. Anyone who sought vengeance on Cain would feel seven times God's wrath. Thus, in the Sermon on the Mount, when Jesus specifically rejected "an eye for an eye" in favor of nonviolence (Mt 5:38–39), he was calling for a *renewal,* just as he did with the divorce laws (Mk 10:2–10).

In his book *Constantine's Sword: The Church and the Jews,* author and former Catholic priest James Carroll points out that Christians have often wrongly depicted Judaism in its most legalistic and inhumane terms in order to portray Jesus as the light that emerged out of shadow. I may be somewhat guilty of overvilifying the Essenes myself, but I stand behind my statement that Jesus was the great pioneer of nonviolence in early Judaism. When Martin Luther King Jr. reintroduced nonviolence to mainstream Christianity after centuries of distortion, it was primarily through the works of Gandhi. When Gandhi learned nonviolence in a political context, it was primarily through the works of Tolstoy, who was Christian. Jesus was the original pacifist. He taught his followers that we should be completely defenseless, that we should "turn the other cheek" and "pray for those who persecute [us]" (Mt 5:39b, 44). He taught that we should not even fight to defend one another. Jesus said to Pilate, "My kingdom is not of this world: if my kingdom were of this world then my servants would fight" (Jn 18:36a). The idea of vengeance itself is transformed so as to become the victory of Christian love. Nonviolence is as radical an idea now as it was then.

Also, Jesus introduced ideas found in other religions that seemed very foreign to Judaism at the time. For example, Jesus made mystical claims of identity with God that even to this day are not well received in Judaism. Buber's mysticism recognized an "I and Thou" relation with God, a relationship of genuine otherness.* But Jesus occasionally made what I would call "I am Thou" claims akin to Hindu nondualism.† In Jesus's day, the Jewish elders considered such forms of mysticism blasphemy worthy of the death penalty (Jn 8:57–59). Neither had any Jew ever claimed the personal authority to forgive sin (Mk 2:6–7).‡ Jesus made faith in himself, not works, the new covenant, proclaiming that he was the fulfillment of the Torah. Jesus laid bare the very heart of Judaism, distilling it to its essence, or *Dao,* as the Chinese call it. The *Logos* in John 1:1–18 is typically translated in Chinese Bibles as *Dao,* and John speaks of Jesus as its very incarnation. I would classify a great deal of Jesus's teachings as *Daoist.* Consider the "effortless action" (*wu wei*) found in this passage: "Therefore, do not be anxious about tomorrow, for tomorrow will take care of itself. Let the day's own trouble be sufficient for the day" (Mt 6:34). Another fact that will help Easterners understand the Bible is that the Greek word translated "yoke" in the following passage is more accurately translated as *yoga,* the Sanskrit term for spiritual union:

> Come to me all who labor and are heavy laden, and I will give you rest. Take my *yoke* upon you, and learn of me; for I am gentle and

---

*It may be wrong to strictly label Buber's "I-Thou" Jewish mysticism. Buber did his doctoral work on Eckhart, the Christian mystic. Thus I wonder how much of Buber's mysticism is his own, and how much is causally related to that first-century Jew named Jesus.

†Jesus's mystical relationship with God is akin to Hindu nondualism, but there are important differences. For instance, most scholars insist that *Brahman*—arguably the Hindu equivalent of God—should be translated as an "It or That, not He." S. Radhakrishan & C.A. Moore, *A Sourcebook in Indian Philosophy* (Princeton, NJ: Princeton U. Press, 1970), 39.

‡*Contra* Vermes, *The Religion of Jesus the Jew,* 192–93, where Vermes offers a spurious interpretation. He wants to interpret Jesus's forgiveness of sin as merely a passive recognition that God had already forgiven a person's sin (Mk 2:5–12 in full context, especially vv. 10–12), where Jesus specifically claims a miraculous healing as evidence of his divine authority. Even Vermes had to admit that the conventional Jews were scandalized at Jesus's declaration (ibid., 193 n. 9).

lowly in heart, and you will find rest for your souls. For my *yoke* is easy and my burden light. (Mt 11:28–30; my emphasis)

In short, Jesus was the ultimate Reform Jew. He introduced a simple lifestyle, practical ethical teaching, revolutionary social order, non-violence, and a wide range of other religious ideas then unheard of in Judaism. Unfortunately, the Essenes were doctrinal purists and would have none of it. That is why the Essenes branded Jesus as the vilest sinner, a "seeker of smooth things" (1QpHab; 1QS; 1QM).

12 THE ESSENES: STILL A MYSTERY

Thus the dilemma I put forth at the outset of this chapter returns. If the Essenes existed at the time of Jesus and were separate from him, and if they were such a prominent sect as to attract the attention of the historians of the era, why do we not find references to the Essenes in the New Testament? Scholars who once thought the Essenes to have been a small sect isolated at Qumran and that Jesus would have had to travel there to meet them were in error. According to Josephus, Philo, and many other historians, the Essenes, together with the Pharisees and Sadducees, made up the three most notable sects of Judaism (*War* 2.119). Josephus also reports that the Essenes were very populous, more than four thousand in number, and that they had a settlement in every town (*Ant* 18.20; *War* 2.124). Bearing this in mind, it is unreasonable in the extreme to think that, in their travels throughout all of Palestine, Jesus and his disciples never once encountered the Essenes; or if the Essenes were encountered, that they completely escaped the attention of all the writers of the New Testament. It is so unreasonable that it could not possibly have happened. That is why the Essenes are indeed found in the New Testament, the Old Testament, and many books of the Apocrypha, too—but not by that name. Biblically, the Essenes were an unbelievably amorphous sect, even given different names by a single writer. It thus requires a keen knowledge of the Bible, the Scrolls, the Mishnah, and other historical writings, one no less than the other, to flush the Essenes out of the New Testament. Fortunately, after years of combined research efforts, we are finally able to make the identification.

13 HERODIANS: A MINOR NEW TESTAMENT NAME FOR THE ESSENES

Many scholars have contributed to the identification of the Essenes in the New Testament. C. Daniel once uncovered a key historical reference to the Essenes that unraveled a great many mysteries.[19] He found that Josephus recorded the story of an Essene named Manaemos (*Ant* 15.371–79). When Herod the Great was still a schoolboy, long before he took the throne, Manaemos predicted that Herod would become king. "And," Josephus writes, "from that moment on, [Herod] continued to hold all Essenes in honor" (*Ant* 15.379). The Essenes became Herod's favorite sect, on whom he would often bestow special favors. For example, Herod excused them from an oath of loyalty (*Ant* 15.371). It is reasonable, then, to conclude that the common people would have nicknamed the Essenes the "Herodians." The scholarly Josephus and other historians would not have referred to them by that name, but the common people, such as Jesus and those who would write our Gospels, would have. Perhaps Josephus had the foresight to know there would be problems of identification. He felt an explanation was needed for his inclusion of the story of Manaemos's prediction: "It will . . . show what the general opinion of these men was" (*Ant* 15.372).

We now have good reason to believe the Essenes were called Herodians. How does that help us? The Gospels of Mark and Matthew contain references to the Herodians (Mk 3:6; 8:14–21; Mk 12:13 // Mt 22:16), and these passages answer a great many open questions. Otto Betz (a leading Dead Sea Scrolls scholar with whom I had the honor of corresponding before he died) commented that New Testament scholars have always had difficulty identifying the

Herodians, for it was assumed that they must have been political delegates of King Herod.[20] But who: Herod the Great? Herod Antipas? Herod's dynasty? None of the interpretations ever made sense. The Herodians we find in the Gospels appear to be a priestly sect in league with the Pharisees against Jesus. The Herodians' interests were not merely political but *religious* in nature, primarily so. Like the Pharisees, they were concerned with what Jesus had to say about the Torah and the prophets.

One of the few New Testament references to Herodians is found in Mark's Gospel. Subsequent to the famous miraculous feeding of the multitudes, Jesus and the disciples were now traveling by boat. When an opportunity to give a parable involving bread presented itself, Jesus did so. He phrased a warning to the disciples in what seems to my generation's eyes just about the most esoteric parable that Jesus ever gave:

> Now they had forgotten to bring bread; and they had only one loaf with them in the boat. And he cautioned them, saying, "Take heed, beware the leaven of the Pharisees and the Herodians."* And they discussed it with one another saying, "We have no bread." And being aware of it, Jesus said to them, "Why do you discuss the fact you have no bread? Do you not yet perceive or understand? Are your hearts hardened? Having eyes do you not see, and having ears do you not hear? And do you not remember? When I broke the five loaves for the five thousand, how many baskets full of broken pieces did you take up?" They said to him, "Twelve." "And the seven for the four thousand, how many baskets full of broken pieces did you take up?" They said to him, "Seven." And he said to them, "Do you not yet understand?" (Mk 8:14–21)

---

*The Greek codices are slightly in disagreement. Vaticanus and Sinaiticus offer "leaven of Herod," but that does not make much sense. Hence, Y. Yadin (see below) chose the translation of the "leaven of the Herodians."

This passage had baffled me for as long as I can remember. These references to the number of baskets left over? What a conundrum! I read commentator after commentator, and the best interpretation anyone could come up with was Kabbalist number mysticism (for example, seven is the number of perfection) that had no direct bearing on the passage. Only when I read the fine work of Yigael Yadin, who published the Temple Scroll found in Cave 11, did I finally discover the accurate interpretation.[21] I doubt the truth would have come to me otherwise, for I lacked the context that a first-century Jew or recently converted Jewish-Christian brought to the page.

Yadin found a passage in the Temple Scroll that dealt with rituals accompanying the Feast of Milluim, a time of ordination, a dedication of the priesthood during the first seven days of the month of Nisan (Ex 29; Ez 43:18–27). According to the Temple Scroll, the Essenes had modified the Torah's procedure for cleansing of the altar during the Feast of Milluim (11Q19 XV, 9–14; cf. Ex 29; Ez 43: 18–27). Instead of offering up twelve baskets of bread for each of the twelve weeks of the Holy Presence in the Temple, as did the Pharisees, the Essenes altered their ritual. On each of the seven days of celebration, the Essenes gathered a basket of bread together with a ram as a waive offering. Thus when Jesus warned the disciples to "beware the leaven of the Pharisees and the Herodians," and then, in that corresponding order, reminded them of the number of baskets gathered after his two feedings (a sympathetic association: Pharisees = twelve baskets, Herodians = seven baskets), he was referring to the respective rituals of each for the Feast of Milluim. Jesus saw himself as the "bread of life" (Jn 6:33–35), who, as God's Son, could offer eternal life. He was both the single sacrificial lamb and single sacrificial loaf of bread the disciples needed (Mk 8:14), by whom they and the multitudes had all just been consecrated as priests of the new era. The miraculous feeding of the multitudes was an ordination from God.*

---

*Yadin concludes that the feeding of the multitude probably took place on the Feast of Ordination, shortly before Passover. I concur; Jn 6:4.

By this parable, Jesus meant that the priests of the Pharisees and the Herodians did not offer the "bread of life," but were consecrated instead by leaven, bread unsuitable for sacrifice (cf. 1 Cor 5:6–7). A *very* rich parable, this, but in addition to its deeper theological meaning, it serves our historical exegesis well. The New Testament's silence on the Essenes has now been broken. They, the Scrolls authors, were called Herodians.

Yadin did not note that Mark and Matthew mention the Herodians in the tribute to Caesar's story, which when fully understood also identifies the Herodians as the Essenes.

> And they sent to him some of the Pharisees and Herodians, to entrap [Jesus] in his talk. And they came and said to him, "Teacher, we know that you are true, and care for no man; for you do not regard the position of men, but truly teach the way of God. Is it lawful to pay taxes to Caesar, or not? Should we pay them, or should we not?" But knowing their hypocrisy, he said to them, "Why put me to the test? Bring me a coin and let me look at it." And they brought one. And he said to them, "Whose likeness and inscription is this?" They said to him, "Caesar's." Jesus said to them, "Render unto Caesar the things that are Caesar's, and unto God the things that are God's." And they were amazed at him. (Mk 12:13–17; cf. Mt 22:15–22)

This story is often cited to show Jesus's creativity in countering his opposition, to show that he had the tact of the sharpest politician. What actually occurred was an ex-Essene holding other Essenes accountable to their own beliefs at a very opportune moment, although we had no way of knowing this fact until now. To find the inspiration for this cunning defense, we need to read the early historians. Josephus is the most widely recognized firsthand historian of the Essenes, but he is often criticized for coloring his accounts for his Greco-Roman audience and not giving us needed details. A more detailed description is found in the lesser-known writings of the early church father Hippolytus. In his *Refutation of All Heresies,* the Essenes emerge as decidedly more Jewish than in the accounts by Josephus and others.* For example, Hippolytus recorded that certain Essenes were fanatical in their intolerance of idolatry. This aversion was unique to Judaism, yet members of the Essenes characteristically took it to the extreme. Hippolytus wrote, "For some observe a still more rigid practice in not handling or looking at a coin which has an image" (*Refutation of All Heresies* IX, 21). Thus when Jesus told his accusers to produce a pagan coin, look at it, and "Render unto Caesar the things that are Caesar's," Jesus was evidently singing out the Herodians/ Essenes for their hypocrisy.

In James H. Charlesworth's *Jesus and the Dead Sea Scrolls,*[22] a chapter written by Otto Betz offers an additional correlation between the Essenes and the Herodians by bringing forth another passage in which they are mentioned, Mark 3:6. In so doing, Betz confronts me with a stunning revelation that appears in chapter 7 (section 73). That one piece of scholarship is the cornerstone for this entire restoration, as you will eventually see. For now it is enough that we confirm the Essenes were called Herodians in the Gospels, where they are in league with the Pharisees against Jesus. This is easily done, for Mark records that Jesus antagonized two Jewish sects in a synagogue, the "Pharisees and Herodians" (3:1–6). The latter sect, the Herodians, was singled out for their extremely rigid observance of Sabbath laws, a characteristic trait of the Essenes (*War* 2.143–49). Betz mentions a parallel citation to this incident found in Matthew,[†] where Jesus cited and ridiculed a stat-

---

*It was at one time believed that Hippolytus drew from Josephus due to the great similarity of their accounts, but this position has been effectively repudiated, and several key Jewish differences pointed out, by M. Smith. See his 1958 article, "The Description of the Essenes in Josephus and the *Philosophoumena," Hebrew Union College Annual* 29:273–323.

†Matthew omits the reference to a second sect and records that only the Pharisees were present. Since he was the only Gospel writer to do so, and since most informed scholars believe Matthew's Gospel to be derivative of Mark's, I conclude that the omission was in error, or, more likely, that the Pharisees and Essenes were so closely allied that Matthew did not feel it necessary to distinguish them.

ute peculiar to the Scrolls, the prohibition against rescuing an animal fallen into a pit on the Sabbath (Mt 12:11; cf. CD XI, 13–14). Betz rightly concludes that the Herodians mentioned in Mark are the Essene Scrolls authors. With this knowledge, we are immediately able to assess Jesus's relation with the Essenes. We are given solid biblical evidence that Jesus directed much of his preaching against the Essenes, just as he did his other well-known spiritual enemies, the Pharisees. Clearly the Essenes/Herodians were opposed to Jesus, as we expected to find given their vast differences in doctrine. But this is just the beginning.

14 A DOOR IS OPENED

The Herodians are very seldom mentioned in the Gospels, so seldom that it seems unreasonable to believe they were the populous Essenes that Josephus, Philo, and other historians record. Could the Essenes have traveled by another name? Could the Herodians have been a derogatory nickname the Gospel writers used only on occasion? It seems so. A parallel citation to Betz's synagogue incident, Mark 3:1–6, is found in Luke 6:6–11. The two groups in league against Jesus are not called Pharisees and *Herodians,* as in Mark's version; Luke calls them Pharisees and *scribes* (Mk 3:6 // Lk 6:7). A little faith that the citations are indeed parallel, that they refer to the same event and persons, and we have just uncovered an unbelievably valuable prooftext. The Essenes/Herodians must have been the same New Testament group as the scribes. What a door has just been opened!

We are now presented with an interpretation problem never before realized. Various New Testament translations suggest that the scribes were servants of another sect. For example, Mark 2:16 is variously translated "the scribes of the Pharisees" (RSV) or "teachers of the law who were Pharisees" (NIV), but see "the scribes and Pharisees" (KJV). The reason? Although they sometimes appear alone or with the Sadducees, the scribes almost always appear alongside the Pharisees. So it has been presumed that the scribes were the latter's servants. But there are too many unanswered questions if this were the case. For example, the Pharisees were the lay people, the "middle class," who had little if any power in the Temple during gospel times. Why would they need scribes? If anything, we would expect to see scribes alongside the sect that was in power, the Sadducees. Also, the numbers fail to match up. Unlike the scribes' infrequent appearances in the Old Testament, where they were merely a handful of secretaries for the Temple cult, in the New Testament, scribes appear more than fifty times in the Gospels alone. This sounds more like a large sect, which is precisely what many scholars believe. Many scholars have concluded that the scribes must have emerged as a large and very important sect during the Persian exile.[23]

The reasons scholars offer for the rise of a large sect of scribes are many. The most obvious is that a large number of scribes were necessary because the Hebrew language was in transition to Aramaic. The displaced Jews were ruled by a theocracy, which meant that every law, every problem that needed resolving in day-to-day life, depended on the accurate translation of the Torah. Obviously Ezra* could not handle the job alone. What he needed was a large class of scribes, a class that in today's society would be known as lawyers, accountants, and bureaucrats. Otherwise Jews would have completely lost their religious identity.

I caution the casual New Testament scholar who has read of the scribes a thousand times unthinkingly, especially if your translation omits certain references to the scribes altogether, as many translations do. We must not be bound by our bad reading habits and collapse the Pharisees and scribes into the same group. On the other hand—please bear with me—I feel it is equally confusing to call the Pharisees and scribes separate *sects*. The relationship of the Pharisees and scribes was a complex one, as the Gospels suggest, an issue we will have to explore as we go along. Not surprisingly, it was the very same relationship that some scholars independently discovered between the Pharisees and

---

*Ezra was a scribe who organized the civil and religious affairs of the Jewish Diaspora exiled in Babylon, then he led about 5,000 of the Diaspora back to Jerusalem in 459 BCE. Ezra is also generally recognized as the author of the Book of Ezra.

Essenes. We must remember that a "sect" is primarily a Christian designation drawn from our particular denominations. It probably creates less confusion and is more accurate to say that the Essenes/scribes were a higher *order* of Pharisee, as, for example, the Jesuits are to Catholics in the present day. Even more precisely, we should probably say, as hinted by the church father Hippolytus, that the Pharisees were a splinter group or reformed order of Essene.

Shortly, I will take up the work of Emil Schürer and Heinrich Gräetz, the nineteenth-century's best Christian and Jewish historians of ancient Judaism respectively. Both maintained that the Essenes were the first Jewish sect from which all other sects formed. Thus it makes perfect sense why we find no sectarian name for the Essenes in the Gospels. If the well-known sects were all defined by their separation *from* the Essenes, you would not expect the parent sect to be named from without, at least not in the beginning. The breakaway sect would probably still identity itself with the parent, or feel it had the true right to claim the parent's title and traditions. Case in point: We Protestants still consider ourselves "catholic," meaning a member of the universal Church or "body of Christ," although we rarely use that self-designation anymore. It is customary to reserve the title "Catholic" for Roman Catholics, a sect Luther nominally and literally brought into being with the Reformation. You will not find the designation "Catholic," meaning Roman Catholic, in the earliest Protestant works. Such arguments, once they have been carefully explored, together with the above parallel reference, produce an inescapable conclusion: "scribes" must be the primary New Testament name for the Essenes. Now the identification is complete. The Essenes emerge not just as bit players in the life of Jesus, but as main characters.

15 SCRIBES: THE PRIMARY NEW TESTAMENT NAME FOR THE ESSENES

I have identified the Essenes as the scribes in the New Testament, albeit by a very roundabout route. I have so far based the identification solely upon a single parallel citation, which may not seem the weightiest of evidence. Actually, we have another parallel citation that points to this conclusion. In addition to the incident in the synagogue, we can also equate the scribes and Herodians as they appear in the previously discussed dialogue concerning tribute to Caesar (Mk 12:13–17 // Mt 22:15–22 // Lk 20:19–26). Add that to the basket reference covered by Yadin, and every single New Testament reference to the Herodians has now been correlated to the Essenes, and all but one of them also to the scribes. I know that consensus Scrolls scholars will not give up their views this easily, however, even if this work is a direct result of their own conclusions. Fortunately, I have other means of identifying the Essenes as scribes at my disposal, arguments that should convince even the most critical scholar.

I will show that the etymology of the name "Essenes" is taken from the *Hasideans* or Greek *Asidaioi,* a sect known as the "pious" that emerged during or shortly after the Persian exile (1 Macc 2:42; 7:13; 2 Macc 14:6). Although it may now be nearly impossible to trace the direct lineage, I believe the Hasideans were the ancient forerunners of the Hasidim, whom Buber studied. What is interesting, given the origins of Christianity that I am now arguing, is that Buber felt the greatest similarity Christianity has with Judaism lies in present-day Hasidism.[24] More important, the dominant consensus of Scrolls scholars—Black, Cross, and Vermes, to name a few—is that the Hasideans either gave rise to the Essenes or were the Essenes once called by a different name. This allows another roundabout way of identifying them, for I will then show that Hasideans are closely allied with, if not inclusive of, the scribes as the latter first appeared as a recognizable group (1 Macc 7:12–14). Not surprisingly, many historians believe the Essenes emerged at the same time. I will discuss the relationship of the Essenes/scribes and Pharisees, two groups with a common origin. The Essenes/scribes and Pharisees eventually grew apart, yet they were closely knit during gospel times. This explains why the Gospel writers always show the Pharisees and scribes traveling together. And finally, I will show so many correlations between the scribes of the

Gospels and the Essenes of the Scrolls by a straightforward Bible study that we need not belabor the identity crisis any longer. The Essenes were the New Testament scribes.

16 ETYMOLOGY: THE ESSENES ARE "THE PIOUS"

The authors rarely refer to themselves by name in the Scrolls published thus far.* This is characteristic of most first-century literature. For example, the New Testament never refers to "Christians." Thus we must seek the etymology for the name *Essenes* in the only other place they appear, the historical writings. The English *Essenes* comes from the Latin *Essenei*, which was used by Pliny the Elder. In the Greek, the order is called *Essaioi* by Philo, and *Essenoi* by Josephus and an early Church father, Hippolytus. Epiphanius, also an early church father, described two divisions of Essenes, the *Nazareans*[†] in the north and the *Osseaens* in the south (*Proem* I 3.1–5; 19.1.1–3). Scholars have determined that these writers are all referring to the same group by examining their common doctrine, location, and similar characteristics. But the etymology still remains an enigma, for the name *Essenes* held no intrinsic meaning in Latin or Greek.

It seems reasonable to conclude, therefore, that the name had meaning in the original Semitic, which has probably come to us as a transliteration, such as *Sadducees,* meaning descendants of the Zadokite priests. If we are lucky, a word will pass meaningfully from one language and alphabet to another. But it can be particularly difficult to

---

*It may still be too early to expect self-designations to appear with many minor scroll fragments not yet translated. I note, however, that references to the Hasidim, "the pious," have been found in 4Q521, line 7: "And [God] will glorify *the pious* on the throne of the eternal Kingdom." In addition to Vermes, an English translation and discussion is found in *Biblical Archaeology Review* November/December 1992, 62; see also Eisenman and Wise, *The Dead Sea Scrolls Uncovered,* 19, 23.

†Epiphanius, Eusebius, Jerome and others record that Jewish Christians were known as "Nazareans" up until the fourth century CE. Charles Page makes a strong case that the Nazoreans preceded Jesus, thus confirming my thesis that Christianity was born of an Essene schism. *Jesus & the Land,* 34.

find meaningful translations of both a word and its root or derivation. Shades of meaning are often lost. In Matthew's Gospel, for example, Jesus made a pun on Peter's name, a pun that rhymed perfectly in their native Aramaic: "You are *Kepha,* and on this *kepha* I will build my Church" (Mt 16:18a). The rhyme is largely preserved in Greek (*Petros* ≈ *petra*) and perfectly in French (*Pierre* = *pierre*), but it is completely lost in English (Peter ≠ rock). Josephus similarly gave a rhyming pun on *Essenoi* that suggests its derivation from the word *semnotes,* meaning "sanctity" or "solemnity" (*War* 2.119–20). But Philo, although he likewise wrote in Greek, derived *Essaioi* from the word *hosiotes,* meaning "holiness" (*Every Good Man Is Free,* 75). Based on these and similar slight disagreements, hypercritical scholars questioned whether the classical historians knew the underlying derivation or were guessing. So many scholars felt free to offer their own guesses—educated guesses usually based on some practice known to the Essenes, but guesses nonetheless. Among the more creative examples are Gräetz, who suggested *assai,* meaning "bathers," and Vermes, who suggested *assayya,* meaning "healers."[25]

Why create confusion where none exists? If we place some faith, as we must, in the scholastic integrity of those who have gone before us, we see that Josephus and Philo were trying to translate as best they could from the original Semitic (which was especially difficult for Philo, as it is fairly clear from his writings that he did not know Hebrew or Aramaic). Do not present-day translators offer slightly different biblical translations, even where they are in complete agreement on the original Hebrew or Greek? The same underlying concept or thesaurus-like "word-field" is captured as consistently among Josephus, Philo, and the other classical historians as we could wish. There is no justifiable reason to go beyond their work on this subject. Clearly the Essenes derived their name from and were known as the "holy" or the "sanctified." Within the same word-field, it is not difficult to imagine that they were known as the "pious," sometimes translated in the Bible as the "faithful ones" or "saints" (1 Sam 2:9a; Ps 30:4a).

It is the last derivation that finally allows us to translate back into the Semitic. The work has already been done. Nearly a hundred years ago, an excellent scholar named Ginsburg collected more than twenty possible derivations from various scholars and concluded that the most logical was the Aramaic *hsa,* whose plural is *hysn,* the equivalent of the Hebrew *hasid,* usually translated as "the pious."[26] Several nineteenth-century scholars had independently arrived at this conclusion—most notably Emil Schürer—and it is still the reigning view. The only apparent weakness of the derivation is that *hysn,* the plural of *hsa,* never occurs in Palestinian Aramaic, but only in Syrian Aramaic, the first Yiddish, the Jewish language of the Persian exile. Yet, as we are about to see, this is hardly a weakness. It only stands to reason that the Essenes originally drew their name from Syrian Aramaic, for it is during the Persian exile that they first emerged.

17 THE SCRIBES EMERGE AS AN ORDER

Etymology alone does not give us a full understanding of the scribes of the late exilic period, the period in which the scribes arose as a recognizable order. For a full understanding, we need to review our history. In approximately 586 BCE, Solomon's first Temple was destroyed and Judah became a *diaspora,* a conquered nation living in exile. Forced to live in Persia, a land where first the Zoroastrian and later the Greek religions flourished, the diaspora faced a serious crisis. Judaism was threatened with extinction due to *syncretism,* the joining together and compromising of diverse ideologies. Thus began a long struggle in which pious Jews resisted their oppressors in order to maintain their religious identity, such as Daniel, who refused to defile himself by eating unclean foods (Dan 1). Then there arose Ezra, "a scribe skilled in the law of Moses" (Ezra 7:6b). Ezra almost single-handedly revived Judaism during the exile by resorting to rigid fundamentalism. Precision in observance of *mishnot,* such as circumcision, honoring the Sabbath, kosher laws, and the like, became the absolute measure of piety. To supply the interpretations necessary for a fundamentalist religion, and to translate the Hebrew Scriptures into Aramaic, an order arose within the diaspora known as "scribes."* Like the prototype scribe, Ezra, this order was dedicated to the study of law as a profession.

The duties of the first-century scribes were similar to those of the pre-exilic scribes, although of greater importance. Their scriptural expertise gave them immense political power, as you would expect in a theocracy. The first scribe identified in the Old Testament is Deborah, who was a muster officer (one who takes an account of troops and their equipment) (Jg 5:14). The chief scribe of the Jerusalem court was a high cabinet officer concerned with finance, policy, and administration (2 Kg 22; Jer 36:10). We read that Jeremiah had a scribe named Baruch who recorded all his words (Jer 36:32). The previous verses generally characterize the scribes of the Old Testament. They were officers of the court, officers of the Temple, or secretaries. But by the time of Ezra, the scribe had taken on so many additional responsibilities that the scribes were no longer humble secretaries. They had become a full-blown order that was the stabilizing force of a theocratic society, similar to the Mullahs in contemporary Muslim countries.

We find a lengthy discourse on the scribes in the apocryphal Book of Sirach. There we find descriptions of their lifestyle and duties, several of which already bear great similarity to those of the Essenes. According to Sirach, "The wisdom of the scribe depends on the opportunity of leisure" (Sir 38:24a). This points to increasing stratification within Jewish society, suggesting that the scribes were the upper class. However, this need not have been the case. Leisure time could have been provided by the well-known Essene practice of communism. At some point, we know certain Essenes began living in communes or monasteries (*War* 2.122). A monastic lifestyle affords a great deal of leisure time. Moreover, Sirach wrote, "[The scribe] will seek out the wisdom of the ancients and be concerned with prophecies. . . . He will seek out

---

*Emil Schürer drew this conclusion, calling the scribes a separate "order." See his *History of the Jewish People in the Time of Jesus* (New York: Schocken, 1961), 13–21.

the hidden meaning of proverbs and be at home with the obscurities of parables" (Sir 39:1–3).

The preoccupation with Scriptures and their esoteric meaning is a well-documented Essene trait (*War* 2.136). Sirach continues, "[The scribe] will set his heart to rise early to seek the Lord who made him" (39:5a). According to Josephus (*War* 2.128), the Essenes were known to arise before sunset and pray toward the sun (*eis*), a practice that scholars once believed to be sun worship. Clearly we are beginning to see that traits and duties of the Old Testament scribes were maintained by the Essenes.

18 THE PIOUS/HASIDEANS ARE THE SCRIBES

As we just saw from the Book of Sirach, a great deal of historical information can be gleaned about the Essenes from a collection of books known as the Apocrypha.* In both First and Second Maccabees, we find the first references to a group known as the "Hasideans." In 1 Maccabees, the Hasideans come to the aid of Matthias, a Jew who lived in the difficult time when Israel had been conquered by Alexander the Great and the Jews driven into exile. Greek culture had penetrated deeply into Palestine, and Judaism was nearly swept from the face of the earth. Matthias responded by leading a revolt against the foreign influence: "Then Matthias cried out in the city with a loud voice, saying: 'Let everyone who is zealous for the law and supports the covenant come out with me!' And he and his sons fled to the hills and left all that they had in the city" (1 Macc 2:27–28). And the Hasideans came to his aid:

> Then there united with them a company of Hasideans, mighty
> warriors of Israel, every one who offered himself willingly for the

---

*The biblical canon recognized by the Roman Catholics is the Douay-Rheims version, consisting of seventy-three books including the Apocrypha. The Apocrypha is recognized by the Greek Orthodox and most Anabaptists too. Mainstream Protestants, however, recognize only the sixty-six books approved by the Archbishop of Canterbury in 1885, known today as the Authorized King James version.

law. . . . They organized an army, and struck down sinners in their wrath; the survivors fled to the Gentiles for their safety. And Matthias and his friends went about and tore down the altars; they forcibly circumcised all the uncircumcised boys that they found within the borders of Israel. They hunted down the arrogant men, and the work prospered in their hands. They rescued the law out of the hands of the Gentiles and kings, and they never let the sinner grab the upper hand. (1 Macc 2:42–48)

Thus the Hasideans emerge on the scene as the strict protectors of the law from the beginning, inflicting exactly the same Jew-on-Jew hatred that we later find in the Essenes. Any Jew not strictly following the law was put to death.

In 1 Maccabees 7, we find further reference to the Hasideans. A group of Jews appeared before the high priest Alcimus and Bacchides, friend of the king Demetrius: "Then *a group of scribes* appeared in a body before Alcimus and Bachides to ask for just terms. The *Hasideans were the first among the sons of Israel* to seek peace from them" (1 Macc 7:12–13a, my emphasis). The editors of *The New Oxford Annotated Bible with the Apocrypha: Revised Standard Version* comment of this text, "The Hasideans (2:42) [are] probably the same as the group of scribes."[27] We are indeed looking at the same group. And this identification points directly to the Essenes, as leading Scrolls scholars have already recognized. None other than Geza Vermes wrote, "It is the Hasidim of the pre-Maccabean and early Maccabean era who best correspond to the earlier and unorganized group [of Essenes] as it is described there."[28]

19 THE CURIOUS COPPER SCROLL EXPLAINED

The scribal duty to oversee finance, in particular, best explains the most curious finding in the Qumran library, the Copper Scroll (3Q15). Written on a sheet of pure copper, the scroll lists more than sixty locations of hidden treasure, an amount so incredible that many Scrolls scholars have taken it to be figurative. That is, they believe this scroll's descriptions of gold, silver, and the like are similar to the spectacular poetry of the mystical Merkabah literature. But other scholars take the descriptions of treasure literally. One scholar concluded that the Copper Scroll must have been a record of the annual tithe.[29] To me, this seems the only reasonable explanation, especially in light of this recent identification of the Essene Scrolls authors as the scribes. According to Nehemiah, a scribe named Zadok was appointed "treasurer of the storehouse" (Neh 13:13). Apparently the Essenes, the "sons of Zadok" (1Q28b III 22), were descendants of those very same scribes.

20 THE SCRIBES ARE THE ESSENES

There is much confusion that remains in this identification, but one thing is clear: The Hasideans are nowhere found in the New Testament, nor can we find references to their extinction in the Apocrypha or any other historical writings prior to the first century. The Hasideans are noticeably absent from Josephus; not one single reference to them ever appears in his writings. He does, however, mention the Essenes as early as the time when Jonathan was high priest (*Ant* 13.171), and numerous times afterward. Where, then, did the Hasideans go? Did they leap off the face of the earth? No, they simply took on different names. The Hasideans were called Essenes by Josephus and other historians, and the Apocrypha and Gospel writers called them by their generic title, scribes.

An example of how an order's name can be made generic is shown by present-day references to the Franciscan monks. Although there are many orders of monks—Benedictine, Franciscan, Dominican, to name a few—the generic designation "monks" has come to replace the "Franciscans" in common usage. Apparently the generic reference to the Hasideans as scribes in 1 Maccabees 7:12–13 was similarly adopted by the Gospel writers. I point out that I am not engaging in wholesale speculation, merely attempting to correct what Scrolls scholar Robert Eisenman called a "distinct failure in criticism."[30] This failure has been the inability to recognize the highly amorphous nature of intertestamental Jewish orders.

Eisenman noted that "terms like: *Ebionim, Nozirim Hassidim, Zaddikim* . . . [these] turn out to be variations on the same theme,"[31] namely, amorphous references to the Essenes. We must recognize not only that Essenes could have taken on different names under various translators; we must also recognize that the Essenes may have actually changed names at some point during their history. This is what makes identifying the Essenes so difficult. By gospel times, the common people must have known and referred to the Essenes as scribes, as they were called in 1 Maccabees.

21 AN EXEGESIS SHOWING THE NEW TESTAMENT SCRIBES ARE THE ESSENES

The scribes appear more than fifty times in the four Gospels alone. A complete exegesis of each and every reference, though surely productive, would exhaust the patience of both author and reader and extend beyond the scope of this work. Thus I will cover only those that correlate the scribes and Essenes the most strongly and leave the systematic exegesis up to the next soul who cares to follow this work.

A Common Messianic Expectation
Unlike most Jewish groups of the first century, the Essenes believed in and eagerly awaited the immediate arrival of "the Messiah."[32] At least one Dead Sea Scroll verse seems to speak of an expected Messiah who will "heal the sick, resurrect the dead, and to the poor announce glad tidings," a passage Jesus quoted nearly verbatim (4Q521 II, 12; Mt 11:4–5 // Lk 7:22–23).[33] It does seem, however, that the Essenes were slow in settling on the idea of a single messianic figure as ultimately did the Christians. Most scholars have noted that the Scrolls speak of

either two[34] or three[35] messianic figures or, as I hold, one King Messiah and two forerunners known as the Prophet and the Priest. This King Messiah, otherwise known as the "Branch of David" or the "Messiah of Israel," was to usher in "the Kingdom of his people" (1Q28b V, 21–25). The parallels with Jesus's self-awareness are striking. The Gospels present Jesus as a direct descendant of King David and maintain that he rightfully laid claim to David's title. Let us not, at this point, take up the ultimate differences in Christian and Essene messianic expectations and their fulfillment, differences that did exist. What is important here is merely that the Scrolls show an Essene preoccupation with Davidic Messiah prophecies. It is the very same preoccupation that the scribes exhibit in the Gospels.

As befitting their title and office, the Essenes/scribes commonly engaged Jesus in dialogues on the fine points of Scripture. On at least one occasion, Jesus engaged his inquisitors in an enigmatic dialogue. According to Mark, Jesus asked: "How can the scribes say that the Christ is son of David? David himself, inspired by the Holy Spirit, declared, 'The Lord said to my Lord, Sit at my right hand, til I put thy enemies under thy feet.' David himself calls him Lord; so how is he his son?" (12:35–37a; cf. Rev 22:16). This passage is paralleled in the other Gospels. Matthew's version shows Jesus addressing only the Pharisees, apparently collapsing the scribes into the Pharisees, as was his custom (22:41). Luke's version shows that Jesus addressed his query directly to the scribes (20:39, 41). Yet whomever Jesus addressed, the point here is that his question notes a scribal messianic concern. The Essenes/scribes had interpreted the Messiah (the Gospel reference to "Christ" is a Greek term) just as did the Scrolls authors, as the "Branch of David." "Branch" means offspring or son (4Q285 v; cf. Mk 12:35).

Elijah as Messianic Forerunner

Again and again the scribes appear in the Gospel narratives as the strongest interpreters and guardians of messianic prophecies. They were sort of a roving scriptural police whose influence, even in their absence, was felt within the circles in which Jesus moved. During an episode known as the Transfiguration, Jesus's disciples were concerned that, according to the scribes, Elijah must precede Jesus if Jesus was to be the true Messiah (Mk 9:11). Jesus replied that indeed the scribes were correct: Elijah had already come in the person of John the Baptist (Mt 11:13–15; 17:11–13; Lk 1:17). It is no wonder that the Essenes/scribes were concerned about Elijah, for the identification of Elijah as John the Baptist was critical not only to Jesus's messianic awareness but also to the objective showing that prophecy was fulfilled. Any Jewish family who still takes the prophets seriously should understand their concern. Malachi prophesied that Elijah would precede the Messiah (Mal 4:5). Therefore, down to this day, a place has been set at the Passover table and the door left ajar awaiting Elijah's literal return. He is the "expected guest."

John's Gospel records that the Baptizer fulfilled the prophetic role of Elijah by proclaiming Jesus as the Messiah (Jn 1:36). Jesus had to rely upon his kinsman John's proclamation, for the Bible strictly prohibits the Messiah from proclaiming himself (see paragraph below); only God can do so via his angels or prophets. The Essenes/scribes, well aware that the true Messiah could not proclaim himself, continually tried to force Jesus into this trap (e.g., Jn 8:13–18). If he ever once openly proclaimed himself, Jesus would have shown unmistakably that he was not the Messiah his followers were claiming him to be. This was the Essenes/scribes' strongest line of defense against a false Messiah. This was a grueling game of cat and mouse. Jesus held out to the bitter end, even though it cost him his life. He could defend himself only by resorting to John's proclamation, which, fatal to their acceptance of Jesus, the Essenes/scribes never recognized (Mk 11:27–33 // Mt 21:23–27 // Lk 20:1–8).

This point is worthy of digression. Read carefully 2 Samuel 7:12–14; Psalms 2:7; also Peter's confession, Matthew 16:15–20. Would-be Christian followers of another fanatic such as David Koresh, the leader of the suicidal Branch Davidian cult in Waco, Texas, are highly encouraged to read these Scriptures to the letter. "And Jesus began to say to them, 'Take heed that no one leads you astray. Many will come in my name, saying, "I am he!" and he will lead many astray'" (Mk 13:5–6). "If I bear witness of myself, my testimony is not true" (Jn 5:31). Jesus never once openly proclaimed himself the Christ,* nor would he ever do so upon his return. If anyone says, as did the misguided gentleman from Waco, "I am Jesus Christ," he has just shown unmistakably that he cannot be who he claims, regardless of his seductive doctrine. In this context, the divine wisdom behind the demand for messianic silence should be self-evident. The real Messiah must show himself by unmistakable holiness and angelic proclamation.

The self-awareness of Jesus has long been debated. It is thought that since the Gospels never record a direct and unsolicited statement of Jesus such as "I am the Christ," he possessed no messianic awareness. On the contrary, Jesus well knew himself and his mission. But he also knew that he was forced to live in a lonely state of concealment, perhaps even in his own home (see my closing comments to chapter 6). When all of Jesus's statements are read with the understanding that Scripture strictly prohibited him from proclaiming himself, Jesus's self-awareness is powerfully evident. The Gospels continually report that Jesus tried to reveal himself by the only means left at his disposal: by the Socratic method—indirect questioning and logic, letting the listener form his or her own conclusions.†

---

*One notable exception is where John records Jesus revealing himself to the Samaritan women at the well (Jn 4:25–26). This was not an open revelation, however, as the listeners were both women and foreigners; thus there was no fear of them passing this information along to Jewish authorities. Ironically, the people who knew Jesus least were probably those with whom he could most easily let down his guard and share his messianic secret.

†See Martin Buber, *Two Types of Faith* (New York: Collier, 1951), 31, 102, 107f. Rudolf Otto also has made great study of the fact that Jesus spoke of himself in "solemn circumlocution," the third person removed. See Otto's *The Kingdom of God and the Son of Man* (Boston: Star King Press, 1957) bk. 1 ch. 17, bk. 2 chs. 6, 8; also James H. Charlesworth, *Jesus Within Judaism* (New York: Anchor-Doubleday, 1988) ch. 6.

"Woe to the Scribes": A Rebuke of Essene Self-righteousness and Lack of Compassion

Matthew devotes the entire twenty-third chapter of his Gospel to an impromptu sermon in which Jesus scathingly rebuked the scribes and Pharisees. Although we must remember that the scribes and Pharisees were intimately linked, there are enough distinctive references to the scribes alone that we can correlate them to the Essenes: "They bind heavy burdens, hard to bear, and lay them on men's shoulders; but they themselves will not lift a finger to move them" (Mt 23:4). Although the Pharisees equally suffered Jesus's criticism, they were lax in legalism by comparison with the Essenes, the scribes in the above passage.

For the reader already familiar with the Scrolls, it is hardly worth mentioning that the most defining characteristic of the Essenes was their rigorous observance of the Torah. For the uninitiated, I suggest a scan of the opening pages of Geza Vermes's *The Complete Dead Sea Scrolls in English*. You will be awed that such a rigidly legalistic and ascetic order ever existed. They make the early New England Puritans seem like slackers. That the Essenes "[bound] heavy burdens" is shown in their numerous statutes in which the Essenes codified the Torah, in addition to which they developed rigid and extensive purity laws now known as *halakhah* (4Q512). That the Essenes "themselves [would] not lift a finger to move" these heavy burdens is also easily shown. Jesus taught us as his disciples to bear one another's burdens (Jn 13:1–15). The Essenes, in contrast, stood absolutely alone against sin. The Essenes' only group support was the fear of harsh penalties inflicted by his fellows if he stumbled (1QS VI, 24–VII, 25; *War* 2.145). Josephus recorded the full measure of compassion the Essenes had for one another. A wretched sinner might be lucky enough to be rescued before dying of forced starvation, for the Essenes sometimes "deem[ed] that torments which have brought them to the verge of death are a sufficient penalty for their misdoings" (*War* 2.144).

A Rebuke of Essene Hierarchy and Formality

"They love the places of honor at feasts and the best seats in the syna-gogues, and salutations in the market places, and being called Rabbi by men" (Mt 23:6–7). The Pharisees and Essenes almost always trav-eled together in the Gospels. Thus I would be hard pressed to distin-guish the Essenes' love of hierarchy from that of the Pharisees, but one must certainly recognize that Jesus here criticized a characteristic trait also of the Essenes. The Essenes were a priestly sect of absolutely rigid hierarchy. Even among themselves, "the Priests [sat] first, and the elders second, and all the rest of the people according to their rank" (1QS VI, 8–9). The sort of hierarchy that depended solely upon one's lineage or caste would have been anathema to Jesus. Jesus taught that honor is bestowed purely by God's grace, not by birthright (Lk 14:7–14). Furthermore, Jesus was of the House of Judah, not that of Levi or Aaron. In taking the role of rabbi upon himself, Jesus rejected not merely a social order, but the entire succession of the Levitical priest-hood (Mt 23:8–10; Lk 6:39–40; Heb 4:14–7:28).

A Rebuke of the Essene Proselyte System

"Woe to you scribes and Pharisees, hypocrites! for you traverse sea and land to make a single proselyte, and when he becomes a proselyte, you make him twice as much a child of hell as yourself" (Mt 23:15). This harsh language by Jesus was again more than likely aimed at the Essenes rather than the Pharisees. Since the Essenes were the only Jews who practiced celibacy and therefore could not replenish themselves easily, logically they were compelled to "traverse land and sea to make a single proselyte." And indeed, Josephus reports that the Essenes replen-ished themselves by prostelytizing children (*War* 2.120). Moreover, Josephus reports, and the Scrolls confirm, a two- or three-year* detailed

---

*It is disputed among scholars whether the Essenes were proselytes for two or three years. See the article on the Essenes in *The Anchor Bible Dictionary*, vol. 2, 623.

admission procedure for the Essene proselyte (*War* 2.137–142; 1QS VI, 14–24). No similar procedure existed for the Pharisees, nor did Josephus ever specifically refer to Pharisee "proselytes" as he did with the Essenes (*War* 2.142). The Essenes were a closed and separatist order. Cut off from the rest of the world, their fanatical observance of the law only multiplied generation after generation. Thus they became "twice as much a child of hell" as their predecessors. The Pharisees, despite their name (Hebrew *Perushim* = separatists), were separatists only in governmental matters and were far less dogmatic. In contrast to the Essenes, the Pharisees, according to Josephus, "cultivat[ed] harmonious relations with the community" (*War* 2.166).

A Rebuke of the Essene Use of Oaths

Jesus preached the abolition of oaths (Mt 5:33–37), which would again seem to reflect his Essene upbringing. According to Josephus, "Everything [the Essenes] say is more certain than an oath. Indeed swearing is rejected by them as being more evil than perjury. For anyone who does not merit belief without calling on God is already condemned" (*War* 2.135). However, the "tremendous oaths" that the Essenes were to take upon admission to their order form a curious exception (*War* 2.139; 1QS V, 7–10). The justification for this inconsistency is found in the legalistic Essene interpretation of the Torah. The Essenes felt it sinful to take YHWH's divine name in vain (Lev 19:12). Swearing was allowed if absolutely necessary, but only by using surrogate terms so as to avoid uttering the divine name (for example, "Adonai"). Vermes notes that these surrogate terms, or *kinnuyim,* as rabbis later called them, were alluded to in the Damascus Document (CD XV, 1) and adopted by the Pharisees according to Matthew 23:16–22.[36] What Vermes failed to note is that the scribes were mentioned in this passage along with the Pharisees. Once again Jesus was condemning an Essene practice, for Jesus preached that the use of kinnuyim was hypocritical.

Woe to you blind guides, who say, "If any one swears by the Temple, it is nothing; but if any one swears by the gold of the Temple, he is bound by his oath." You blind fools! For which is greater, the gold or the Temple that has made the gold sacred? . . . So he who swears by the altar, swears by everything on it; and he who swears by the Temple, swears by everything in it; and he who swears by heaven, swears by the throne of God and by him who sits upon it. (Mt 23:16–22)

The heart of Jesus's message is that no oaths at all are necessary. A simple "yes" or "no" will suffice.

Sowing the Seeds of Wrath

There are additional correlations that show Jesus referred to the Essenes as scribes in this lengthy rebuke passage. Jesus went on to criticize the scribes and Pharisees ever more scathingly, citing them for their just appearances but inner hypocrisy. He compared them to "whitewashed tombs" full of "rotting corpses" (Mt 23:27). It is very possible that by "whitewashed" Jesus was alluding to the distinctive Essene dress. According to Josephus, the Essenes wore long white robes (*War* 2.137). *"Beware of the scribes who like to go about in long robes"* (Mk 12:38a, my emphasis). Finally, Jesus unleashed his ultimate rebuke, a warning mixed with insult and born of utter disgust: "Fill up, then, the full measure of your father, you serpents, you brood of vipers! How are you going to escape being sentenced to hell?" (Mt 23:32–33).

I cannot leave this lengthy passage of Matthew's Gospel without noting that this sort of open animosity on Jesus's part clearly shows the relationship between him and the Essenes was totally severed at this point. And, as one might imagine, the Essenes were equally infuriated with Jesus. Jesus furthered the rift, driving the Essenes/scribes to the point of rage when he drove the money changers from the Temple:

And they came to Jerusalem; and Jesus went into the Temple, and began to cast out those that bought and sold in the Temple, and overthrew the tables of the money changers. . . . The *scribes* and chief priests heard it and sought how they might destroy him, because the people were astonished at his doctrine. And when evening fully came, he left the city. . . . And [Jesus and the disciples] came again to Jerusalem; and as he was walking in the Temple, the chief priests, the *scribes*, and the elders approached him. And they said, "By what authority do you do these things?" (Mk 11:15–18, 27–28; my emphasis)

We find reference to the same Temple incident in the Scrolls, in a Habakkuk pesher (see chapter 3 for an explanation of pesher) where the Essenes/scribes spoke of Jesus as a "Wicked Priest":

Because of the blood of the city and the violence done to the land . . .
(Hab 2:17)
Interpreted, *the city* is Jerusalem where the Wicked Priest committed abominable deeds and defiled the Temple of God. (1QpHab XII, 7–9)

What finally became of this struggle? Predictably, the Gospels and Acts tell us that the scribes were key figures behind Jesus's crucifixion (Mk 14:1; 15:31; Lk 22:2, 66; 23:10; Acts 4:5, 10), which will be explored more fully in chapter 7. But first I must complete this process of identification.

22 WE HAVE ALL MISSED THE FOREST FOR THE TREES

If anything characterizes present Dead Sea Scrolls research, it is that scholars are exceptionally reluctant to form a general consensus behind any restoration that would correlate to Jesus and the gospel period. And politics and ideological commitments have only worsened the problem. Thus it would come as a great surprise to me if I were to pick up a newspaper and find that the entire community of scholars instantly accepted my restoration. Swift paradigm shifts are rare in academia. But you, the reader, need not wait for the experts to decide. The beauty of the hard-won academic freedom in Scrolls research is that anyone is free to research the Dead Sea Scrolls for themselves, to make up their own minds. For the lay reader and community of scholars alike, I have one final argument that will have to be reckoned with.

In Hebrew, the scribe was called a *soper* (plural *sopherim*), which comes from the Semitic root *spr*, originally meaning a written message that was sent, or "writing." Hence, a *soper* meant a "writer." In New Testament Greek, the scribes were called *grameteus,* which comes from the word *gramma,* likewise meaning something drawn, most commonly written letters.[37] What relevance, this? Forget the minutiae of texts for the moment. The entire corpus of the Qumran library *itself* is the most compelling reason we must identify the Essenes as the scribes of the Gospels. Unlike Jesus, who apparently wrote nothing, the Essenes were forever busy writing and copying. *That is why the relatively uneducated Gospel writers called them scribes,* as was probably the custom. Whatever other roles the scribes took on, their name *sopherim* implies, and is literally defined as, a group of writers.

The abundance of Jewish literature in the intertestamentary period has long been cited as evidence of the growing number of scribes. For example, in 1 Enoch, Enoch, the supposed author, is twice referred to as a scribe, as was Ben Sira and the prototype of the exilic scribe, Ezra (1 En 12:4; 15:1; see also Sir 38:24–39:11). We have all the more reason to accept that the Essenes were called scribes since these very texts were found at Qumran.* Moreover, there is handwriting evidence in

---

*In his article on the scribes, Saldarini made an interesting comment: "The scribal activity and separatist tendencies of the Enoch traditions were intensified . . . in the Qumran's community's traditions." *The Anchor Bible Dictionary,* vol. 5, 1013.

the Scrolls that should have put up a red flag years ago. That same evidence is more than sufficient to support the identification I now offer.

What is that evidence? Norman Golb, a Hebraist who has studied the Scrolls since the late 1960s, offers this astute observation:

> In the autumn of 1969, soon after personally examining the Khirbet Qumran site . . . I undertook a review of all the texts that had become available. Noticing that virtually each new one was in a handwriting different than all the others, I began to see that the growing number of scripts was starting to pose . . . a problem for [the de Vaux team's sectarian hypotheses, namely that all the Scrolls were produced at Qumran]: How many scribes, after all, could have lived together at Khirbet Qumran at any one time, or even over three or four generations? . . . With a total of over one hundred and fifty scribal handwritings already identifiable by the mid-1960s, it was evident that each new text being published was in a different hand than that of its predecessors. Meanwhile, by that time, several popular books by scholars who were part of Pére de Vaux's team— J. T. Milik, J. Allegro, and F. M. Cross—had appeared, all describing the fact that fragments of at least *four hundred* different compositions had been discovered in Cave 4. Assuming roughly the same ratio of handwritings to text in the unpublished scrolls as in those published, this would imply that there were as many as three to four hundred more scribal handwritings preserved among the Cave 4 manuscripts alone. If so, this would be a fact of the deepest significance. For by no stretch of the imagination could it be thought that, even over two centuries [the time allotted for the texts to have been produced at Qumran according to the de Vaux team], as many as four or five hundred scribes had worked in the room that de Vaux had so confidently labeled a "scriptorium.". . . If verified, this very large number of scribes would in itself require a different explanation.[38]

In Golb's view, so many scribes would have been required to produce the Dead Sea Scrolls that Qumran must have been something of a Judean "Library of Congress." I really doubt the Essenes shared their texts with other Jewish sects given their secretive nature (*War* 2.142). But what Golb's observation does suggest is two things. First, Qumran was a depository of texts produced elsewhere.* Second, if the Essenes were the primary if not sole producers of these texts, as I believe they were, then they were a *very* large scribal class, so large that we are now compelled to identify them as the scribes of the New Testament.

Let us look at this problem from another perspective. James H. Charlesworth noted how strange it is that a characteristic of the Essenes is never perceived, or is perhaps considered too obvious to mention. No similar library to Qumran has ever been found or is likely to be found in Israel, for "the Essenes," said he, "were the writing group in Early Judaism."[39] If a large library's worth of texts exists such as those found at Qumran, and if we know that the Essenes were the only writing group in early Judaism, then it follows that the perennial residents of Qumran, the Essenes, were the scribal class of the period. Knowing this, how could the Essenes have possibly been any other group than the scribes of the New Testament? If it were otherwise, if there were another equally large scribal class mentioned in the New Testament

---

*In addition to Golb's handwriting observation, several facts point me toward this view. One is that the events of chapter 7 took place in Capernaum, where the Teacher of Righteousness actually lived, not Qumran. Another is that I suspect Qumran changed hands between the Essenes and early Christians several times, though likely settling in the hands of the Essenes before the fall of Israel to the Romans in 74 CE. I believe that Saul/Paul's "Damascus" (Acts 9) was a pesher code name for Qumran. See Michael Baigent and Richard Leigh, *The Dead Sea Scrolls Deception* (New York: Touchstone, 1991), 146–49. Although Baigent and Leigh seem to have been the first to make the Paulinian connection, F. M. Cross and others of de Vaux's original editorial team first put forward "Damascus" as a pseudonym for the Qumran settlement. See Norman Golb, *Who Wrote the Dead Sea Scrolls?* 81–88.

but elsewhere unaccounted for, then we would expect to find another library rivaling Qumran, or at least the remnants of one.

Let us not stare so long at the trees that we fail to see the forest. Surely there is no reason to belabor the point further. By using bits and pieces of the work of virtually the entire community of Scrolls scholars, I have correctly identified the Essenes in the New Testament. From this point forward, the entire community of Scrolls scholars should join me in exploring the full implications of their own work.

3

Understanding the Essene Pesher Method

Most first-time readers of the Dead Sea Scrolls will be confused by its many scriptural commentaries, which are done in a style known as *pesher*. The word *pesher* (plural *pesharim*) is derived from the Hebrew *pishro,* meaning "its interpretation is." Exceptionally learned scholars have been confused by pesharim too. During the fourteen years it took for me to research and write this book, there were significant shifts in pesher methodology among Scrolls scholars. As James H. Charlesworth points out, the early tendency was to treat the pesharim as if they were straightforward Jewish histories like 1 Maccabees or Josephus's *War* and *Antiquities.*[1] This method proved to be fatally flawed, because most references to persons, places, and events recorded in pesharim were never intended to be read literally. So for the next twenty years, scholars generally called for a moratorium on historical interpretations of pesharim.

During this period, many advances were made in *hermeneutics*—the science of textual interpretation. Slowly but surely, the highly creative literary methods used in pesharim began to be understood. Consequently, we are now entering into a third phase, a "middle course," as Charlesworth put it, where a growing group of scholars believe that some historical data may be gleaned from pesharim, provided we keep in mind two things. First, historical references in pesharim must be decoded hermeneutically in order to make sense. Second, the history presented in pesharim must be seen from the author's point of view. Happily, Charlesworth and other Scrolls scholars are finally coming around to a methodology I discovered when I began this project.

What mainly characterizes Dead Sea Scrolls pesharim is that they are intensely apocalyptic. The Essenes believed that they were living at the end of the old age and at the beginning of a new age, at a time when all God's promises in the prophecies were due and owing. Thus, their pesharim focused upon the drama unfolding before their eyes, upon their heroes, their avenging angels, and their leader, whom they called the Teacher of Righteousness, as well as their enemies, including a man called the Wicked Priest or Man of a Lie. Since the Essenes understood themselves as the "elect," for whom the apocalypse was their own personal happening, they feared their pesharim would be discovered by the Greeks, the Romans, or any other opponents. They had good reason to fear, because most of their pesharim had a very militant tone.

The classical sources seemed to indicate that the Essenes were pacifists. For example, Philo records that the Essenes never trafficked in weapons (*Every Good Man Is Free,* 78). This is one of the main reasons that nineteenth-century historians, like Renan, concluded Christianity was an Essenism that survived. However, in *The Dead Sea Scrolls Deception,* authors Michael Baigent and Richard Leigh point out numerous difficulties with this notion.[2] Josephus reports that the Essenes were brutally tortured during the revolt against the Romans (*War* 2.152–53). Obviously the Romans considered them a threat. Moreover, the ruins of Qumran reveal a defensive tower and a probable forge; arrows have even been found there during excavations. Therefore some of the Essenes, at least, were much more closely related to the Zealots than the classical historians report. There was a spiritual dimension to their warfare, too. But it was never a wholly pacifist spiritual war, as the early Christians would soon wage. If the Essenes were not actively taking up the sword against the Greeks or Romans, it was because they were quietly biding their time until the long-awaited Messiah would help them deliver Israel from its occupiers with supernatural force. This, ironically, is the same view held by some misguided Christians today who think Jesus will engage in ethnic cleansing upon his return.

The War Scroll leaves no doubt that the Essene Scrolls authors were militant. It speaks of war between the "sons of light" (the Essenes) and "sons of darkness" (practically everyone else) in graphic detail (1QM). If the Essenes had written openly of war against Israel's occupiers, many Essenes would likely have been tried and executed for sedition if these texts were ever discovered. Accordingly, each pesher was written in a highly developed esoteric format. Some texts were written in code or mirror image. Yet even the commonly drafted texts are difficult to understand. The reason is that, like the terms "sons of light" and "sons of darkness" used in the War Scroll, one seldom finds real names in the Scrolls, either of persons, places, or events. This has led to confusion among even the ablest Scrolls scholars, which is why a plethora of interpretations has emerged.

But there is one point upon which we can all agree. Robert Eisenman wrote, "[Pesharim] usually involved a high degree of esotericism: [it drew from] a passage or some vocabulary from older texts like Isaiah, Nahum, Hosea, Habakkuk or Psalms, and it developed in the most intense and imaginative manner conceivable, relating it to the present life of the community, its heroes and enemies, and to the people of Israel."[3] To my knowledge, every respected scholar agrees with Eisenman that the pesharim found in the Scrolls referred to the *present* life of the Essene community. Although there is disagreement concerning what events or persons a particular pesher is referring to, if the accurate interpretation can be determined, it would fix the date of the writing of that pesher precisely. *This is very, very important.* Radiocarbon dating can reliably fix the date only within a time frame of a hundred years or so. Therefore, if the persons, places, and events referred to within a pesher have been incorrectly interpreted, its composition will be erroneously dated. This is how the Essenes' role in emergent Christianity has completely escaped most scholars.

23 THE FURIOUS YOUNG LION

The best way to get a feel for pesharim is to read some. The following pesharim are taken from the prophet Nahum:

> *The Lion tears enough for its cubs and it chokes prey for its lionesses.*
> (Nah 2:12a)
> Interpreted, this concerns the Furious Young Lion who strikes by means of his great men, and by means of the men of his council.

> [*And chokes prey for its lionesses; and it fills*] *its caves* [*with prey*] *and its dens with victims.* (Nah 2:12a–b)
> Interpreted, this concerns the Furious Young Lion [who executes revenge] on those who seek smooth things and hangs men alive, . . . formerly in Israel. Because of a man hanged alive upon [the] tree, He proclaims, *"Behold I am against* [*you, says the Lord of Hosts*]." (4Q169 3–4 I, 4–9)

The current consensus view is that the Furious Young Lion in the above pesharim refers to a tyrannical king named Alexander Jannaeus, who crucified eight hundred Pharisees while their wives and children were disemboweled before their dying eyes (*War* 1.96–98).[4] If this interpretation is correct, then the Nahum pesharim should be dated in the Hasmonean period, approximately 88 BCE, safely removed from Jesus and the gospel period. If, however, the Furious Young Lion were another, then the reference to the "seekers of smooth things" who followed a "man hanged alive upon [the] tree" should be carefully rethought. For reasons consistent with my entire restoration, I am convinced that the Furious Young Lion was persecuting Christians and that the "man hanged alive on [the] tree" was none other than Jesus. This puts me squarely in the dissident camp of scholars such as Barbara Thiering and Robert Eisenman, of which Geza Vermes offered this comment, "Only the sensation-seeking media have been taken in by their theories."[5]

It is unfortunate that these types of comments characterize much of consensus scholarship. If the main camp had resorted to fewer *ad hominem* arguments and stopped covering up their own anomalies, much more might have been accomplished through the years. One such anomaly was cited by the late Yigael Yadin, who held that the Essenes chose to write pesharim on Nahum, for it speaks not of the persecution of the Essenes, but of Essene persecution of *their* enemies, the "seekers of smooth things."[6]

24 PESHER AS SYMPATHETIC MAGIC

Yadin's interpretation is the right one. I say this not only because it fits within my overall restoration, but because he rightly picked up on the fact that the Book of Nahum has historically been used as inspiration in warfare against Israel's enemies. Yadin recognized this perhaps because, in addition to being an archaeologist like his father, he was also a military commander of Israel. Yadin was operations officer of the Haganah, and he devised and implemented many of the strategies used in the War of Independence. The Nahum pesharim speak of the utter annihilation of God's perceived enemies, just as the prophet Nahum spoke of the annihilation of the Assyrians almost seven hundred years earlier.

A theme is now presented that will prove very useful to explore. The Australian Scrolls scholar Barbara Thiering wrote:

The Scroll writer takes an Old Testament book such as the minor prophet Habakkuk, which deals with events in 600 BC, when armies of Babylonians were marching towards Judea, inspiring fear and terror. He goes through it verse by verse, and after quoting each passage adds "Its pesher is . . . ," then explains that it is really about events in his own time. The Babylonians stand for "Kittim," by which he means the Romans. Some Romans were currently marching across the land, inspiring fear and terror. Other verses, he says, refer to the Teacher of Righteousness and his troubles with the Wicked Priest/Man of a Lie.[7]

Thiering correctly perceived, as did Yadin, that what one finds in Scrolls pesharim is what anthropologists who study primitive religion refer to as the practice of *sympathetic magic.*

The term was coined by the anthropologist James Frazer in his famous work *The Golden Bough* (1922). Sympathetic magic usually involves some form of shamanic healing or fertility rites. One finds sympathetic magic in the Bible in the story of Rachel and Leah. Rachel, the wife of the patriarch Jacob, was barren and desperately wanted children. Leah, Jacob's other wife, had a houseful of children, one of whom, Reuben, was in possession of roots called "mandrakes." Mandrakes (known better today as gingerroots) resemble the human body, especially the male, and were therefore thought to bring the birth of a son. Rachel traded Leah a night with Jacob for her son's mandrakes and went on to have her first son (Gen 30:14). One should not be surprised to find sympathetic magic in the Bible, for ancient Judaism was in many respects little different from primitive religions still found throughout the world. The most common forms of sympathetic magic use roots or herbs, like the mandrakes, or a similar imitative object. For example, the Malay make wax figures imitative of a human subject. They believe that any action upon the wax figure will bring a resulting and similar action upon its human likeness. Though Scrolls pesharim have nothing to do with objects or charms, the more common practice, they involve sympathetic magic nonetheless. The underlying principle involved, said Frazer, is the "association of ideas by similarity," the idea that "like produces like."[8]

What makes Scrolls pesharim sympathetic magic is that when an Essene reads Scripture, he deeply believed that recorded events were meaningfully related to his own, and thus by understanding scriptural history, he could predict a current event's outcome. One could perhaps call their pesher method "divination" as well, since divination involves forecasting the future. Since the Essenes saw Scripture as the unfolding of God's plan, and since historians report and the Scrolls confirm that they were strict predeterminists (*Ant* 13.172; 1QS III, 13–25), they very likely saw their pesharim as divination. The Essenes were famous for predicting the future, according to the historians (*Ant* 15.371–79), and they were also famous for the scrutinizing of Scripture. One now sees how the two practices were related. The Essenes believed history was cyclical—not necessarily cycled in the literal sense, but cycled in the figurative or archetypal sense.* Future events were predictable if you were able to correlate present events with past events to know where you were in the cycle. Essene pesharim correlated seemingly unrelated cycles of history by means of sympathetic connection.

I realize how difficult it may be for the modern westerner to assimilate this material. It is difficult to free ourselves of the prejudice that sympathetic magic is nonsense. Even Frazer, who coined the term, could not break free of his ethnocentrism in his descriptions. He spoke of the associations made in sympathetic magic as "wholly irrational" and

---

*See Mircea Eliade, *The Myth of the Eternal Return* (Princeton, N.J.: Princeton University Press, 1971), especially ch. 3. Eliade did not specifically discuss the Essenes, for when he wrote this essay in 1949 the relevance of the Essenes to the Dead Sea Scrolls had not yet been established bringing the Essenes into scholarly focus. But he did discuss the ancient Hebrew, Babylonian, and Pythagorean traditions that made up the Essene milieu. The cyclical view of history, or the "repetition of archetypes," as Eliade worded it, ran strong in these traditions, a belief structure that survived even the dawn of messianic Judaism. Eliade wrote, "Under the 'pressure of history' and supported by the prophetic and messianic experience, a new interpretation of historical events dawns among the children of Israel. *Without finally renouncing the traditional concept of archetypes and repetitions,* Israel attempts to 'save' historical events by regarding them as active presences of Yahweh" (ibid., 106; my emphasis).

"spurious," a "disastrous fallacy."[9] But if we are ever to understand the pesharim literature of the Essenes, who lived in a completely different culture, in a time so different from our own, we have to place ourselves within their mind-set. Once we do, their pesharim will begin to make sense.

Subsequent to Frazer's publication of *The Golden Bough* (1922), the study of sympathetic magic reemerged in a guise more palatable to the westerner. Carl Jung introduced us to the study of *synchronicity,* the phenomenon of meaningful coincidence between an internal psychological event and an external objective event. Synchronicity involves the very same sort of mental working one finds in sympathetic magic. The "meaning" of the meaningful coincidence involves what Jung called "active imagination,"[10] whereby the mind associates persons, places, and events that have no rational connection whatsoever, at least according to our modern-day notions of science and causality. The Essene pesher method is very similar. Thus to unravel the contemporaneous events recorded in an Essene pesher, one must know the subjective mind of the Essene in order to know the wellspring of his imagination. And that basically means knowing their favorite Scripture, inside and out.

In many ways, the Essene pesher method comes quite naturally for me. Students of Origen, the third-century church father, will see many parallels. But long before I ever read Origen, I had already been exposed to an Essene-like pesher method in the Bible-belt South of my upbringing. In many grassroots Protestant churches, the eldest of the elders meet in elite Sunday school classes and are known by the figurative term "Bereans" (cf. Acts 17:10–11). With one eye on the current headlines and the other on the Bible (some have called this "newspaper exegesis"), the Bereans tediously study the prophecies looking for esoteric clues as to when, where, and how Christ will return.

As the reader might well imagine, pesher methods can go off upon the wildest allegorical speculations if left unchecked by reason. To make sense of Essene pesharim, one must think as the Essene thought, read the same literature as the Essene read, and with the same sharp eye for details. It is important to understand that the Essenes practiced a *pneumatic* theology. That is, their scriptural interpretations were, to their eyes, Spirit based, just as the New Testament authors likewise believed their scriptural interpretations were Spirit based.[11] Because both the Dead Sea Scrolls and New Testament authors often use the same terminology, the reader must be careful not to read back into an Essene pesher his or her own theology. If Essene messianic expectations were nationalistic, for example, one does great harm to the interpretation by trying to extrapolate Christian messianic ideas back into them. One also does great harm in searching out the Scrolls for excessively esoteric interpretations, such as one finds in Barbara Thiering's research.

Thiering has broken much ground for this work. Without her, I doubt many of the technical arguments for redating the Scrolls would have ever come forward. Although Thiering and I differ on a lot of details, such as the identification of the Righteous Teacher or the extent of Jesus's break with the Essenes, I am very much in agreement with her overall views. Yet I am not the only scholar who is uncomfortable with Thiering's pesher method. The problem is that instead of reconciling the Scrolls with the Gospels, she has often used the Scrolls to completely rewrite the Gospels. She has Jesus crucified at Qumran instead of Jerusalem, for example. And she also believes the Scrolls support a "Passover plot," the notion that Jesus was not raised from the dead but instead faked his own death. Thiering's work is blasphemy in the eyes of many Christians, and understandably so, because the resurrection is the central tenet of our faith. The idea of a Passover plot is nothing new. Due to the fact that the Gospels were written between forty and seventy years after Jesus's death, countless critics through the centuries have alleged that the resurrection was invented by the early Christians or Gospel writers. Ultimately, belief in the resurrection is a matter of faith, but it is not nearly the leap many suppose. What is often overlooked is that Paul was the first to document the resurrection, most scholars say just twenty years after the fact. Paul claims to have received his report directly from Peter and James, who were eyewitnesses

(1 Cor 15:3–7). And let us not forget the most outstanding fact of history. Hundreds of early Christians were put to death for their belief in the resurrection. They may have been deluded, but they could not possibly have been hypocrites. No one knowingly and willingly dies to perpetuate a lie.

Thiering is often guilty of interpreting the Scrolls and Gospels in what I would classify as a Gnostic manner, not necessarily in terms of Gnostic doctrines but in terms of the Gnostic hermeneutic method. Gnosticism was one of the greatest dangers that the Church ever faced. The Gnostics found unusually esoteric meanings in all the Scriptures and even offered versions of their own making, supposing themselves to have received secret revelations. As a defense against Gnosticism the canon was fixed; otherwise, we might have forever lost all reliable accounts of the historical Jesus. The New Testament is remarkably well preserved when compared with other ancient literature, and even from a purely scholastic viewpoint, it is highly trustworthy. I doubt Plato's writings could have withstood the scrutiny of Bultmann's form criticism as successfully as did the New Testament. The heavily edited and reedited Gnostic literature could not have withstood Bultmann at all. Granted, I do, as do many biblical scholars, recognize some spiritual and historical validity in literature not found in the orthodox canon. For example, I am perfectly comfortable endorsing the collection of books known as the Apocrypha and many works of Pseudepigrapha. The point is that one should not rewrite the cannon to make sense of Essene pesharim. Essene pesharim is indeed highly esoteric, but there is an objective rationale to it. Its sympathetic associations are very reasonable and easy to understand once we grasp Essene ideological commitments. Because many scrolls were written from the perspective of Jesus's enemies, naturally one would not expect to find support for the resurrection. But they do harmonize with the Gospels and Acts in that they give us the reverse perspective on many of the same events.

25 INTERPRETING THE NAHUM PESHARIM

Let us look at a few key examples. The Nahum pesharim describe a struggle between two figures called the Teacher of Righteousness and the Wicked Priest. Scholars are in agreement that the Teacher of Righteousness was the leader of the Essenes, but so far only a few of us agree that the Wicked Priest was Jesus. When one uncovers the true meaning of the Nahum pesharim, this identification will become undeniably clear. It is obvious from the texts themselves that the Nahum pesharim concern events immediately following the struggle between the Teacher of Righteousness and the Wicked Priest. The Nahum pesharim speak of enemies of the Essenes known as Manesseh and Ephraim. I hold that these esoteric names refer to the followers of Jesus and, as Robert Eisenman discovered, his half-brother James. Manesseh and Ephraim did not, as the majority of scholars now believe, refer to Pharisees and Sadducees, a conclusion that must logically follow if the Furious Young Lion is identified as Alexander Jannaeus, as I covered earlier.

Consistent with the misdating of the Habakkuk Commentary in the Hasmonean period, and therefore the misdating of Wicked Priest and Teacher of Righteousness, another key figure in the Scrolls has been misdated by the consensus of Scrolls scholars. The Nahum Commentary (4Q169) describe an era immediately following the struggle between the Wicked Priest and the Righteous Teacher. The principal character therein is called the Furious Young Lion, who executed judgment upon the "seekers of smooth things" by "hanging men alive," an obvious reference to crucifixion. The Furious Young Lion was also designated as one of the "last Priests," which should be interpreted as meaning one of the last priests of the true Jerusalem in the Essene scheme of eschatology (4Q167 ii). Unfortunately, this is not how consensus scholars have interpreted the Furious Young Lion. In the attempt to show that the Nahum pesharim were written concerning events in the late Hasmonean period, Geza Vermes, among many others, interpreted the Furious Young Lion as one of the Hasmonean priests who reigned from 134 to 63 BCE. Said Vermes, "There can be little doubt that the 'Furious Young Lion' . . . was one of [the Hasmonean priests], namely Alexander Jannaeus."[12] Jannaeus would, at first glance, seem to fit the bill, for in 88 BCE he had eight hundred Pharisees crucified "and their wives and children butchered before their very eyes, while he looked on, drinking, with his concubines reclining beside him" (*War* 1.96–98).

One may equate references to the Furious Young Lion in the Psalm and Nahum pesharim to find that his opposition, the "seekers of smooth things," are also given the cryptic reference "Manneseh" and "Ephraim." In the attempt to build his reconstruction of the Furious Young Lion as Alexander Jannaeus, Vermes interprets Manneseh and Ephraim as enemies of the Essenes, which is quite correct. But he then proceeds to interpret the Manneseh and Ephraim, respectively, as the Sadducees and the Pharisees, which is in error.[13] This misinterpretation has seriously clouded the understanding of the relationship of the Essenes to the other groups. The names Manneseh and Ephraim do not refer just to groups *per se,* but to actual persons and their followers, as I will discuss shortly. But first, I must determine the enemies of the Furious Young Lion as a general class.

26 UNACCEPTABLE ANOMALIES

The consensus view must be overturned. It must be overturned not only because 1QpHab and 4Q169 must be redated during the Herodian period, consistent with my identification of the Essenes as the scribes of the New Testament in chapter 2, but also because of internal and external inconsistencies that, upon closer examination, fail to square with specific texts of Nahum pesharim. The pesher that shows the biggest anomaly is the following:

[*And chokes prey for its lionesses; and it fills*] *its caves* [*with prey*] *and its dens with victims.* (Nah 2:12a–b)

Interpreted, this concerns the Furious Young Lion [who executes revenge] on those who seek smooth things and hangs men alive, . . . formerly in Israel. Because of a man hanged alive on [the] tree, He proclaims, "*Behold I am against [you, says the Lord of Hosts].*" (4Q1693–4 I, 4–9)

The code name "Furious Young Lion" is thus drawn from the prophetical language of the Book of Nahum itself. Before we can understand this pesher of a brief passage in Nahum, and the role of the Furious Young Lion therein, we need to understand the Book of Nahum as a whole.

The Book of Nahum was written between roughly 626 and 612 BCE as a triumphal ode predicting the overthrow of Nineveh by Israel. The Assyrians had dominated the Near East for centuries. With the fall of Nineveh, Assyrian domination seemed to be ended at last. Nahum penned a graphic picture of Nineveh's utter destruction at the hand of God, for, according to Nahum, Nineveh was deserving of God's wrath for its many sins against Israel. That is why the Furious Young Lion in the above pesher should not be understood as an *outside* enemy, a harbinger of doom *against* God's nation. Rather, the Furious Young Lion must be understood as the instrument *of* God's wrath *upon* his enemies. The Essenes believed themselves to be the true Israel. By invoking the prophecies of Nahum, the Essenes found justification and inspiration for utterly destroying those whom they perceived to be God's enemies. Thus, the Furious Young Lion cannot be viewed as an enemy of the Essenes. He must be an Essene himself or an agent friendly to the Essenes. He certainly cannot have been Alexander Jannaeus, the Hasmonean Priest. The Hasmonean were hellenizers, corrupters of Judaism whom the Essenes had vigorously opposed since Maccabean times.

Note the following pesher, which appears directly before The Furious Young lion pesher in the Nahum Commentary manuscript:

Whither the lion goes, there is the lion's cub, [with none to disturb it].
(Nah 2:11b)
Interpreted, [this concerns Deme]trius king of Greece who sought,
on the counsel of those who seek smooth things, to enter Jerusalem.
[But God did not permit the city to be delivered] into the hands
of the kings of Greece, from the time of Antiochus until the coming
of the rulers of the Kittim. But then she shall be trampled under
their feet. (4Q169 3–4 I, 1–3)

The references to the Seleucid kings Demetrius and Antiochus are rare
instances where the Essenes depart from their cryptic writing style
and actually use historical names (likely Demetrius III Eucaerus, d. 88
BCE, and Antiochus XIII Asiaticus, d. 64 BCE). But note the reference to the Kittim in the last line. Why did the author bother to use
an esoteric reference here when he spoke openly of the Greeks earlier?
It stands to reason that the Kittim were the next occupying power of
Israel, the Romans. The Greeks were gone at this point, so there was no
need for the clandestine reference; the Romans were the new military
threat. The reason the author chose the Kittim reference is because the
Romans, like the Greeks, were a great western sea power, and Numbers
24:24 predicts that the Kittim, a great western sea power, will be
destroyed. The author was prophesying that the Romans would fail in
their conquest of Israel, just as the Greeks did (this is a good example of the sympathetic magic "like produces like" aspect of the Essene
pesher method).

Thus, by using these internal references, we may fix the date of
this and related pesharim concerning the Furious Young Lion within
an exact chronological window. The first Roman to occupy Israel was
Pompey in 63 BCE (*War* 1.19–29, 141–58). Therefore, if Vermes has
translated the tenses correctly in the Nahum pesharim, the current consensus view results in an anachronism. The Nahum pesharim generally
speak of the Furious Young Lion in the present tense, which must place

him at a *later* date than the Roman occupation, for the latter event is spoken of in the past perfect tense. Yet Alexander Jannaeus died in approximately 76 BCE, seven years *before* Pompey's occupation (*War* 1.106). Furthermore, to reconcile the two above pesharim, the "seekers-of-smooth-things" must be hellenizers sympathetic to King Demetrius or a similar group. A Hasmonean priest cannot very well have persecuted himself, could he? Nor can one suppose that the enemies of the Furious Young Lion were the eight hundred crucified Pharisees who were devoutly Orthodox Jews, not Hellenists. The "seekers of smooth things" must be understood in a more general sense. In the Nahum and other pesharim, they must be understood ideologically as recurring enemies of pious Judaism, as any person or group who strayed from Essene fundamentalism. That is why the individual "seeker of smooth things," and also the Wicked Priest of the Habakkuk pesharim, referred to Jesus. Since the Nahum pesharim describe an era immediately after the Wicked Priest, its references to the "seekers of smooth things" refer to the early Christian Church.

Sure enough, if one carefully reexamines the Nahum pesher I have been analyzing, there is a reference which points without a doubt to the early Christians: "Because of a man hanged alive on [the] tree, He proclaims, *'Behold I am against [you, says the Lord of Hosts]'*" (4Q169 3–4 I, 7–8). Before the verse *"Behold I am against you . . ."* (Nah 2:12), the Essenes inserted their own interpretation that God was against the "seekers of smooth things" because they followed "a man hanged alive on [the] tree." Note that it was a *single* man hanged alive upon a tree. This is another significant anomaly that in and of itself should cause the consensus view to fail. Jannaeus crucified eight hundred men, not just one. When in the course of Israel's history has there ever been a significant group of followers of a single crucified leader other than the Christians? The above pesher also gives us a powerful reason why the Furious Young Lion would have persecuted the early Christians. To first-century Jews, belief in a crucified Messiah was not only a dangerous superstition, it was blasphemy: "for a hanged man is accursed by God" (Dt 21:23a).

27 WHO IS THE FURIOUS YOUNG LION?

Is there now sufficient information for identifying the Furious Young Lion of the Nahum pesharim? Let us look at what we know. He must have been an Essene, an Essene proselyte, or somehow a close ally of the Essenes, possibly a Pharisee. He must have viewed the early Christian movement from a pious Jewish point of view, must have thought the belief in a crucified Messiah to have been blasphemy, and must have persecuted the early Christians shortly after Jesus's time on earth. Also, he would doubtless have been antagonized by the Greek-speaking element of the early Jewish-Christians, the "seekers of smooth things" and traditional enemies of the Essenes. Stephen, the foremost of the hellenized Jewish-Christians, would have particularly incensed him (cf. Acts 6–7). Finally, it is quite reasonable to expect, given the numerous references to his persecution of the Christians in the Scrolls, that references to this young man would also have appeared in the Book of Acts, the New Testament history of the early Church. Could the Furious Young Lion have been Saul of Tarsus, also known as Paul after his conversion? He seems to fit the facts. The pesher rationale might have been his name. The name Saul would have evoked a sympathetic association with King Saul, who, at the outset of his reign, was the archetypal Furious Young Lion (1 Sam 13).

28 PAUL'S "DAMASCUS"

Thiering has hypothesized that the authors of the New Testament continued in the esoteric Essene pesher tradition. If she is right, and I believe a strong case can be made that she is (but within reason: I think Thiering sometimes goes too far and forces esoteric interpretations where they do not belong), then there is a geographical reference in the Bible that needs rethinking. In Acts, Paul, or Saul as he was then called, was en route to Damascus to persecute Christians when he was converted. He then spends three years at Damascus in prayer and meditation. For centuries, New Testament scholars have assumed that this Damascus should be read literally, that Luke was referring to the city in Syria. But this interpretation has never made much sense. Syria was a Roman province at the time. And if Paul were on his way there to murder Syrian citizens, he likely would have met with a Roman sword, especially since he was traveling solely under the authority of the high priest of Jerusalem.[14] Occupying powers do not tolerate infighting among countries under their control. A few early Scrolls scholars immediately picked up on the fact that the early Christians, like the Essenes from whom they broke, may have been referring to Qumran as Damascus, a Qumran that by then likely had fallen into the hands of the Christians.

The Essenes/early Christian converts probably made a sympathetic connection. According to the Damascus Document, one of the first Dead Sea Scrolls discovered at Qumran, the Essenes traced their origins back to Damascus in Syria.[15] Thus it seems that they symbolically named the Qumran community "Damascus" in imitation of the scriptural events that had played out centuries before. Having grown up in the Bible-belt South, in which many towns or small communities around me were given biblical names—Mount Moriah, Bethel, Pisgah, Hebron; the list goes on and on—it was easy for me to understand how the Essenes and early Christians may have followed the same practice.

29 IDENTIFYING THE MANNESEH AND EPHRAIM

As I stated earlier, I believe I have correctly identified these two references, Manneseh and Ephraim, as alluding to Jesus and his half-brother James, respectively, and their followers. This is a very important identification for my entire restoration. Why would the Essenes have chosen these precise references? Because it was in the nature of their pesher method to make sympathetic associations. Bear in mind that the identification of the Essenes as the scribes of the New Testament shows them to be Jesus's spiritual archenemies who planned and carried out his crucifixion. Following on this theme, the Bible mentions a Manesseh, a wicked king of Judah in the sixth century BCE who was crucified for his sins (2 Kg 21:1–18; 24:3–4; 1 Chr 7:20–22; 2 Chr 33:12–13; see also the apocryphal Prayer of Manesseh). Because Jesus relaxed the rigid asceticism practiced by the Essenes, they would have referred to him and his followers as "seek-ers-of-smooth-things" (4Q169). Likewise, the evil King Manneseh "seduced Judah and the inhabitants of Jerusalem, so that they did more evil than the nations whom the Lord destroyed before the people of Israel" (2 Chr 33:9). Jesus's miracles would have been perceived by the Essenes just as Manneseh's "soothsaying and augury and sorcery" (2 Chr 33:6a). There is also an earlier Manneseh mentioned in the Bible who was the eldest son of Joseph (Gen 41:51), just as Jesus would have been popularly perceived: "Is not this the carpenter's son?" (Mt 13:55a). This same Manneseh had a younger brother, Ephraim, who was born in Egypt (Gen 41:52), just as Jesus's half-brother James would likely have been born in Egypt due to Joseph and his family's flight there to escape Herod's persecution of the firstborn (Mt 2:13–23).*

These sympathetic associations are complex, to be sure, but once the Essene pesher method is understood, they are quite natural. Note the following pesher:

> *Woe to the city of blood; it is full of lies and rapine.* (Nah 3:1a–b)
> Interpreted, this is the city of Ephraim, those who seek smooth things during the last days, who walk in lies and falsehood. (4Q169 3–4 II, 1–2)

---

*Obviously I reject the Catholic teaching that Mary never bore other children besides Jesus and that she remained a perpetual virgin. After centuries of debate between Catholics and Protestants, we have finally come to the point in which Mary's perpetual virginity must be rethought for a purely pragmatic reason. To continue to subscribe to it would now seriously impede our vital understanding of early Christianity.

Robert Eisenman showed that the Scrolls speak of the region near Jericho, where James fled during his persecution by the Essenes.[16] The city of Ephraim was located about ten miles northwest of Jericho. Thus, the above pesher reference may have been literal in this instance, though still highly esoteric in its application. It was esoteric in that Ephraim not only referred to James, the half-brother of Jesus, but also to his followers, "those who seek smooth things," which is how the Essenes would have seen the nonascetic Christians.

30 A NEW PARADIGM

I trust I have shed some valuable light on the Essene pesher method. Henceforth, dissenting scholars such as Thiering, Eisenman, and myself should be able to show that our late dating of 1QpHab and related Commentaries deserves a serious look. Consensus scholars must recognize that a paradigm shift is now in order, and many of their old conclusions are no longer valid. For example, Otto Betz once offered this criticism:

> Was Jesus the "wicked priest" of the Damascus Rule and the Habakkuk pesher? Not at all. Thiering's late dating of the Qumran writings and identification of their main figures with John the Baptist and Jesus are as false as Eisenman's attempt to identify the anonymous "Teacher of Righteousness" with James the brother of the Lord. . . . Thiering's book is an insult not only to the Christian faith but to serious scholarship. She and Eisenman show the by-ways one gets into with the alleged transmuted meaning of the Qumran texts. Both claim to have cracked the Qumran code, but each solution excludes the other. Their methods do not open up the texts, but only make way for whimsy. By Thiering and Eisenman's methodological aberrations one can claim whatever one likes about Qumran, Jesus and the Early Christians, from whatever motives.[17]

I have similar problems with the lack of objectivity in Thiering's pesher method myself, as I pointed out earlier; especially her willingness to rewrite the canon so recklessly. Perhaps consensus scholars will be more accepting of this present work. Why? If for no other reason, *they should accept it because my work is based primarily on their very own findings.* But for Betz's identification of the Essenes as traveling under the name "Herodians" in the New Testament, found in the chapter he contributed to James H. Charlesworth's *Jesus and the Dead Sea Scrolls,*[18] this book would not have been possible. Throughout this book, I tie up similar loose ends in the work of other consensus scholars who have been just as critical of the Jesus as Wicked Priest theory. For sure, there are differences between Eisenman, Thiering, and myself, just as there are differences among the main body of scholars. But that is no reason to cast aside groundbreaking work. Recall the epistemological standard I set forth in my introduction: If radiocarbon science cannot conclusively prove or disprove my restoration, its correctness should be judged by whether it is coherent, and internally and externally consistent. By comparison, I believe I have shown the consensus restoration to be random guesswork, containing one unacceptable anomaly after the other.

4

The Lost Christian Doctrine
of Reincarnation

———————•———————

Christianity is the only major world religion without an official doctrine of reincarnation. It is well known that reincarnation is taught in
the Eastern religions; reincarnation and karma are their principal concerns. Reincarnation is taught in Judaism and Islam, too. Hasidic Jews
teach *gilgul,* literally translated, "turning in a circle." And Sufi and
other Muslim sects teach *rajat,* "going up and down." But not a single
mainstream Christian sect currently teaches reincarnation. It was not
always so. This chapter will show that the early Christians and the
Essenes from whom they sprang unmistakably taught reincarnation, but
the doctrine was lost in history. Although space does not permit me to
completely revitalize this lost doctrine, I can shed enough light to show
that reincarnation was originally and properly a Christian teaching. It
is a teaching that adds a completely new dimension to both the New
Testament and the Dead Sea Scrolls. It is a teaching that also adds new
insight to the person of Jesus and how he saw himself and his place in
the divine plan of history.

I suspect that many orthodox Christians will be uncomfortable
with this chapter and my work in general, for I will shake up their belief

systems. But it is always better to seek the truth. Indeed, the further-ance of the gospel is the very reason that I take up this lost doctrine. In his book *Rescuing Jesus from the Christians,* Clayton Sullivan voiced a sentiment that is very popular in this age of pluralism. He wrote that Christians should accept the idea that Christianity is merely one among many paths to truth. Sullivan pointed out that Eastern faiths teach reincarnation, but the Bible exhibits no apparent evidence of the doctrine.[1] Thus it seems "East is East, and West is West, and never the twain shall meet," as Kipling put it. Sullivan and I are old friends. In fact, I was his teaching assistant in graduate school. He is an excellent New Testament scholar, but I disagree with his pluralist approach. If one is to take seriously universal truth claims ascribed to Jesus in the Gospels, that he is "the true light that enlightens every man" (Jn 1:9), then one must adopt the inclusivist approach of the early Christian apologist Justin Martyr. Namely, we must not be afraid to incorporate overlapping teachings. To paraphrase Justin: If anywhere there is found even a single existential truth that cannot be found in Jesus's teach-ings or an organic outgrowth thereof, Jesus was not the Christ. That is the demanding standard Justin set for Christianity, a standard we Christians cannot shy away from and be true to our faith. If reincarna-tion does occur and Jesus is the "true light that enlightens every man," then he must have addressed it.

Empirical evidence for reincarnation is abundant. Many past-life memories are well documented, evidence that is clear and convincing to any open mind.[2] The standard Christian apologetic against past-life memories and hypnotic regression is that these are explainable as demonic possession by disembodied spirits. How easy it is to label as demonic everything that conflicts with your personal theology! I am reminded of a similar argument I once heard against evolution, or more specifically against archaeological evidence that the earth is much older than the Bible appears to support by adding up the ages of the patriarchs. Fundamentalist Christians have actually argued that the earth only *appears* to be billions of years old because God is playing tricks with the rocks to test our faith. For Christians so arrogant in their doctrines as to be willing to worship a malicious trickster idol, there is very little chance any arguments in this chapter will change their minds. But for Christians not willing to commit cognitive suicide, who believe God is "not the author of confusion but of peace" (1 Cor 14:33a), please keep reading.

It is estimated that three-quarters of the world's population believes in reincarnation and struggles with the issues of karma, but officially Christianity has nothing whatsoever to offer them. This is a mistake whose correction is long overdue. Moreover, there is a direct apologetic concern for Jews who ask if Jesus could have been the Messiah. At Jewish Passover tables down to this day, an empty place is set for the "expected guest," Elijah. Nearly every Jewish family still pays homage to the tradition that the literal, bodily return of Elijah is expected before the Messiah can come (Mal 4:5). Jesus's disciples knew this too, which is why they asked of him, "Why do the scribes say that Elijah must first come?" (Mk 9:11). Jesus answered that the expected guest had already come in the person of John the Baptist: "For all the prophets and the law prophesied until John; and if you are willing to accept it, he is Elijah who is to come. He who has ears to hear, let him hear" (Mt 11:13–15). This is as plain a teaching of reincarnation as one will find in the entire Bible. The early Christian fathers knew of this and similar teachings of reincarnation in the Bible but suppressed them. Why they did so is the starting point of our investigation.

31 A BRIEF HISTORY OF REINCARNATION WITHIN CHRISTIANITY

Like Buddhism, which split into the Theravada, Mahayana, and Zen schools, Christianity also is known for three major schisms in its history. The third and latest was the Protestant Reformation in the sixteenth century; the second, the eleventh-century split between the Latin and Byzantine churches; and the first, the fifth-century excommunication of the Gnostics—the Syrians, the Copts of Egypt, and other Oriental sects. We would suspect that doctrine preceding the fifth-century schism would be common to the remainder of Christianity. And this is largely true: common to Protestant, Greek Orthodox, and Roman Catholic alike is some form of the Nicene Creed resulting from the first four Ecumenical Councils (325–381 CE). But with the excommunication of the Gnostics, Christendom left most Gnostic doctrine behind, including reincarnation.

Reincarnation was officially condemned as anathema by the Fifth Ecumenical Council in 553 CE. Also known as the Second Council of Constantinople, this council was a highly political one, headed by the emperor Justinian, which Pope Vigilius did not even attend. Vigilius later deferred to the findings of the Second Council, but only after vacillating, and then for mostly political reasons. Justinian had hoped to reconcile the Eastern and Western churches, which were split on the issue of Monophysitism versus Nestorianism—whether Christ is possessed of one nature or two. The Latin and Byzantine churches ultimately split over this very issue, with the former basically adopting Nestorianism.* The seeds of schism were already planted, and the "unity at all costs" approach of Justinian in order to tell his soldiers

---

*Nestorius's teaching of the two natures of Christ was condemned in the Latin church because it rapidly degenerated into the idea of two distinct God-man persons. Nestorius himself repudiated this account; thus there is a distinction between Nestorius and the doctrine that came to be known as Nestorian. Cyril favored the language that the two natures of Christ were in "hypostatic union." For fuller explanation of this complicated period in Christian doctrinal history, see J. N. D. Kelly, *Early Christian Doctrines* (HarperSanFrancisco, 1978), 310f. The early fathers struggled with such ideas because they were caught up in Platonism and could not understand how God could be born, suffer, and die in human form. For a process theologian, which is how I would probably classify myself, a suffering God presents no problem at all; this is basic panentheism. I scathingly refer to Dyophysitism as "Nestorian" because any discussion of Christ's "two natures" or "two essences" necessarily leads to the idea that God and humankind are essentially separate. The Bible clearly states that human nature is essentially divine, although we suffer existentially due to sin. This is how Jesus defended his own claims to deity when he quoted the Psalmist: "You are gods, all of you, sons of the Most High; yet you die like men" (Ps 82:6, quoted in Jn 10:34).

what to pray did not help matters. Himself a Monophysite, Justinian attacked the Nestorian school of Antioch. Unfortunately for the doctrine of reincarnation, the school of Antioch was vigorously opposed to Alexandrian Christianity, whose strongest representative was the early father Origen (185–254 CE).

As the saying goes, "The enemy of my enemy is my friend." To gain political support for Monophysitism, Justinian attacked Origen, whose name was already suspect among conservatives, for he had come to be synonymous with syncretism. The Anchorite monks who broke away from the New Laura monastery in Jerusalem were seeking an authority figure in Origen, as were many other Gnostic sects. Ironically, Origen was the most prolific anti-Gnostic apologist the Church has ever known (see his *Against Celsus*), but at this point in history he was perceived as the Gnostics' greatest ally. As early as the fourth century, Origen was condemned by the fathers Epiphanius, Jerome, and Theophilus, the latter of whom called Origen "the hydra of heresies." Although he himself never taught reincarnation, Origen's respect for Plato led to belief in the Greek doctrine among the Gnostics. Thus, by the time the Second Council of Constantinople wrote in 553 CE, "Whosoever shall support the mythical doctrine of the pre-existence of the soul and the consequent wonderful opinion of its return, let him be anathema," Origen was wrongly condemned a heretic for having supported the doctrine.

Such is the story of Christendom's rejection of reincarnation. Gnostic Christians continued to hold the doctrine until their disappearance, just as syncretic Christians do today—for example, the New Age movement. But since the split with the Gnostics occurred so early in Christianity's history, the vast majority of Christendom has never given reincarnation a second thought. When the issue reappeared in medieval times, the Council of Lyons (1245–1274 CE) and the Council of Florence (1438–1445 CE) took for granted that reincarnation had already been discarded. Each held to the already familiar scheme that human beings live once only and upon death go immediately to an eternal heaven, hell, or purgatory.* Yet, as we have seen, reincarnation was never more than a lateral concern for council Christianity. The Second Council of Constantinople was so besieged with political interests that it lacked the theological scrutiny to properly deal with the issue. Present-day Catholic scholars rightly question whether its anathemas should still bind the conscience. And as I am a radical Protestant, I certainly do not feel bound by the theology of a sixth-century emperor or a vacillating pope, but instead feel free to search out the issue for myself.

32   ORIGEN'S UNIQUE VIEW OF REINCARNATION

Perhaps the greatest tragedy of the Second Council lies not in its oversimplification of the reincarnation question, but in the slander of a truly great thinker, Origen, who had already considered the question in depth. Of all the early Christian fathers, none dealt more rigorously with the complicated question of reincarnation than Origen of Alexandria. Well read in Greek philosophy, Origen was Christianity's first systematic theologian. The depth and breadth of his thought have been compared to Paul, Aquinas, and Luther. Origen is unique among the early fathers in that he held a complex doctrine of the preexistence of souls. Specifically, he held a Neoplatonic view that souls "emanated" or "cooled" into this world by prior workings of their free will (*First Principles* 3.5). In other words, the Fall for Origen is precosmic. In anticipation of Augustine's question, "What was God doing prior to the creation of the world?" Origen claimed that God was creating world upon world for the wayward soul to cycle through en route to salvation, a process that Origen termed *apocostasis* (roughly translated, "the end is like the beginning"). Origen reversed the usual thinking of reincarna-

---

*The purgatorial scheme is the Christian theological attempt to deal with what happens in the interim of postmortem individual judgment versus a historical collective judgment, the latter of which is expected at "judgment day" (1 Th 4:13–18).

tion: Instead of the soul revolving around a single world, there are multiple worlds that revolve around a single soul. A soul never incarnates within the same world twice—except, according to apocostasis, back in the world in which the soul was created, which is precisely the contradiction I find in Origen's system.* Understandably, Origen's version of reincarnation is often confused. Both the Gnostic Origenists and the church fathers who excommunicated them wrongly believed Origen taught an earthly form of reincarnation, as do some uninformed writers today.† But this clearly was not the case. Origen said in one commentary, "[It would be error for me to] fall into the dogma of transmigration, which is foreign to the church of God, and not handed down by the Apostles, nor anywhere set forth in the Scriptures" (*Commentary on Matthew* 3.1).

Note that Origen had two main reasons for rejecting reincarnation. The first is that reincarnation is not supported by what Christian scholars now call *apostolic succession,* meaning that the doctrine flows continuously back to Jesus and the apostles. The second is that reincarnation is not supported by the Bible. The first claim is a matter of historical inquiry, the second a matter of biblical exegesis. With the aid of the Dead Sea Scrolls, I now attack both claims.

Without question, my Dead Sea Scrolls restoration reopens the issue of apostolic succession for this and many other doctrines. The Scrolls authors, the Essenes, were the Jewish sect from whom Christianity took much of its doctrine and personnel, including Jesus and many of the apostles. And it is easily shown by Scrolls prooftexts, which I will soon cover, that the Essenes believed in reincarnation. It is outright laughable that Origen claimed reincarnation is found nowhere in the

---

*To clarify: My belief is that it is this world, and no other, in which the soul (*psyche*) is created and into which the spirit (*pneuma*) returns repeatedly until the end times; Gen 2:7; 3:19.

†A commentator in an edition of the *Tibetan Book of the Dead* wrongly stated, "Origen . . . held the doctrine of rebirth and *karma* to be Christian." W. Y. Evans-Wentz (3rd ed., London: Oxford University Press, 1960), 234.

Bible. Origen, as an anti-Gnostic apologist, worked very hard at creating unnatural explanations to explain away numerous biblical references to reincarnation wherever he found them. Biblical references to reincarnation are there as they have always been, and many are quite obvious. But few sympathetic Christian theologians have ever seriously worked through them.

33 THE ESSENE BELIEF IN REINCARNATION

Essene doctrines are well described in several classical sources apart from the Dead Sea Scrolls. For example, the historian Josephus claimed that their belief in reincarnation helped the Essenes endure the hardship of war with the Romans:

> Smiling in their agonies and mildly deriding their tormentors, they cheerfully resigned their souls, *confident that they would receive them back again.* For it is a fixed belief of theirs that the body is corruptible and its constituent matter impermanent, *but that the soul is immortal and imperishable.* Emanating from the finest ether, *these souls become entangled, as it were, in the prison-houses of the body,* to which they are dragged down by a sort of natural spell; but when they are released from the bonds of flesh, then as though liberated from a long servitude, they rejoice and are born aloft . . . while they relegate base souls to a murky and tempestuous dungeon. (*War* 2.153–55; my emphasis)

These are very Platonic ideas. The Greeks would have understood the soul to be immortal by nature. By contrast, the Hebrew Bible does not support the natural immortality of the soul, only its conditional immortality. Adam and Eve were expelled from the Garden of Eden before they could partake of the Tree of Life, which would have made him immortal (Gen 3:22–24). And elsewhere Elihu utters to Job, "The

Spirit of God has made me, and the breath of the Almighty gives me life" (Job 33:4). The Greeks would also have understood the soul to have a pre-earthly origin. But although the Hebrew Bible teaches that the *soul* is created simultaneously with the body (Gen 2:7), in other verses it appears that the *spirit* returns to God whence it came (Ec 12:6). It is possible that Josephus distorted Essene theology somewhat out of ignorance or the attempt to appease the Graeco-Roman audience to whom he was writing. Yet I believe Josephus to have been accurate in regard to the Essene belief in reincarnation in general.

Josephus's statements regarding the Essene belief in reincarnation are confirmed in the Dead Sea Scrolls. The clearest examples are found in Scroll fragments that have been referred to as the "Physiognomic Horoscopes" (4Q186; 4Q534; 4Q561). The Horoscopes were so named by Scrolls scholars because they give astrological references to the forecasted births. For example, "his animal is the bull" meant that the person mentioned would be born under the sign of Taurus. It should not surprise Jewish and Christian readers that early Jewish sects wrote of astrology. Similar references are found in the New Testament, for example, where John's Revelation makes reference to an angel who "planted his right foot on the sea and his left foot on the land" (Rev 10:2b), which I believe is a subtle reference to Cancer, the sign of the crab. But in addition to the astrological references, certain of the horoscopes contain unmistakable references to reincarnation. Let us look at 4Q186 in full context.

Fragment 1

II . . . and his thighs are long and lean, and his toes are thin and long. He is of the second Column. His spirit consists of six* in the House of Light and three in the Pit of Darkness. And this is his

---

*Vermes inserted the word "parts" at this point in the texts in an attempt to make sense of these passages: "His spirit consists of six (parts) in the House of Light." I think it is more responsible scholarship to pull the interpretive comment altogether and let the reader draw his or her own conclusions based on the surrounding context.

birthday in which he is to be born in the foot of the Bull. He will be meek. And his animal is the bull.

III . . . and his head . . . [and his cheeks are] fat. His teeth are of uneven length. His fingers are thick, and his thighs are thick and very hairy, each one. His toes are thick and short. His spirit consists of eight in the House of Darkness and one from the House of Light . . .

Fragment 2

I . . . order. His eyes are black and glowing. His beard is . . . and it is . . . His voice is gentle. His teeth are fine and well aligned. He is neither tall, nor short. And he . . . And his fingers are thin and long. And his thighs are smooth. And the soles of his feet . . . [And his toes] are well aligned. His spirit consists of eight [in the House of Light, of] the second Column, and one [in the House of Darkness. And this is] his birthday on which he is to be born: . . . And his animal is . . .

The physical characteristics of each man correspond to his spirit's migration history. Characteristics that reflect wickedness—like shortness, fatness, and teeth of uneven length—correspond to the number of times his spirit was imprisoned in the House of Darkness. Likewise, virtuous characteristics—like glowing black eyes and well-aligned teeth—correspond to the number of times his spirit was perfected in the House of Light. That one's physical characteristics reflect prenatal sin (or karma in Eastern religions) is a very common reincarnation belief, found the world over. Although he rejected it, Jesus even encountered this belief among his disciples when they asked him if a man was born blind because of his prenatal sin (Jn 9:2).*

In 4Q534,[3] Noah's physical characteristics were expected to be

---

*This is a complicated passage and deserves more attention that I can give it here. Briefly: Jesus shifted the focus away from the man's sin and upon the opportunity to work God's miracles (Jn 9:3). Yet, once the subject of prenatal sin had been opened, Jesus expounded on upon himself as he who could bring deliverance from all sin, even prenatal (Jn 10).

near-perfect—except for a reference to a mysterious "birthmark," which will never be fully understood because of the poor condition of the texts—and he is said to be the "Elect of God" (4Q534 I, 10). Curiously, we find no language concerning his spirit's migration to the House of Darkness. Perhaps this is because Noah was "perfect in his generations" (Gen 6:9, KJV). Many Scrolls scholars have determined that this horoscope of Noah describes the long-awaited leader of the Essene congregation. I will return to this important text in the next chapter. For now, we must explore more fully why reincarnation was rejected from Christianity.

34　DID PYTHAGORAS LEARN REINCARNATION FROM THE ESSENES?

Let us review the fact that when the early church fathers rejected reincarnation, they did so primarily because they feared the doctrine was a corrupting Gnostic influence imported from the Greeks, and it lacked any proper foundation in Judaism and Christianity. This is the standard orthodox argument against reincarnation today. However students of philosophy will find that reincarnation was not originally a Greek doctrine. Pythagoras appears to have introduced the doctrine to the Greeks in the fifth century BCE.[4] What is most interesting is that many scholars now believe Pythagoras may have picked up the doctrine on his journeys to the East, where he may have traveled as far eastward as Persia.[5] Many Jews would have been exiled in Persia during this time. Origen believed Pythagoras got most of his ideas from the Jews. He wrote, "It was from the Jewish people that Pythagoras derived the philosophy which he introduced among the Greeks" (*Against Celsus* 1.15). It thus appears the Greek doctrine may have originated with the Essenes. For it was precisely during the Persian exile that the scribes/Essenes were emerging as a recognizable sect. And Essene practices were far more similar to those of the Pythagoreans than to those of any other Jewish sect. Diogenes Laertius, a Greek historian, records of Pythagoras:

Being asked, once, when a man ought to approach a woman he replied, "When you want to lose what strength you have."

Some say that he was satisfied with honey alone, or a bit of honey-comb and bread (he did not touch wine during the day); or for a treat, vegetables boiled or raw. Seafood he ate but rarely. His robe, which was white and spotless, and his bedclothes, which were also white, were of wool; for linen had not yet reached those parts. He was never observed to relieve himself, or to have intercourse, or to be drunk. He used to avoid all pandering to scurrilous jokes and vulgar stories. (*Lives of Eminent Philosophers* 8.9)

The asceticism in matters of food, drink, and sexual relations with women; the white robes; not relieving oneself in public; reincarnation: these are all doctrines characteristic of the Essenes.[6] Josephus even said of the Essenes, "These men live the same kind of life as do those whom the Greeks call the Pythagoreans" (*Ant* 15.371). How ironic it would be if reincarnation were rejected by the early Christian fathers as a Greek doctrine when it may have originated with the Jews all along.

35 REINCARNATION IN JUDAISM AND EARLY CHRISTIANITY

There are three basic views of the afterlife in contemporary Judaism. There is the view that there necessarily is no afterlife *per se,* that one's memory is all that lives on through children and friends. There is the orthodox view that each person lives once only and upon death and judgment goes to an eternal heaven or hell. And finally there is the view held by most Hasidic Jews that each of us reincarnates in a cycle known as *gilgul* until final judgment. The scriptures that would eventu-ally form the Hebrew Bible have provided continuity from one genera-tion of Jews to the next. Accordingly, if there are three different views of the afterlife in Judaism today, these same three views are likely to have been held by the major Jewish sects in Jesus's time.

A brief analysis shows this to have been the case. The first view was apparently held by the Sadducees (Mk 12:18–27 // Mt 22:23–33 // Lk 20:27–40). According to the historian Josephus, "[The Sadducees] take away the belief of the immortal duration of the soul, and the punishments and rewards in Hades" (*War* 2.165). Orthodox Judaism as we know it today arose largely out of the Pharisee sect, from the Mishnah and other rabbinical writings. The orthodox beliefs have been well explored, so there is no need to duplicate them here. But the Essene afterlife beliefs have not been so well explored, primarily because until now there was little reason to do so. Prior to the discovery of the Dead Sea Scrolls, the Essenes were little more than a footnote in history. And prior to this present book, no one had significantly identified the Essenes in the New Testament. As I pointed out in chapter 2, the word *Essene* appears to be a Latinized term for Hasid, suggesting that the Essenes are the ancient forerunners of the present-day Hasidim. So in response to the early Christian fathers who claim reincarnation lacked a biblical foundation, let us explore both contemporary and historical Hasidism to determine whether their belief in reincarnation is biblically based.

36 HASIDISM AND THE KABBALAH

Orthodox Judaism has historically had great problems understanding the Hasidic belief in reincarnation because most of the Hasidic texts on the subject are found in the Kabbalah. The Kabbalah is a collection of highly mystical and esoteric Jewish works that until fairly recent times were kept secret. The Kabbalah contains and has spawned numerous works on reincarnation. For example, reincarnation sequences of Moses and others are found in the Zohar and other mystical works, such as the *Sepher hag-Gilgulî* (Frankfort, 1684). It is reported there that the ancient Samaritan doctrine of the *taheb* taught the reincarnation sequence of Moses to be Seth, Noah, and Abraham.[7] But can such a reincarnation sequence possibly be Bible based? Yes, it can.

We must first understand that reincarnation is a very ancient doctrine, and that references to it are found throughout the Bible from the very beginning. We will not find the term *reincarnation,* of course, for the term is French and came into use around the seventeenth century. We will not find the term *reincarnation* in Buddhist texts either; although it is well understood that is what is meant when the ancient texts speak of "rebirth." Perhaps it was equally clear in context that Jesus was speaking of reincarnation in his conversation with Nicodemus, when Jesus said one must be "reborn" (Jn 3). I will return to this important text shortly. The point is that biblical references to reincarnation are there, provided one has eyes to see them. For example, the serpent is understood as a graphic symbol of reincarnation the world over. The serpent sheds its skin, which is symbolic of the death-and-rebirth cycle. In this light, the whole Fall myth takes on a new meaning: Had Adam and Eve not sinned, they would not have fallen into the cycle of death and rebirth like their tempter.

Not only is reincarnation the most natural reading of certain texts, there are combinations of texts that are absolutely impossible to reconcile without reading them in the context of reincarnation. The most obvious is found in the Ten Commandments, where the word of God came to Moses: "I the Lord your God am a jealous God, visiting the iniquities of the fathers upon the sons, to the third and fourth generation of those who hate me" (Ex 20:5b). How can one reconcile this text with the word of God as it came to Ezekiel? "The soul that sins shall die. The son shall not suffer for the iniquity of the father, nor the father for the iniquity of the son. The righteousness of the righteous shall be upon himself, and the wickedness of the wicked shall be upon himself" (Ez 18:20).

The only way it is possible for God to visit the iniquities of the father on the son and also for each to bear sole responsibility for his own sin is for one's sin to pass to oneself through reincarnation. Note carefully that in Exodus God said the sins of the father would pass to the "third and fourth generation," *but not the second.* Your second-generation descendant is your son. Because a father must necessarily be living in order to sire a son (at least prior to artificial insemination, which raises a whole new concern never contemplated by the ancients), it is physically impossible to be the reincarnation of one's own father. However, it is possible to be the reincarnation of one's own grandfather or great-grandfather, as many African cultures know when they name a newborn "Father has returned." In Ghana, the name *Ababio,* "He has come again," carries the same meaning.[8] The idea that we reincarnate back into the same family is a very common cross-cultural belief, which is probably the reason that in eastern Europe, children never used to be named after the living.

Returning to the reincarnation sequence of Moses: What are some biblical passages that would have suggested to ancient Kabbalist writers that Moses was the incarnation of Seth, Noah, and Abraham? Let us take them in reverse. To begin with, there is a passage Jesus quoted to the Sadducees in support of the idea that the dead were being raised (Mk 12:26–27 // Mt 22:31–32 // Lk 20:37–38). Jesus quoted from Exodus the passage in which God spoke to Moses from the burning bush, saying, "I am the God of Abraham" (Ex 3:6). Abraham was living in the person of Moses. That is why God said, "*I am* the God of Abraham," not "*I was. . . .*" In *On the Resurrection of the Flesh,* the early church father Tertullian argued at length that Jesus spoke only of a resurrection in spirit as opposed to the flesh. But Jesus said, quite simply, "[God] is not God of the dead, but of the living" (Mk 12:27). The whole passage loses its context unless Jesus was speaking of a bodily resurrection, at least in general (Mk 12:18 // Mt 22:31 // Lk 20:27). And if that is the case, we cannot overlook the verb tense Jesus used. If the Orthodox view is correct, "resurrection" would take place only in the final judgment. But the verb tense Jesus used indicated that the dead were constantly being raised. Here is the proper translation:

But the dead   that   they are raised (Mk 12:26a)
De   ton nekron oti   egeirontai

But are raised the   dead (Lk 20:37a)[9]
De   egeirontai oi   nekri

If Abraham were incarnate in Moses, it would certainly explain why God visited upon him the awesome responsibility of delivering the children of Abraham from Egypt. Note the following passage, where Moses asked difficult questions of God: "Why hast thou dealt ill with thy servant? And why have I not found favor in thy sight, that thou dost lay the burden of all these people upon me? Did I conceive these people? Did I bring them forth, that thou shouldst say to me, 'Carry them in your bosom as a nurse carries a suckling child, to the land which thou didst swear to give to their fathers'?" (Num 11:11–12).

Or perhaps the sequence will be revealed to the reader's satisfaction in other passages. The baby Moses was found in an ark (*te-vah*) among the reeds and bulrushes of the Nile River (Ex 2:1–10). He was miraculously delivered from death by drowning, a fate that befell every other Hebrew son (Ex 1:22). The name given by Pharaoh's daughter, who rescued him, together with the above circumstances, is an identification of Noah incarnate in Moses by the hand of providence: "And she named him Moses (*Mosheh*), for she said, 'Because I drew him out of the water'" (Ex 2:10b). An even more suggestive translation was given by Josephus: "For the Egyptians call water *môu* and those who are saved *esês*; so they conferred on him the name compounded of both words" (*Ant* 2.228). Therefore, Moses means the one who was saved from the water. Another revealing passage is found in the Book of Joshua: "[Thus says the Lord, the God of Israel], And I took your father Abraham from the other side of the flood, and led him throughout all the land of Canaan, and multiplying his seed, and gave him Isaac" (Jos 24:3, KJV). Taken "from the other side of the flood" signifies that Abraham was aboard the ark of Noah, which, reconciling the above passages, leads us to the conclusion that Moses was the incarnated patriarchs Noah and Abraham. As for the reincarnation of Seth, we could look at the fact that Genesis speaks of Noah as having been perfected: "Noah was a just man, perfect in his generations" (Gen 6:9b, KJV). Curiously, according to Genesis, both Adam and Seth survived all their progeny, except that both died prior to the birth of Noah (Gen 5:1–32). Thus we may choose between Adam and Seth as a possible candidate for the reincarnation. God promised Adam that his children would be at enmity with the serpent (Gen 3:15), so Seth became the "new Adam" in Noah.

Obviously, reading Bible passages in this esoteric way is a bit of an art.* In fact, it is a lost art for all but a select handful of Hasidic Jews. But this is exactly the technique used in the Kabbalah as well as the Essenes' writings. It is the same literary tradition.

37 ANGELS IN THE DEAD SEA SCROLLS AND OTHER JEWISH LITERATURE

Many Dead Sea Scrolls mention reincarnation in the context of angels. Josephus wrote of the Essenes, "[They] carefully preserved the books of the sect and the names of the angels" (*War* 2.142). In 1QS, 1QH, 1QM, and the Enoch literature, a cosmological battle is described wherein the angels and all humanity are divided into the forces of Light and Darkness, with the angels commanding the way. Many scholars have studied angelology in the Scrolls.[10] What remains unexplored is the

---

*Origen attempted to give guidelines for the appropriate use of allegory and metaphor in scriptural reading (*First Principles* 4), which are still quite useful. In defense against the contemporary critical scholar who has no taste for interpretations of this sort, I point out that Jesus constantly interpreted Scripture in this multidimensional way.

integral role of reincarnation in angelology.* The Essenes believed that this cosmological battle was not a distant event; rather, it was playing out around them, and the angels were walking among them in human form. *"Do not neglect to show hospitality to strangers, for thereby some have entertained angels unawares"* (Heb 13:2, my emphasis).

It may be surprising to some that a monotheistic religion would have a tradition of angels. This tradition did not originate with the Essenes, however, but within Judaism as a whole. The word *angel* is best translated as a mediator or messenger. The Hebrew God is an invisible God, who must reveal himself through his angels. The earliest references to angels are found in the Bible. According to Exodus 23:20, "Behold, I send an angel before you, to guard you on the way and bring you to the place I have prepared." This angel is said to bear the "name of God" (Ex 23:21b). Likewise, an angelic figure is described seated upon the throne of God in Ezekiel 1 and Daniel 7 bearing the "name of God" and sharing in his glory. In Jewish literature known as Merkabah or Pseudepigrapha,[11] this principal mediating angel is often referred to as Metatron, one who stands next to the throne. Metatron is often identified with the angel Michael and sometimes the mysterious figure Melchizedek. This figure is particularly important in the Dead Sea Scrolls, for Melchizedek was the exalted leader of the angelic armies (11Q13).

The current popular belief is that angels are celestial beings, but this was not always so. Ancient Jewish texts describe angels in human form. In some Jewish texts known as *Pseudepigrapha*, we find that

---

*See Gustav Davidson, *A Dictionary of Angels* (New York: Free Press, 1971), an amazingly detailed sourcebook for practically every angelic reincarnation sequence in all of Jewish literature. (Davidson does not explicitly discuss reincarnation, but when he "identifies" one figure with another, this is usually how it should be interpreted.) Davidson put in some fifteen years of research in Talmudic, Kabbalist, and other texts. I am not saying all the reincarnation sequences given in the book are complete and correct—many of them are not. But for readers gifted with spiritual maturity and the appropriate discernment, it is recommended as a place to start your inquiry into this highly esoteric subject. I guarantee it will pique your curiosity. See especially the entry for Metatron.

biblical patriarchs are explicitly identified as angels. *Pseudepigrapha* is a scholarly term taken from the Greek words *pseudos,* "false," and *epigrapha,* "inscriptions." Texts are classified as Pseudepigrapha if the claimed authors could not possibly have written them. The Testament of Abraham, for example, dates to the first or second century CE, but we know that the patriarch Abraham died nearly two thousand years earlier. Personally, I believe the authorship of Pseudepigrapha should be rethought, given that many of these texts were found at Qumran, and the Essenes believed in reincarnation. The authors likely believed themselves the reincarnations of the ascribed patriarchs. Regardless, Pseudepigrapha invariably describe angels in human form, such as in the following passage taken from the Testament of Abraham (note that Abel is presented as the angel of judgment, presiding over all creation):

> Do you see, Abraham, the frightful man who is seated upon the throne? This is the son of Adam, the first formed who is called Abel, whom Cain the wicked killed. And he sits here to judge the entire creation, examining both righteous and sinner. For God said, "I do not judge you, but every man is judged by man." On account of this he gave him judgment to judge the world until his great and glorious Parousia. And then, righteous Abraham, there will be perfect judgment and recompense, eternal and unalterable, which no one can question. (Testament of Abraham [A] 13:2–5)

Similarly, in the Prayer of Joseph, Jacob describes himself as "an angel of God and a ruling spirit," the "firstborn of every living thing," and the "first minister before the face of God," ([A] 1, 3, 9).[12] Thus, according to this description, these two angels are twin brothers, for Cain was the firstborn of every living thing, and Abel was his second-born twin (Gen 4:1–2; note that Adam knew Eve only once before both births; cf. 3:15; 25:21–26; 32:24–30; see also the twin brothers Ahriman and Ormuzd in Zoroastrian lore).

38 MELCHIZEDEK

Melchizedek is one of the most important angelic figures described in the Dead Sea Scrolls. Scroll 11Q13 contains thirteen fragments describing how Melchizedek would fulfill eschatological hopes and deliver the captives. As Vermes put it, "Identical to the archangel Michael, he is the head of the 'sons of Heaven' or 'gods of justice' and is referred to as *elohim* or *el*." He added, "This manuscript sheds valuable light not only on the Melchizedek figure in the epistle to the Hebrews vii, but also on the development of the messianic concept in the New Testament and Early Christianity."[13] Indeed it does. Although only fragments of the scroll remain intact, they provide valuable understanding. Bear in mind that the Essenes believed they were living in a time when the fulfillment of all eschatological prophecies was at hand. Therefore, the following pesher was aimed at interpreting how Melchizedek himself would fulfill these prophecies, a figure they believed would soon be living among them, if he were not already.

> *This is the day of* [*Peace/Salvation*] *concerning which* [*God*] *spoke* [*through Isa*]*iah the prophet, who said:* "[*How*] *beautiful upon the mountain are the feet of the messenger who proclaims peace, who brings good news, who proclaims salvation, who says to Zion*" *Your* ELOHIM [*reigns*]. (Is 52:7)
>
> Its interpretation; *the mountains* are the prophets . . . and *the messenger* is the Anointed one of the spirit, concerning whom Dan[iel] said [Until an anointed one,] a prince (Dan 9:25) . . . (11Q13 II, 15–18)

Paul cited this very same verse from Isaiah in reference to Jesus (Rom 10:15). It is from a passage known as the Servant Songs, very similar to another Isaiah passage Jesus quoted in reference to himself at his home synagogue in Nazareth:

He opened the [scroll] and found where it was written: "The Spirit of the Lord is upon me, because he has anointed me to preach good news to the poor. He has sent me to proclaim release to the captives and recovering of sight to the blind, to set at liberty those who are oppressed, to proclaim the acceptable year of the Lord." And he closed the [scroll], and gave it back to the attendant, and sat down; and the eyes of all in the synagogue were fixed on him. And he began to say to them, "Today this Scripture has been fulfilled in your hearing." (Lk 4:17–21)

How relevant was the mysterious figure Melchizedek to early Christians? Very. As Vermes pointed out, the Epistle to the Hebrews mentions Melchizedek in great detail. It is ironic that when most Christians quote the Bible against reincarnation, they cite: "And just as it is appointed for men to die once and after that comes judgment, so Christ, having been offered once to bear the sins of many, will appear a second time, not to deal with sin but to save those who are eagerly waiting for him" (Heb 9:27–28). Little do they realize this verse, in full context, actually supports reincarnation.

Theologically, the Epistle to the Hebrews is about as complex as it gets. It speaks of reincarnation in esoteric terms. That is because it is "solid food" and not "milk," as the author puts it. It is solid food for the "mature, for those who have their faculties trained by practice to distinguish good from evil" (Heb 5:14). The point of the Epistle to the Hebrews is to show the superiority of Jesus to the prophets (1:1–3), to the angels (1:5–2:18), to the Levitical priesthood (4:14–7:28), and, most importantly, to Moses himself (3:1–6). But what is puzzling is that the author also covers the mysterious figure Melchizedek at great length. And instead of downplaying Melchizedek to show Jesus's superiority over him, he instead equates Jesus with Melchizedek. That is because the author is trying to make the subtle point that Jesus is Melchizedek's reincarnation. Jesus was "designated by God a high priest after the order of Melchizedek.

About this we have much to say which is hard to explain" (5:10–11a).

The author brings forth Melchizedek's first appearance in the Bible from Genesis 14:17–20, where he met and blessed Abraham: "He is first, by translation of his name, king of righteousness, and then he is also king of Salem, that is, king of peace. He is without father or mother or genealogy, and has neither beginning of days nor ending of life, but resembling the Son of God he continues a priest forever" (Heb 7:2b–3). Note that Melchizedek was the bearer of bread and wine (Gen 14:18), which is the great and mysterious Christian sacrament, the Lord's Supper, or *Communion,* as it is otherwise known (Mk 14:22–24 // Mt 26:26–28 // Lk 22:14–20; 1 Cor 11:23–26). That Melchizedek has "neither beginning nor ending of days" is later cited in reference to Jesus to substantiate his authority over the Levitical priesthood: "This becomes even more evident when a priest arises in the likeness of Melchizedek who has become a priest, not according to a legal requirement concerning bodily descent but by the power of an indestructible life. For it is written of him, 'Thou art a priest forever, after the order of Melchizedek'" (Heb 7:15–17). If the reader doubts that the author is identifying Melchizedek with Jesus, note how he amplifies the earlier verses:

> And it was not without an oath. Those who formerly became priests took their office without an oath, but this one was addressed with an oath, "The Lord has sworn and has not changed his mind, 'Thou art a priest forever.'" This makes Jesus the surety of a better covenant.

> Now the point of what we are saying is this: we have such a high priest, one who is seated at the right hand of the throne of the Majesty in heaven. . . .

> Christ has obtained a ministry which is as much more excellent than the old as the covenant he mediates is better, since it is enacted on better promises. (Heb 7:20–22; 8:1; 8:6)

If I am correct in my conclusion that many of the early Christians were Essene converts, then it is no accident that the Essene reverence for Melchizedek found in the Scrolls made its way into the Epistle to the Hebrews in reference to Jesus. Early Christians believed Melchizedek and Jesus were one and the same.

39 ENOCH

Several caves at Qumran have yielded for the first time Aramaic copies of a major Pseudepigrapha work known as the Book of Enoch (4Q201–2; 204–12). The Book of Enoch was also cited in the New Testament's canonized Book of Jude (v. 14, quoting 1 En 1:9). Enoch first appears in Genesis as the seventh descendant from Adam. Like Elijah, Enoch was translated directly into heaven without seeing death: "Enoch walked with God; and he was not for God took him" (Gen 5:24). And that is practically the last we hear of him in the orthodox Protestant canon (but see the Wisdom of Solomon 4:10–17 in the Apocrypha). The Book of Enoch describes what happened to Enoch after being taken into heaven: he ascended to the throne and was seated at the right hand of God. Then it expressly identifies Enoch as the Messiah. It says specifically, "You are the Son of Man, who art born into righteousness and upon whom righteousness has dwelt. The righteousness of [God] shall not forsake you. He added and said to me, 'He shall proclaim peace to you in the name of the world that is to come. For from here proceeds peace since the creation of the world, and so it shall be unto you forever and ever'" (1 En 71:14–15).

The Book of Enoch is known to have existed as early as the first century. Although it was directly quoted in the canonized Epistle of Jude, the Book of Enoch was itself never placed in either the Hebrew or Christian canon, for obvious reasons. The book was too Christian-sounding for the Jews, and its references to a preexistent Messiah posed far more doctrinal difficulties than Christians were then prepared to deal with. Scholars generally agree that the Son of Man passages found in the Book of Enoch (1 En 37–71) are missing from the Qumran copies.[14] This confirms that the Son of Man passages are probably later Christian additions; if so, that gives Christian theologians all the more reason to explore them, for it implies they were specifically intended to apply to Jesus.

In John 3, the Pharisee Nicodemus comes to Jesus at night and asks him, "Rabbi, we know that you are a teacher come from God; for no one can do these signs that you do, unless God is with him." Jesus responds, "Truly, truly, unless one is born from above he cannot see the kingdom of God" (Jn 3:2–3). Contemporary Jewish scholars such as R. Yonassan Gershom have read that Jesus was speaking of reincarnation in this passage when he speaks of being born from above, or "born again," as some translators term it. That is a very astute reading, for the Christian idea of being born again by accepting Christ as one's personal savior was completely unknown to Nicodemus at the time. Jesus explained:

> "That which is born of flesh is flesh, and that which is born of the spirit is spirit. Do not be surprised that I told you you must be born from above. The wind (*pneuma*) blows as it wills and you hear its voice, but you cannot tell where it comes from, nor where it goes: so it is with everyone that is born of the spirit [*pneuma*]."* Nicodemus said to him, "How can this be?" And Jesus said to him, "Are you a teacher of Israel, and yet you do not understand this?" (Jn 3:6–10)

Jesus was speaking of a doctrine Nicodemus should already have been exposed to. Note that the point of the discussion was for Jesus to explain how he *personally* was able to do the marvelous signs from God in response to Nicodemus's question. To miss this is to miss the context of the entire passage. Thus, we need to carefully read John 3:13, paying particularly close attention to the verb tense: "No one *has*

---

*Wind and spirit are the same word in Greek and Hebrew. In Hebrew, the word is *ru'ach*.

ascended [*anabebeken*] into heaven but he who descended from heaven, the Son of Man" (my emphasis). Jesus's glorious ascension into heaven to sit at the right hand of the Father did not occur until after his death, burial, and resurrection (Mk 16:19). However, here Jesus says that he had *already* gone up into heaven before his birth. Prior to the historical Jesus, there are two and only two figures in all the Bible who were taken up into heaven while still living.* They are Enoch (Gen 5:24) and Elijah (2 Kg 2:11).

Elsewhere in the New Testament, Jesus had identified John the Baptist as Elijah (Mt 11:14; 17:1–13). Therefore, in John 3:13, Jesus effectively announced himself as the reincarnation of Enoch. The use of the title "Son of Man" in this verse is also important, for it is the same messianic title ascribed to Enoch in the Book of Enoch passage above. His prior ascension as Enoch is therefore what Jesus meant when he asked the disciples, "Then what if you were to see the Son of Man ascending to where he was before?" (Jn 6:62).

40 CHRISTIAN REINCARNATION DOCTRINE

I trust I have done a good job of revitalizing the lost doctrine of reincarnation in Christianity by pointing out that the Essenes and early Christians believed in it. Since I am one of the few Christian theologians who take reincarnation seriously, I shall close out this chapter with a short biblical study of reincarnation. Many will assume that since I believe in reincarnation, I encourage the wholesale importation of reincarnation doctrine from other faiths. That is not true. In some cases, there is no harm in searching out other faiths for doctrines that Christians have left unexplored. If we take the idea that Jesus was the full and complete incarnation of the Logos seriously (Jn 1:1–18), then we would expect to find similarities in other faiths, for the Logos is the

---

*Moses was taken into heaven by God *after* death, which is also important, but to avoid confusion I thought it best to go into that detail at the end of chapter 7. Jewish texts refer to these three figures as the "elect" of God (Mt 17:3–5; Mal 3:1; 4:5–6).

common seed of truth in all the world's religions. In many respects, however, the Bible's teachings on reincarnation are unique, which is why they must be studied in their own right.

Anthropology

The New Testament, in continuation of the Hebrew Bible, teaches a distinctive anthropology. It teaches that human beings are composed of mind (*nous*), body (*soma*), soul (*psyche*), and spirit (*pneuma*). The Greeks believed that the spirit was merely an animative force that perishes with the body. They also believed the soul is immortal by nature. Much of this Platonic body/soul dualism was incorporated into Christianity by the early fathers. But it is directly contrary to biblical teaching.[15]

Note that although Adam was created a living soul (Gen 2:7), he was forbidden to eat of the Tree of Eternal Life, which would have given him unconditional immortality (Gen 3:22–24). The soul is not immortal by nature, as the Greeks taught, nor does the Bible teach a body/soul dualism. For example, the Bible often attributes bodily functions to the soul. It hungers (Ps 107:9; Pr 10:3; 27:7) and thirsts (Pr 25:25), it hates (Ps 17:19), loves (Gen 34:3; Jer 2:24), or seeks vengeance (Ps 27:12). The soul knows and remembers (Ps 139:14; Lam 3:20). And it even dies (Ez 13:19; Rev 16:3). In short, the Bible teaches that the soul and body are completely unified. The soul is created with the body, and it ceases to be upon death.

Although the soul dies, we never find an instance in the Bible where the spirit dies. When death comes, "the silver cord is snapped, the golden bowl is broken . . . the dust returns to earth as it was, and the spirit returns to God who gave it" (Ec 12:6–7). The spirit in human beings, not the soul, is the enduring supernatural part of us. It is also the part of us that enables us to engage in dialogue with God's Spirit: "The Spirit itself bears witness with our spirits that we are children of God" (Rom 8:16). Note this passage from the Wisdom of Solomon: "As a child I was by nature well endowed, and a good soul fell to my lot; or rather, being good, I entered an undefiled body" (8:19–20). The editors of *The New Oxford Annotated Bible with the Apocrypha* commented that this text speaks of "the platonic view of the soul as preexistent."[16] But they got it slightly wrong. Yes, the author is discussing reincarnation. But his views on reincarnation are Hebrew, not Platonic. He says "a good soul fell to my lot," and that he was awarded "an undefiled body" for "being good." His soul is therefore not preexistent. He took on both a new body and a new soul in that life. The Greeks taught that the soul migrated from life to life, but the spirit dissipated upon death.

In Hebrew thought it is exactly the opposite. The Bible teaches that the spirit migrates, not the soul.* Thus, when Luke reported that John the Baptist would go before Christ in the "spirit and power of Elijah" (1:17a), this is all the information we need to ascertain that John was Elijah reincarnated, just as Jesus so identified him (Mt 11:14; 17:1–13). To ask whether John bore the soul of Elijah is not a properly formed question in Biblical anthropology. The spirit of Elijah *is* Elijah. It is all of him that remains. Consistently, the Dead Sea Scrolls also show that the Essenes believed it is the spirit that migrates, not the soul: "His spirit consists of six in the House of Light and three in the Pit of Darkness" (4Q186, 1 II, 7–8).

Heaven, Hell, and Final Judgment

As the Scroll fragment just quoted indicates, heaven and hell play an integral part in one's migration history. The Bible teaches two types of reincarnation. First there are those who reincarnate to help humankind, such as when Paul addressed the Galatian church: "My little children, of whom I travail in birth again until Christ be formed in you" (Gal 4:19, KJV). Paul also wrote, "Are they ministers of Christ? (I speak as a fool) I am more; in labors more abundant,

---

*It may helpful for me to coin a new term, *metempneumosis,* meaning the specific form of reincarnation the Bible supports, as opposed to *metempsychosis.* See also John 3, where Jesus discusses migration of the spirit (*pneuma*).

in stripes above measure, in prisons more frequent, *in deaths oft*" (2 Cor 11:23, KJV). Second, there are those who reincarnate as a necessary consequence of their sin, like the serpent in the Garden of Eden, who are caught in an endless cycle of death and rebirth until the Day of Judgment. Their bodies and souls are destroyed in hell (Mt 10:28), and their still-polluted spirits come back again: "Fill up, then, *the measure of your fathers*. You serpents, you brood of vipers. How are you going to *escape* being sentenced to hell?" (Mt 23:32–33; my emphasis).

Inasmuch as angels are the spirits of humans who reincarnate (see the dream of Jacob's ladder, Gen 28:12), likewise the brood of serpents are the spirits of humans who reincarnate. For the latter, hell is the first form of death. It is not the second and final form of death, which comes at the Day of Judgment in the end times: "Blessed and holy is he who shares in the first resurrection! Over such the second death has no power" (Rev 20:6). For the righteous, final judgment means no longer having to endure the hardship of rebirth: "Him that overcomes I will make a pillar in my Temple and he will go out no more" (Rev 3:12, KJV). Just as the Hasidim today believe, orthodox resurrection of the dead also occurs at the end times for those not already incarnate, and the Lord will "swallow up death forever" (Is 25:8). Note that the purgatorial scheme, a man-made theological attempt to deal with what happens in the interim between individual death and final judgment, is completely unnecessary. Upon death, one goes immediately to heaven or hell, just as Scripture reports (Lk 16:22–23; 23:43; Acts 7:59).

As to whether those who have made it to heaven *must* reincarnate until the end times, or whether it is left up to each individual whether he or she *wants* to return, it is hard to say. Very likely God leaves that question for each of us to decide, based on our love of humankind versus our need to replenish. The Bible does not seem to give express instruction one way or the other, except to say that Christ himself will return only at the end times (Heb 9:27–28, which can now be understood in its full context). The Buddhists are split right down the middle on this very question. The Mahayana or "greater vehicle" school of Buddhism teaches that Siddartha Gautama returns again and again until all humankind is enlightened. The Hinayana or "lesser vehicle" teaches that Siddartha Gautama is no more, that he has reached Nirvana and no longer exists as an entity.

While we are on the subject, I do not believe that the Buddhist *anatta* or "no-self" doctrine can easily be reconciled with Christianity, due to the fundamentally different views on existence. The no-self doctrine is Siddhartha Gautama's answer to suffering.[17] In Buddhism, existence is generally considered a tragedy to be overcome, whereas the Bible teaches that existence is a good thing in and of itself (Gen 1:31). A certain form of ontological separation from God is necessary and natural for us to exist as individual entities. To deny that would be to deny God's very reason for creating us. In contrast, sin is an *unnecessary* and *unnatural* form of separation, both from God and oneself. In other words, as opposed to Buddhism, where subjective immortality has no value, the mystical dialogue with God is one that makes a person increasingly whole as an individual, not less.[18] That is why Buber referred to our dialogue with God as an "I-Thou" and not an "I-It,"[19] because an "I-It" does not recognize a relationship of genuine otherness. For example, Jesus, who is the very measure of our perfection as Christians (Lk 6:40), still exists as an entity apart from the Father (Mk 16:19). Jesus did not pass into nonexistence, as some believe of the Buddha.

Here is another point that, incidentally, was missed in the formulation of the erroneous original-sin doctrine. In the Bible, existence precedes the Fall (Gen 1–3); existence is not itself the Fall, as many Buddhists believe. Buber made the astute observation that unless the Fall is interpreted as a recurring myth, we fail to grasp its deeper meaning: "Man always begins again and again as God's creature, although henceforth under the burden of a humanity cast out from Paradise into the world and history. . . . That he sins belongs to his condition, that he turns back belongs to his holding his own in it. He sins as Adam sinned and not because Adam sinned."[20] The only thing I would change of Buber's statement is to amend the last sentence to read: "He sins as Adam sinned and not *strictly* because Adam sinned." But for temptation, there would be no sin, and vice versa. Sin is its own "dependant co-arising," to borrow a useful term from the Buddhists.* In other words, sin is primarily a problem of human history, not human nature. Our children are not born racists, for example; that is something we teach them with each passing generation. The serpent in the Garden of Eden story is merely a mythological symbol for those wretched old dragons (human beings) who continue to pollute the world with their bad karma.

However, as the early church father Pelagius knew but was unable to convince the rest of Christendom, each and every child is born as innocent as Adam and Eve in the primordial Garden.† Thus, we have always been but a single generation away from the Promised Land. God said to Moses when he denied him and that entire generation of Israel the right to cross the Jordan, "Your children, who this day have no knowledge of good and evil, shall go in there, and to them I will give it, and they shall posses it" (Dt 1:39). That is why Jesus said, "Whoever does not enter the kingdom like a little child shall not enter it" (Mk 10:15).

The Calvinist doctrine of "once saved, always saved" takes on a new dimension in a reincarnation context. This is another question to which I will not attempt to give an absolute answer, for to do so would surely distort the issue itself. In other words, it comes down to

---

*The cause and effect of sin are so closely related they are practically inseparable, which leads us to the extremely valuable conclusion that sin effectively is its own cause. I know this will be difficult for westerners to accept, for we tend to see causality only in linear terms, which means we usually want to make God responsible for evil.
†Original sin doctrine is still deeply entrenched. In 1989, the Vatican censured Catholic priest Matthew Fox for his teachings on "Original Blessing," which eventually led to his expulsion from the Dominican Order. See his *Original Blessing: A Primer in Creation Spirituality* (Santa Fe, NM: Bear & Company, 1983, rev. ed., 1996).

free will. As for myself, I have never believed the Calvinist doctrine applies to one life, let alone multiples, for it makes a joke of our free will. Lord knows I have seen many a "backsliding" Christian (and have even been one, on occasion). Jesus gave a parable that seems to me to speak directly to the issue. The setting for this parable is that Jesus came into Jerusalem and was hungry: "Seeing a fig tree in leaf, he went to see if he could find anything on it. When he came to it, he found nothing but leaves for it was not the season for figs. And he said to it, 'May no one ever eat fruit from you again.' And his disciples heard it. As they passed by in the morning, they saw the fig tree withered away to its roots. And Peter remembered and said to him, 'Master, look! The fig tree you cursed has withered'" (Mk 11:13–14; 11:20–21).

The fig tree was a perennial. It bloomed every year and produced figs; it just happened not to bear figs at the very moment Jesus came upon it seeking its fruit. Thus Jesus cursed it to death to make a point. Regardless of how righteous each of us may have been in our past lives, all that matters is the "eternal now," as Paul Tillich put it. That is why we must always be on the ready for judgment and not delay our salvation, even for one moment: "Take heed, watch; for you do not know when the time will come" (Mk 13:33). I will give this concession to the Calvinists: The principle of karma means that we tend to reap in accordance with the character we sow, not only from life to life but also within each life. But the fact that there is judgment and recompense at the end of each life means that each life is, for the most part, a closed book (Heb 9:27; but see Wis 8:19–20).

Karma

Finally, we may think that the purpose of reincarnation is to be a better person so that we might eventually balance the negative karma we have accumulated through several lifetimes. However, this would reduce reincarnation to a doctrine of "works" and justify such wrongs as the oppressive caste system that arose in India. Any theologies that bless and ordain social injustice as God's will are monstrous. Being a "better person" has nothing whatsoever to do with the Bible's plan of salvation. As the Epistle of James makes clear, good works naturally follow salvation, but works are not a means to an end. The Bible's teachings on karma, to borrow the term, are very different from the karma of Hinduism or Buddhism. Popular Hinduism essentially teaches that we reincarnate until our good works have overcome our bad, a feat impossible to achieve until after many lifetimes. Buddhism teaches that we reincarnate out of ignorance, because we have not perceived what Siddhartha Gautama deemed as truths about the cause and effect of physical existence—the "Four Noble Truths," the "Eightfold Path," and so on. Technically, in Buddhism you could still have sins upon you yet achieve full enlightenment. The fact that you have sinned against someone is irrelevant; what matters is that you grasp and experience the Buddhist philosophy. The Buddhist approach is to bypass sin by undoing the structures of the self. The Hindu meditative tradition found in the Upanishads is very similar. Experiential knowledge of the *Atman-Brahman* is supposed to liberate you regardless of the sins upon you. In contrast, the Bible teaches that our sins remain until they are *forgiven*. And that is purely a matter of grace (cf. Jn 9, especially vv. 1–5, 39–41). Our sins are interwoven into a moral and social context, which is to say they are objectively real. We cannot work or meditate them away.

Note carefully the Lord's Prayer: "And forgive us our debts, *as we also have forgiven our debtors*" (Mt 6:12, my emphasis). Note also this key passage: "Judge not, and you will not be judged; condemn not, and you will not be condemned; forgive, and you will be forgiven; give, and it will be given to you; good measure, pressed down, shaken together, running over, will be put into your lap. For the measure you give will be the measure you get back" (Lk 6:37–38). And also this passage: "Therefore I tell you, whatever you ask for in prayer, believe that you have received it and it will be yours. And when you stand praying, if you hold anything against anyone forgive him, so that your Father in heaven may forgive your sins. But if you do not forgive, neither will your Father who is in heaven forgive your sins" (Mk 11:24–26; cf. Mt 18:23–35). These are the karmic laws of the New Testament, and they are unique in the entire comparative religious landscape. We Christians often think that as long as we ask Jesus for forgiveness, we are home free. We think we can begrudge our trespassers and seek all the retribution we want, yet rely upon the blood Jesus shed on the Cross to cleanse us. This is a mockery of the Cross. Jesus will indeed forgive us for each and every sin we have ever committed, but only if we do likewise for everyone who has ever sinned against us. Jesus asks nothing more, nothing less. Contrary to popular opinion, universal love and forgiveness are not empty, feel-good "works," they are the necessary and sufficient conditions of being Christian—the very means of accepting Jesus as one's personal Savior.

Jews practice the Day of Atonement. On that day, each Jew is obligated to seek atonement for every sin he or she has committed throughout the year. There is a bifurcated concept of sin in Judaism that survives to this day. Sin against God is readily forgiven by asking forgiveness of God. God forgives, and the relationship is restored. Sin against another human being, on the other hand, is forgiven only by asking forgiveness of the one you have wronged. And, of course, winning human forgiveness is much more difficult. There is believed to be a final Day of Atonement, a day when all humankind will mutually forgive one another, and we can begin anew in Paradise. This concept survives in Christianity: the final Day of Atonement is identical to the fulfillment of the Kingdom of God on earth. Christians accept the Atonement of Jesus based on faith: faith in him, faith in each other that the Kingdom will actually come to pass. A similar concept is Jubilee. Every fifty years, the ancient Jews released indentured servants, returned land held for indebtedness, and otherwise mutually forgave all financial debts (Lev 25:8–24). Jesus announced the Jubilee at his home synagogue as a way of proclaiming that the messianic age was at hand (Lk 4:18–19). Yet the Jubilee Jesus had in mind extended far beyond forgiving financial debts. Jesus intended that we forgive all sins against one another, and he knew he would light the way. Jesus is the one man in history who can bring about the Atonement and Jubilee of all humankind, because he alone has that moral authority; in his enigmatic words, he is the one and only "door" (Jn 10:6–7). Let me point out that, under this bifurcated concept of sin, the idea that Jesus is the incarnation of God does not quite answer how Jesus can offer complete forgiveness. As the Son of God, he can offer forgiveness of sin against God. But it is only as the Son of Man that he can offer forgiveness of sin against man.

Reincarnation means our sins are far more interconnected with each other than most of us realize. Eastern faiths refer to this as the problem of *collective karma*. Because temptation causes sin and sin further temptation, the effects of a single unforgiven sin can spread out among all humankind, even circle back to you in another life. And it has been so since the beginning of time. When Cain slew Abel, Abel's blood cried out from the ground for vengeance, and that unforgiven sin has haunted the family of man ever since.* Death seemingly closes the door for the opportunity to win forgiveness, for, as Camus put it in *The Fall*† we "cannot catch time by the tail." Yet Jesus takes it all away. Just like the sweet wine of Communion, the blood of Jesus "speaks more graciously than the blood of Abel. See that you do not refuse him who is speaking" (Heb 12:24–25).

---

*No gender bias is intended by the phrase "family of man" because in context the "family of man" refers to the family of Adam, meaning the entire human family. Adam means "man" in Hebrew.

†The tragedy in Camus's *The Fall* is one the author did not explicitly reveal, for in true Socratic fashion, he knew it is always better for the reader to come to knowledge on his or her own. The main character, Clamence, is racked with guilt because his girlfriend has drowned herself over him. Clamence is in existential angst because he wrongly believes he is beyond the grace of God.

5

The Teacher of Righteousness Revealed

The Teacher of Righteousness was the high priest and charismatic leader of the Essenes, the authors of the celebrated Dead Sea Scrolls. Although the Teacher is the central figure found in the Scrolls, his identity has thus far eluded Scrolls scholars. The task has always been a difficult one, for, like most figures found in the Scrolls, the Teacher is never mentioned by name. Although more references are made to him than to any other person, he is always referred to in a cryptic manner, such as "the Teacher of Righteousness, to whom God made known all the mysteries of the words of His servants, the prophets" (1QpHab VII, 4–5). Therefore I cannot identify the Teacher from the Scrolls alone and doubt whether anyone on earth will ever be able to do so. Such references simply are not there to be found. The Teacher's identity can only be recovered through a combination of Scrolls, Bible, and other historical research, together with a lot of deductive reasoning. Given that many early Scrolls scholars speculated that the Teacher was Jesus, the true identity of the Teacher is anticlimactic by comparison. His actual name is really little more than a footnote of history. What is not anticlimactic is the Teacher's self-understanding and role in prophecy, for they show how deeply rooted in Judaism Christianity truly is.

41 THREE MESSIANIC FIGURES EXPECTED BY THE JEWS

Origen noted in his commentary on the Gospel of John that when John the Baptist was asked by what authority he was baptizing, the Pharisees asked first whether he was the Christ; second, whether he was Elijah; and third, whether he was "the prophet" (Jn 1:19–21). John denied that he was all of these, but he did not deny he was *a* prophet, for that would have denied even his own limited understanding of his role; John merely denied he was *the* prophet. The distinction must be carefully maintained. Otherwise, we miss the fact that when the Pharisees asked, "Then why are you baptizing, if you are neither the Christ, nor Elijah, nor the prophet?" (Jn 1:25) they were speaking of *three separate figures*. Christians have been so caught up in defending John the Baptist as the forerunner of Jesus, we have missed another equally important forerunner altogether.

"The prophet" emerges from this passage as a term of art used by the Pharisees in expectation of a messianic forerunner, if not the Messiah himself (Jn 7:40–41). The Pharisees seemed ignorant of his identity. And rightly so, for the Bible nowhere mentioned "the prophet" by name, as it did the return of Elijah. Origen, with his characteristic sharp eye for Scripture, noted a key reference to the anonymous prophet in the Book of Deuteronomy, a reference found in Moses's final address to Israel: "[And the Lord said to me], I will raise up for them a prophet like you from among their brethren; and I will put my words in his mouth, and he shall speak all that I command him. And whosoever will not give heed to my words which he shall speak in my name, I myself will require a reckoning of him" (Dt 18:18–19). It is of great relevance that this passage from Deuteronomy is found in the Messianic Anthology from Cave 4 at Qumran as the

first of three prooftexts (4Q175 I, 7–8). The Essenes doubtless interpreted this prophetical passage to speak of their expected Teacher of
Righteousness. This reveals the Teacher's self-understanding to me as
clearly as I could wish, although this is a matter I should take the
time to rightly develop.

42 THREE MESSIANIC FIGURES EXPECTED BY THE ESSENES: THE PROPHET, THE KING, THE PRIEST

I should first note the messianic theme found in the Scrolls. Geza
Vermes mentions in his introduction to *The Complete Dead Sea
Scrolls in English* that the messianic theme is prominent: "Complex
and *sui generis,* [the Scrolls] envisage sometimes one messianic figure,
royal, Davidic, triumphant . . . again and again two, and once possibly even three Messiahs."[1] Though Vermes is aware of more than one
messianic figure expected in the Scrolls, he seems unable to decide
upon the actual number. Here is the heart of the problem. A great
deal of confusion over the identity of the Teacher has resulted from
mistakenly limiting the number of messianic figures expected by the
Essenes to two. That is why the attempts by dissident scholars to
identify the Teacher as either Jesus or John the Baptist have rightly
failed. I have just shown that three messianic figures were expected
by the Pharisees. I must now establish that the same three messianic
figures were expected by the Essenes.* For ease of exposition, I shall
address each figure in the order given above. I ask the reader not to
draw ideas of hierarchy from this.[2] The Essene hierarchy of the three
almost certainly differed from that of the early Christians, a complicated issue that will emerge shortly. The first order of business is to

---

*It may have taken the Scrolls authors some time to formulate the idea that three messi-
anic figures were expected. One of the earliest manuscripts, the Damascus Rule, seems to
combine references to the Messiahs of Aaron and Israel as one (CD XIV, 9). See Vermes,
The Dead Sea Scrolls in English (4th ed., New York: Penguin, 1995), 96.

correlate the Prophet, the King, and the Priest, the three messianic figures of the Scrolls, with the three messianic figures of Pharisaic inquiry: Elijah, the Christ, and "the prophet."

43 JOHN THE BAPTIST, THE PROPHET

The first messianic figure I will discuss is the Prophet. In the scrolls and fragments that have been translated so far, he is apparently mentioned directly only once, but that is sufficient to show that he is a separate and third messianic figure. His arrival is expected together with that of the two other messianic figures, the Priest and the King, who are called "the Messiahs of Aaron and Israel" (1QS IX, 11). The Prophet, the third figure who was expected to appear with the Messiahs of Aaron and Israel, may cause the reader confusion. He should not be confused with "the prophet" referred to by the Pharisees in John's Gospel. In the context of the Scrolls, mentions of the Prophet should be interpreted as cryptic references to another who was eagerly expected by Jews in Jesus's day, namely Elijah incarnate. The reason I believe this reference by the Essenes differs from the similar usage by the Pharisees is that the former, being "perpetually conversant in the discourses of the prophets" (*War* 2.159), would have known the identity of "the prophet," whereas the Pharisees would not have. It can be shown analytically how these two references differ from each other, but such an argument would exhaust the conclusions of this entire chapter. I ask the reader to trust me at this point and keep reading.

44 ELIJAH COME TO LIFE

I believe the Scrolls authors, or at least the highest priests among them, perceived the Prophet to be Elijah, who was incarnate in John the Baptist (Mal 4:5; Mt 11:13–15). Perhaps the strongest connection to show that John the Baptist was expected by the Essenes is recorded in Luke's Gospel, where the angel Gabriel appears and announces to John's father, Zechariah the priest, his son's role: "[John] will go before [the Lord] in the spirit and power of Elijah" (Luke 1:9–19). Although I do not believe Barbara Thiering's identification of Gabriel to be complete, I endorse her assessment that he was a living human being, an Essene high priest believed to be the angel Gabriel (cf. Dan 9:21).[3] Hence, at least Zechariah's understanding of his son's role and the Prophet as expected in the Scrolls would have been one and the same, since an Essene high priest actually announced this expectation, largely bringing it to pass. We also know of John's continued association with the Essenes. The Essenes were known to "adopt other men's children, while yet pliable and docile, and regard them as their kin and mold them in accordance with their own principles" (*War* 2.120). We can deduce that Zechariah either was one of their priests already living among them, or deferred the raising of his son to the Essenes. There can be no other reasonable possibility, for Luke's account of John's birth ends with this astonishing statement: "And the child grew strong in spirit, and *he was in the wilderness until the time of his manifestation to Israel*" (Lk 1:80, my emphasis). John obviously could not have survived the wilderness as an infant. Therefore, reason suggests that the "wilderness" Luke referred to was the area in and around the Qumran settlement in North Judea.[4] The Qumran settlement was more or less a monastery where the Essenes withdrew in eager preparation for the Messiah.

When John began baptizing at the Jordan River where Elijah was taken up (2 Kg 2:5–11; Mt 3:4), he was a few scant miles or so from Qumran, which has suggested to many Scrolls scholars over the years that John once lived there.[5] In light of the above references to his upbringing, there is no doubt in my mind that he did. John would one day leave the settlement to live the rough-and-ready hermetical life of an Old Testament prophet, just as did Elijah, dressing in camel's hair and eating wild honey (2 Kg 1:8; Mt 3:4). We cannot be sure exactly when John left the settlement. But it is likely John struck out on his hero's walk with God and began his baptismal ministry at age thirty, the age at which an Essene was considered fully mature and able to participate in ministerial affairs (1Q28a I, 13–16). This would accord nicely with the Gospel of Luke, for we know that Jesus was about thirty years old when he began his public ministry, and that he was born six months later than his cousin John (Lk 1:24–26; 3:23). Thus, the idea that both John and Jesus began their ministries purely by mystical direction will have to be modified. More than likely, each was merely following the dictates of the Essenes.

45 ESSENE BAPTISM AS EARLY CHRISTIAN BAPTISM

Much ado has been made of the fact that John was baptizing repentant sinners at the River Jordan and that the Essenes are well known to have been "bathers," to have practiced ritual baptism for just such a purpose. For the ancient Essenes and Christians alike, baptism was the rite by which a proselyte gained admission into the community of believers (1QS III, 9–10; V, 13–15). Largely for this reason, the Jewish historian Gräetz concluded that John the Baptist was an Essene attempting to bring in the new age by baptizing all of Judea into his order.[6] I concur; I believe this was precisely what John was doing. Interestingly, Gräetz gave this interpretation based on classical sources alone, nearly a hundred years before the Dead Sea Scrolls were found. But surprisingly, Scrolls scholars have thus far rejected Gräetz's interpretation. James H. Charlesworth concluded that it is misleading to label the Essenes a baptismal cult. He rejects the notion that Christians derived the doctrine of baptism from the Essenes, and therefore from John. He draws this conclusion on the basis that Christian baptism occurs only once, whereas Essene baptism was a continual ritual.[7]

Yet I think Charlesworth and a great many other scholars have fallen into an anachronism by failing to recognize Christian baptism in the form it once existed. *The Gospels never assert that John practiced solitary baptism* (Mk 1:1–8 // Mt 3:1–12 // Lk 3:3–16 // Jn

1:25–33). There is one notable exception: Jesus himself was given a solitary baptism. John preached that he baptized with water only, but Jesus would baptize with the Holy Spirit and with fire (Mt 3:11).* Jesus's own baptism was the latter, a wholly different type of baptism than John had been practicing (Mk 1:9–11). Unlike the Essenes, Jesus probably understood himself to need only one baptism, for what is clean is clean (cf. Jn 13:9–10). It is very likely Jesus himself reformed this Essene practice, for we have solid scriptural evidence that the baptism as practiced by Jesus's disciples conflicted with John's. Note this brief but revealing reference found in John's Gospel: "Now a discussion arose between John's disciples and a Jew over *purifying*. And they came to John, and said to him, 'Rabbi, he who was with you beyond the Jordan, to whom you bore witness, here he is baptizing and all are going to him'" (3:25–26; my emphasis). "Purifying water" was the term applied to baptism by the Scrolls authors (1QS III, 9). It is probably at this point in history that solitary baptism was introduced, triggering the discussion over it by John's disciples and other Jews.

There exists today a small but fascinating group of people, found mainly in southern Iraq and Iran, called *Mandaeans*. The Mandaeans claim to be directly descended from disciples of John the Baptist, who never converted to Jesus. More correctly, they would say they preceded John the Baptist, that he grew up with them, learned from them, and taught according to their customs and traditions. Some scholars believe the Mandaeans are perhaps the last living descendants of the Essenes.[8] How that is relevant to this discussion is that the Mandaeans practice baptism continually throughout their lives. They are baptized in running water at least once each Sunday, in the same manner as they

---

*Charlesworth believes that the Essenes coined the use of the term "Holy Spirit," which appears nowhere in the Old Testament. See his *Jesus and the Dead Sea Scrolls*, 20f. I concur. John's use of the phrase indicates an Essene upbringing. However, Charlesworth is hesitant to draw connection between John and the Essenes because of Acts 19:1–6, see ibid., 22. I distinguish this verse in the following discussion.

believe John the Baptist baptized more than two millennia ago in the River Jordan.

At whatever point in history solitary baptism was introduced, reason simply begs for the connection. "One baptism for the remission of sins," as a present-day Christian would understand it from our various creeds, is undoubtedly an evolved version of this Essene ritual. Perhaps solitary baptism was slow to take hold among the early Christians, given what we now know of James the Righteous, Jesus's half-brother. James became leader of the Jerusalem church, where we know Essene practices lingered. Or perhaps Paul was ultimately responsible for the change. Paul could have modified Essene baptismal practices in imitation of the Holy Spirit anointing of Jesus, and in imitation of the crucified and resurrected Christ (cf. Acts 19:1–6, note the double baptism which was not refused; Eph 4:4–5; Col 2:12).

46 TELLTALE ESSENE LIFESTYLE AND DOCTRINES

As for John's lifestyle and preaching, the Gospels give several references to doctrines known to be held by the Essenes. John "did not eat or drink" as instructed by the Essene high priest Gabriel (Mt 11:18; Lk 1:15). That is, John led a rigid ascetic lifestyle that the Essenes were known to follow, abstaining from rich foods and hard wine. We also find in John's preaching a call for primitive communism. He preached, "He who has two coats, let him share with him who has none; and he who has food, let him do likewise" (Lk 3:11). The historian Josephus records the very same doctrine of the Essenes: "[T]heir community of goods is truly admirable; you will not find one among them distinguished by greater opulence than another. They have a law that new members on admission to the sect shall confiscate their property to the order, with the result that you will nowhere see either abject poverty or inordinate wealth; the individual's possessions join the common stock and all, like brothers, enjoy a single patrimony" (*War* 2.122).*

And finally, the last general similarity I wish to note between John and the Essenes is the vocabulary John used in his preaching. One finds the same apocalyptic dualism in both. John called the unrepentant hypocrites who came to him for baptism "a brood of vipers" (Mt 3:7a). Otto Betz found this to be a term of art unique to the Essenes. In Hebrew, it is *ma'ase eph'eh,* meaning "creatures of the snake." The same term is found in the Thanksgiving Hymns (1QH III, 17). "In short," Betz concluded, "the prophetic language of John the Baptist was enriched by the polemics of the Qumran community of the Essenes."[9] Betz was absolutely correct. John was brought up in and still strongly influenced by the same breed of apocalyptic fervor as the Essenes at the time of his ministry. It is possible, even, that some of John's apocalyptic fervor rubbed off on Jesus. In the popular movie adaptation of Nikos Kazantzakis' *Last Temptation of Christ,* Jesus begins his ministry with a message of love that is almost too pure to be grasped. After Jesus encounters his cousin the Baptist (Jesus and John were maternal cousins of unknown degree, Lk 1:36), he begins to take up some of John's fire-and-brimstone approach to get his message across (cf. "The axe is laid to the root of the trees," Mt 3:10a).

While Jesus often emerges from the Gospels as an extremely complex figure due to the opposition he encountered, it is all the more difficult to get inside the head of the Baptist. Both John and Jesus were a generation removed from the radical apocalyptic dualism that characterized the Righteous Teacher and his support group. Yet John

---

*Josephus may be speaking of a different group of Essenes than those who lived monastic existences, namely those who lived among towns. Vermes notes that there seems to be some difference in the property laws for the Qumran sectaries, CD XIV, 12–16, yet this would be only a matter of degree. Since John was later to separate himself from the Qumran sectaries, these slight variations do not outweigh this characteristic Essene doctrine. See Vermes, *The Dead Sea Scrolls in English* (4th ed., New York: Penguin, 1995), 15.

was still close enough that many of their doctrines are recognizable in him. He was living as the human center of both the old and the new. I believe we can understand Jesus only in terms of his personal calling and unqualified dedication to God, and likewise the heroic walk of his prophet, John. This is probably why scholars have been so hesitant to mechanically identify John as an Essene. Nevertheless, once it is granted that John's personal relationship with God was dynamic, his Essene background seems too clear to ignore. Too many Essene doctrines are found in the Baptist's preaching for it to be otherwise.

47 AN IDENTIFYING EXEGESIS

There is a reference to the Prophet that may give us enough information to point directly to John. In 1QS IX, 12–X, 26, we find a listing of precepts by which "the Master" is supposed to walk. The entire scroll, known as the Community Rule, consists of such precepts. The Community Rule probably applied to the Masters and Guardians of the community in general. If the passage that mentions the third prophet was about John, if he was the particular Master in question, then it parallels nicely John's self-understanding as fulfilling the prophecy of Isaiah. John cited the prophet Isaiah to the Pharisees to show by whose authority he was preaching: "I am the voice of one crying in the wilderness, 'Make straight the way of the Lord,' as the prophet Isaiah says" (Jn 1:23). And found in the Scrolls is: "*This is the time for the preparation of the way into the wilderness,* and he shall teach them to do all that is required at that time and to separate from all those who have not turned aside from ungodliness" (1QS IX, 19–21; my emphasis). This Master was also supposed to be "a man zealous for the Precept" (1QS IX, 23), who would "bless Him [with the offering] of the lips at the time ordained by Him" (1QS IX, 26). In other words, he was to make known the time of Messiah, a role that seems to have been specifically reserved for John. He alone, and no other Essene, proclaimed openly to the masses, "Repent, for the kingdom of heaven is at hand! . . . I baptize you with water for repentance, but he who is coming after me is mightier than I, whose sandals I am not worthy to carry; he will baptize you with the Holy Spirit and with fire" (Mt 3:2, 11). And where would Christianity be without John's famous identification of Jesus, "Behold, the Lamb of God, who takes away the sin of the world!" (Jn 1:29)?

I should note that John does not seem to have been informed that he was Elijah incarnate by the Essenes (Jn 1:21), an identification that Jesus later made (Mt 11:13–15). It is possible his father, Zechariah, never told him of the circumstances of his birth—the announcement by Gabriel, the Essene high priest, that he was Elijah. Perhaps Zechariah loved his son too much to reveal the horrors, foretold in the prophecies that awaited him (Mt 17:12–13 cf. Gen 40). Thus, John's rational or "earthly" self-understanding was likely limited to the above passage known to him from his Essene upbringing. All the self-understanding he needed to fulfill his mission as recorded in the Gospels can be found there.

48   JESUS THE KING

The second messianic figure I will discuss is the King. He is referred to in the Scrolls as the "Messiah of Israel," the "Branch of David," and the "Scepter." He was to usher in "the Kingdom of his people" (1Q28b V, 21). These references are so suggestive of Jesus to the Christian reader that, when delivered from the radical doubt of the present scholarly consensus, they produce a presumption to be rebutted that Jesus was *not* this one who was foretold. They are that obvious. Jesus was a descendant of the line of Judah, the royal line of David (Is 7:13–14; 9:6–7; 11:1, 10; Zech 3:8; Mk 12:35–37; Mt 1:1; Heb 7:14). He was also born in Bethlehem, the birthplace of the Davidic Messiah as prophesied (Mic 5:2–6; Lk 2:1–11). Make no mistake, the birth of Jesus is foretold in the Dead Sea Scrolls. Preparing the way for the Messiah was the very purpose of the Qumran settlement's existence, as well as any other of the Essene settlements at the turn of the era. Scrolls scholars Eisenman and Wise have rightly called the Essenes who wrote the Scrolls a "messianic élite retreating or separating into the wilderness."[10] This is why on the Qumran Isaiah scroll, we find highlighted and separated from the rest of the text: "A voice cries in the wilderness, 'Prepare the way of the YHWH'" (1QIsa XL, 3).[11] The Essenes knew themselves to be personally fulfilling this prophecy. Found in the Community Rule, one of the oldest scrolls of the Qumran community, is: "[T]hey shall separate from the habitation of unjust men to go into the wilderness to prepare the way of Him; as it is written, 'Prepare in the wilderness the way of YHWH'" (1QS VIII, 14, quoting Is 40:3).

The reader might become confused in that the Scrolls refer to Jesus both as a King and a Wicked Priest. "Wicked Priest" is generally how the Essenes referred to Jesus after his break from them, especially in the Habakkuk Commentary (1QpHab). Otto Betz criticized the Jesus as Wicked Priest theory because 1QpHab specifically refers to this figure as a "Priest" (*cohen*), and Jesus was born of the House of David, a nonpriestly line.[12] This is a valid objection, but I do not think it fatal to the whole theory. If my restoration is correct, 1QpHab should be dated shortly after the first Easter. Early Christians certainly referred to Jesus as a "Priest" (Heb 7–8). Therefore it seems likely to me that the Essenes took their cue from them. Christians came to know Jesus both as a King and a Priest.

There is also internal evidence in 1QpHab that indicates the Essenes blurred the lines between the roles of King and Priest for this figure:

> *Moreover, the arrogant man seizes wealth without halting. He widens his gullet like Hell and like Death he never has enough. All the nations are gathered to him and jeer at him saying "Woe to him who amasses that which is not his? How long will he load himself up with pledges?"* (Hab 2:5–6)

Interpreted, this concerns the Wicked Priest who was called by the name of Truth when he first arose. But when he ruled over Israel his heart became proud and he forsook God and betrayed the precepts for the sake of riches. He robbed and amassed the riches of men of violence who rebelled against God, and he took the wealth of the peoples, heaping sinful iniquity upon himself. And he lived in the ways of abominations amidst every unclean defilement. (1QpHab VIII, 3–13)

Keep in mind that this text was written by Jesus's enemies, so we should not be surprised if it slanders him. It portrays exactly the reaction we would expect. The Essenes had groomed Jesus to be a royal figure. But at some point, Jesus broke from the Essenes, both ideologically and financially. He therefore had to solicit funding from those sympathetic to his cause to fuel the early Church. The Gospels report that Jesus was friendly with Roman soldiers and tax collectors (Mt 8:5–13; 10:3). Since the Essenes were puritanical Zionists, this accounts for the description of those who supported Jesus's ministry as "men of violence" who "rebelled against God." It may surprise some that Jesus could have been widely known as a "ruler over Israel," but this is just what the Gospels report.

Jesus was a social revolutionary. He preached the Kingdom of God, which his followers understood to embrace all aspects of life, including politics. Although he taught nonviolence instead of traditional military resistance to Israel's occupiers, Jesus was nonetheless popularly believed to be the Messiah of Israel. And Jesus took every opportunity he could to live up to that role. At the close of his ministry, Jesus made a triumphal entry into Jerusalem during Passover, an event now celebrated as Palm Sunday (Mk 11:1–10 // Mt 21:1–9 // Lk 19:28–38 // Jn 12:12–18). Jesus entered through the royal gate riding a colt, thus announcing himself as the Davidic Messiah in a very deliberate and dramatic fashion, with the specific intent to fulfill prophecy (cf. 1Kg 1:28–40; Zech 9:9). Mark's Gospel reports that a multitude called out, "Blessed is the kingdom of our father David that is coming! Hosanna in the highest!" (11:10). Some of them placed their garments in front of Jesus, others lined his path with palm branches (Mk 11:8; Jn 12:13). What is important about the palm branches is not only that they signified royalty (1 Kg 6:29, 32, 35), but also that palm trees have never been found in Jerusalem due to its high altitude. Mark's Gospel reports that the palm branches were "cut from the fields" (11:8), most likely from the banks of the Jordan near the Qumran settlement, where palm trees were and still are abundant. The point is, Jesus's triumphal entry into Jerusalem was not a spontaneous event. It had all the makings of a carefully planned and executed coronation. It is no wonder that Jesus caused such a reaction among the elders of Israel and the Romans.

49 A DIVERGENCE IN DOCTRINE: EARLY GNOSTIC INFLUENCES

While it is true that the coming of Jesus is foretold in the Scrolls, it is not easy to recognize this fact for those unfamiliar with Essene doctrines. In fact, even when one is well versed in their doctrines, it is very difficult. The Scrolls bear witness to an intense apocalyptic dualism, the like of which is unfamiliar to contemporary Judaism. When the angel Gabriel appeared to Daniel at the end of his vision, he told him that he had to return to fight against the patron angel of Persia (Dan 10:20). On the spiritual battlefield, that meant Israel was fated to clash with the doctrines of Zoroaster that had blended with Judaism during the Persian captivity. Texts are found in the Temple Scroll at Qumran that bear the unmistakable mark of Zoroastrian dualism:

> [God] has created man to govern the world, and has appointed for him *two spirits* in which to walk until the time of His visitation: the spirits of *truth* and *falsehood*. Those born of truth spring from a fountain of light, but those born of falsehood spring from a source of darkness. . . . The *Angel of Darkness* leads all the children of righteousness astray, and until his end, all their sins, iniquities, wickedness, and all their unlawful deeds are caused by his dominion in

accordance with the mysteries of God. . . . But the God of Israel and His *Angel of Truth* will succor all the sons of light. For it is He who created the spirits of Light and Darkness and founded every action upon them and established every deed [upon] their [ways]. *And He loves the one everlastingly* and delights in its works for ever; but the counsel of *the other He loathes forever* and hates its ways. (1QS III, 17–IV, 1; my emphasis)

These texts show the harmful effects of syncretism. It is hard enough for one religion to fight its way clear of error, but when foreign doctrines are introduced without the cultural understanding from which they arose, it usually always spells disaster. The dualism that took hold of the Essenes was even more pronounced than that of the Zoroastrianism of its day.[13] The Essenes have God creating two spirits and, most illogically, hating his own handiwork. In Zoroastrianism, it was implied, though never expressly stated, that the evil spirit chose to do evil by his own free will. But the Essenes rejected free will. They were such strong monotheists they fell into predestination (*Ant* 13.172). Since they believed some of humankind were created and predestined to be evil, not surprisingly, the Essenes felt divinely empowered to curse their enemies:

And the Levites shall curse all the men of the Lot of Belial, saying: "Be cursed because of all your guilty wickedness! May He deliver you up for torture at the hands of the vengeful Avengers! . . . Be cursed without mercy because of the darkness of your deeds! Be damned in the shadowy place of everlasting fire! May God not heed your call when you call upon Him, nor pardon you by blotting out your sin! . . ." And after the blessing and the cursing, all those entering the covenant shall say, "Amen, Amen!" (1QS II, 4–10)

Such are the ugly doctrines of the Essenes. Eisenman and Wise note that this harsh spirit of religious militancy may be unfamiliar to contemporary readers. It is very similar to the Puritans of seventeenth-century Europe, particularly Oliver Cromwell's bloody persecution of royalists and Catholics, and shortly thereafter the witch hangings in Salem, Massachusetts.[14] It is the same militant spirit found in today's Taliban or in some ultraconservative Christian groups. This type of militant spirit always arises in religion whenever there is found a good/evil dualism in which the "in-crowd" of believers feels divinely authorized to judge and punish God's enemies.

Because the Essenes have God creating a dualist cosmology to explain the origin of evil, many of their doctrines closely resemble those of Gnosticism. Readers of this book will likely be familiar with the Gnostic literature found in the Nag Hammadi documents. They are very important for understanding early Christianity. Although the Nag Hammadi documents were discovered about the same time as the Dead Sea Scrolls, research on the former has seriously lagged behind the latter due to the same sort of tight scholarly controls that once hindered Scrolls research. Elaine Pagels was one of the first Nag Hammadi scholars to publish, and she continues to be one of the most prolific scholars in the field. She points out that one of the key questions the Nag Hammadi documents present is how early the Gnostic movement began.[15] At one time, Gnosticism was believed to be a purely Christian movement. The theory was that Gnosticism was born of Greek-speaking Christians who created a hybrid religion by incorporating wholesale amounts of Platonic philosophy.

In the early twentieth century, however, New Testament scholar Wilhelm Bousset traced Gnosticism to ancient Persian sources. In other words, he believed Gnosticism arose from the same Zoroastrian influences that I just pointed out in the Scrolls. Hopefully my work will shed some valuable light on this question. It is common knowledge among philosophers that Plato was heavily influenced by Pythagoras. In chapter 4, I pointed out that Pythagoras likely got many of his ideas on reincarnation and asceticism from the early Essenes who were exiled in Persia during his travels there, many of the same ideas that eventually influenced Plato. Therefore a directly causal link between Platonism and Gnosticism is no longer necessary. It now appears from the Dead Sea Scrolls that Gnosticism arose indigenously within Judaism, at least initially.

Hence we now have a better understanding of how Jesus would have viewed the Gnostics. Like Essene doctrines, Gnostic doctrines are sometimes agreeable with Jesus's teachings and sometimes not. In many respects, the Gnostics interpreted Jesus's teachings correctly. For example, Gnostics believed that self-knowledge was a worthy path to God. They also believed that Jesus was not uniquely the Son of God in a way that forever excludes the rest of humanity. Orthodoxy rejected both these ideas, but they are solidly in accordance with the orthodox canon. Jesus taught, "The kingdom of heaven is within you" (Lk 17:21). And he also taught, "A student is not above his teacher, but everyone who is fully trained will be like his teacher" (Lk 6:40). But there were elements of Gnosticism that were sharply in disagreement with Jesus's teachings. Most Gnostics taught a doctrine that came to be known as *Docetism*. Docetism (from the Greek word *dokeo,* meaning "to appear") is the idea that God was not truly incarnate in the flesh. Rather, if Jesus was truly the Son of God, then an illusory phantom of Jesus appeared on earth; he only appeared to be crucified and resurrected. The second letter of John warned early Christians to steer clear of Docetism: "For many deceivers have gone out into the world, men who will not acknowledge the coming of Jesus Christ in the flesh; such a one is the deceiver and the antichrist" (2 Jn 7; cf. 1 Jn 4:2–3).

But this explanation is oversimplified. One Gnostic teacher wrote a letter found at Nag Hammadi, called the *Treatise on Resurrection,* in which he explained Docetism to one of his students: "Do not suppose the resurrection is an apparition. It is not an apparition; rather, it is something real. Instead, one ought to maintain that the world is an apparition, rather than the resurrection."[16] I cite this passage to show the real dangers of Docetism that still haunt us today. The Gnostics did not merely believe Jesus was an apparition. They believed in an existential alienation from the material world itself, similar to the maya teachings found in Shankara's monistic interpretation of nondualism (*advaita*) in Hindu philosophy.

Why is Docetism so harmful? Most of the problems with Christianity today can be traced back to this doctrine in one form or another. New Testament authors condemned Docetism because it reduced Christianity to a mystery religion devoid of practical worldly application, such as ethics and politics (1 Cor 2:14–3:1; 1 Jn 4:1–6). But generations of Christians have failed to heed their warnings. For instance, the Constantinian Fall and Docetism are very closely related. When the early church fathers took it upon themselves to distort Jesus's teachings on nonviolence, they typically did so by resorting to an "otherworldly" eschatology. Augustine's *City of God* is a prime example. Before his conversion, Augustine ascribed to Manichaeism, which is very similar to Gnostic Docetism and perhaps derived from the same source.* Augustine argued that as long as we inhabit a material body, we are incapable of living in perfect accordance with the gospel, so the Kingdom of God would have to wait. The Kingdom of God was interpreted as ahistorical, a realm that exists outside normal space and time. Augustine's *City of God* was instrumental in establishing the heretical "just war" doctrine. Therefore, to this day, most Christians do not take Jesus's teachings of "turn the other cheek" seriously.

It is also utterly impossible to practice meaningful environmental ethics when one believes the physical world should be destroyed so that Christians will be swept up to heaven in a glorious apocalyptic rapture. James Watt, the secretary of the interior during the Reagan administration, reportedly based his anticonservation policies on this heresy. And there is growing evidence that President Reagan himself based his nuclear arms buildup on the same heresy, specifically

---

*Upon deeper examination, Manichaeism will probably turn out to be a direct ideological descendant of Essene theology by way of the Mandaeans. Mani's father was a Mandaean, and contemporary Mandaeans revere John the Baptist as their last great prophet.

John Darby's peculiar brand of apocalypticism now taught by Hal Lindsey in his *Late Great Planet Earth* and *The 1980s: Countdown to Armageddon.*[17] The physical world may very well be destroyed if our leaders continue on their present course. But to *actively seek* the world's destruction to hasten the Kingdom of God? And to label peacemakers antichrist, as the "rapture ready" often do? I cannot think of a greater abomination.

The doctrine of original sin is another good example of docetic error grown cold. Docetism holds that we live in an imperfect world born of an imperfect creator, which is essentially the same worldview one still finds in orthodoxy. Incidentally, Anabaptists like the Amish and Mennonites realized long ago that the original-sin doctrine directly contradicts nonviolence, which is one of the reasons they rejected original sin. What is the relation? Once, at an honors forum at the University of Southern Mississippi, I asked Mohandas Gandhi's grandson, Arun Gandhi, if his grandfather believed human nature was basically good. He replied, "Yes, he did believe human nature was basically good, and so do I. The entire philosophy of nonviolence rests on that principle." Indeed it does. Laozi, Socrates, Jesus, Menno Simons, Leo Tolstoy, Mohandas Gandhi, Martin Luther King Jr., Dorothy Day, Oscar Romero, the Dalai Lama: what all these teachers of nonviolence have in common is a deep and abiding faith in the basic goodness of human nature. Nonviolence is an utterly nonsensical approach without that faith. It depends solely upon the transforming power of love to restore a wrongdoer to humanity. In contrast, original sin is a self-fulfilling prophecy. It expects the worst in human nature and thereby causes it and excuses it, even while it judges and punishes it. Ultimately, original sin puts the responsibility for evil on God instead of on us, where it belongs.

The problem of evil was addressed in one of the most thought-provoking books of the Bible, the Book of Job.[18] Those who struggle with the problem of evil usually fail to grasp that it was not God who punished Job; he merely allowed Satan to punish him acting as his own free agent (Job 1:12). The best way to understand the problem of evil is that God's omnipotence has to be "qualified," as process theologians put it. Namely, since we were created in the all-powerful Creator's very image and likeness (Gen 1:26), *God is no longer the only creator in the process.* It is thus up to us to take evil away, to co-create a world without evil in it. Adam said to God, "The woman whom *you* gave to be with me, *she* gave me the fruit of the tree, and I ate." Then Eve said, "*The serpent* beguiled me, and I ate" (Gen 3:12–13, my emphasis). There lies the heart of the Fall. It is the failure to accept existential responsibility for oneself before God and join God as a full partner in the creative process.[19]

In answer to those whose hatred is focused on the devil and desire his destruction, I say, let go of it. That kind of devil does not exist, except in the mind of Captain Ahab. I am not saying that there are not evil spirits set on our destruction, or even that there is not a most evil spirit. There certainly are and is, at least for the time being. What I am saying is that God has no opposite; there is no absolute Badness in opposition to God's perfect Goodness. For those of philosophical backgrounds, I am saying that evil has no *ontological grounding.* There are no perfectly evil beings whose existence we can eradicate to bring about harmony and justice. In contrast to the Gnostics and Essenes, who saw themselves in existential alienation from God as long as they lived in the mortal coil, Jesus taught perfection in the flesh was possible. Moreover, he not only taught that it was possible, but that it was required of us: "Therefore, be perfect, even as your Father in heaven is perfect" (Mt 5:48). How could Jesus command such a thing? His approach to perfection was wholly different from that of the Gnostics and Essenes. Both the Gnostics and Essenes identified the material part of our existence as sinful. Thus their path to perfection was based on strict asceticism: forbidding hard wine, forbidding natural intercourse with one's mate except for procreation, and the like.

The problem with this approach is self-evident: *It never works.* For example, whenever fundamentalist Christians come close to having a lock on political power in the United States, their leaders inevitably self-destruct by using prostitutes or illegal drugs or engaging in pedophilia—whatever behavior they condemn the most. Jungian psychologists tell us that the more forcefully we try to suppress our "shadow," the more forcefully it erupts, and usually at the most embarrassing times. When Jesus said, "My yoke is easy and my burden light" (Mt 11:30), he spoke of an entirely different and better way. He spoke of what is really best termed "wholeness" and not perfection.* The best way to deal with sin is to understand it for what it is. Sin is what results when our God-given passions are out of harmony with one another, a result of "good tortured by its own hunger," as the poet Kahlil Gibran so elegantly put it. Gibran continued, "You are good when you are at one with yourself. Yet when you are not one with yourself you are not evil. For a divided house is not a den of thieves; it is merely a divided house."[20] Precisely as Gibran recognized, Jesus and the early Christians taught that sin is nothing more than our own misrelation to ourselves, therefore ultimately a misrelation to God, in whom we are all grounded (Jn 10:34; Acts 17:28; Rom 7:15–25, especially v. 22; Jas 4:1–8).

50 A DIFFERENCE IN MESSIANIC EXPECTATIONS

When the Dead Sea Scrolls were first discovered, the great similarity in language between the Scrolls and the New Testament, particularly between the Temple Scroll (11Q19) and John's Gospel, immediately grabbed everyone's attention. It was perceived that the hidden origins of Christianity had been discovered. As Scrolls research matured, however, the harsh apocalyptic dualism shown above became evident,

---

*For a very rewarding discussion of this concept, see Erich Neuman, *Depth Psychology and a New Ethic* (London: Hodder & Stoughton, 1969). Incidentally, the verse "Therefore, be perfect" (Mt 5:48) is better translated "Therefore, be complete." The Greek word is *teloi*, from the root *telos*.

and scholars then realized how different Essene doctrines were from true Christian doctrines. For this reason, most scholars are now hesitant to think that Christianity had any Essene origins whatsoever. Yet this is also a scholarly attitude that has not matured. Eisenman and Wise have probably been the strongest advocates of the interpretation that the authors of the Dead Sea Scrolls withdrew into the wilderness specifically for the coming of Jesus. But even they realize that this is very difficult to show.

51 A "PIERCED" OR "PIERCING" MESSIAH?
(4Q285 v)

Vermes	Eisenman and Wise
1 Isaiah the prophet: [The thickets of the forest] will be cut [down]	1 […] Isaiah the prophet […]
2 with an axe and Lebanon by a majestic one will [f]all. And there shall come forth a shoot from the stump of Jesse […]	2 […] The Scepter shall go forth from the root of Jesse […]
3 the Branch of David and they will enter into judgement with […]	3 [the] Branch of David and they shall be judged [ ]
4 and the Prince of the congregation will kill him […]	4 And they shall put to death (possibly too "shall put to death") the leader of the community, the Bran[ch of David]
5 [by stroke]s and by wounds. And a priest [of renown (?)] will command […]	5 […] with wounds (also "stripes" or "piercings"), and the Priest (the High Priest) shall order […]
6 the [s]lai[n] of the Kitti[m]	

A scholastic battle was waged in the technical journals between Vermes (who published the Scrolls translations I have been using) and Eisenman and Wise. The competing translations above appeared side by side in the *Biblical Archaeology Review*.[21] Scrolls scholars referred to this as the battle over the "pierced" or the "piercing" Messiah. Note in line four: In the Eisenman and Wise translation, the Branch of David is put to death. Vermes probably offers the better translation. Prior to the actual crucifixion of Jesus, which I cover in chapter 7 (section 81), I doubt seriously that the Scrolls speak anywhere of a Messiah who is *pierced,* rather one who *pierces;* not one who is slain on an eschatological battlefield of the spirit, but one who slays on the battlefield of men. This fragment was a commentary on Isaiah 11:1–5, a passage that Paul would later use to speak of Jesus (Rom 15:12). While a true-to-the-gospel Christian pacifist today would interpret the Isaiah passage "He shall strike down a land with the rod of his mouth and shall slay the wicked with the breath of his lips" spiritually and non-violently—for example, he slays the wicked intentions of the heart with his loving words of peace—the authors of the Scrolls did not. Their expectations were worldly and militant. Similar expectations are found in the Blessing of the Prince of the Congregation, which interprets the Messiah as one who is expected to destroy the earth and slay the wicked (1Q28b V, 24–25), as well as the controversial "Son of God" fragment (4Q246) that presents the Messiah as a traditional military leader.

Evidently Essene messianic expectations were mostly drawn from chapters 1–39 of Isaiah, sometimes called *First Isaiah.* There, the Messiah is presented as a military leader who would conquer the occupiers and restore Israel to its lost glory. But Jesus specifically rejected this narrow interpretation, opting to include the later chapters known as *Second Isaiah* in his understanding of Messiah. For example, Isaiah 49:6 reads: "It is too light a thing that you should be my servant to raise up the tribes of Jacob and to restore the survivors of Israel; I will give you as a light to the nations, that my strength may reach the ends of the earth." Jesus understood himself to be the *Suffering Servant* of Isaiah 52:13–53.12, who "poured out his soul to death, and was numbered among the transgressors; yet he bore the sins of many, and made intercession for the transgressors" (53:12b). *Jesus allegorized the Zionist prophecies in First Isaiah, whereas the Essenes interpreted them literally*—a lesson woefully lost on Christian Zionists today. In fact, Jesus rejected a worldly kingdom as a temptation of Satan (Mt 4:8–11). Jesus did not behold himself as a king, but as a lowly slave, and asked the same of those who would follow him: "You know that those who are supposed to rule over the Gentiles lord it over them, and their great men exercise authority over them. But it shall not be so among you; but whoever would be great among you must be your servant, and whoever would be first among you must be slave of all. For the Son of Man came not to be served but to serve, and to give his life as a ransom for many" (Mk 10:42–45).

The Jesus we know from the Gospels, the Messiah who suffered and was crucified for the sins of the world, was the herald of a new way completely unknown to the Essenes and to first-century Jews in general. In fact, Jesus utterly astonished them, just as it was prophesied (Is 52:13–15; Mt 13:13–16). Even Jesus's disciple Peter, who knew him intimately, was totally unprepared for the fate of his master and tried to discourage him from meeting the Cross. Peter surely thought his master was insane (cf. Mk 8:31–33, 9:10; Mt 16:21–23). Jesus did not perceive his coming to be the end, but the beginning of a new Kingdom: "For God sent his Son into the world, not to condemn the world, but that the world might be saved who believes in him" (Jn 3:17).

52 THE TEACHER OF RIGHTEOUSNESS, THE PRIEST

The third messianic figure is the Priest, who, as I will show, was the Teacher of Righteousness. He is referred to in the Scrolls also as the "Messiah of Aaron," the "Elect," and the "Interpreter of the Law." Unsurprisingly, the Essenes, themselves of priestly descent, held him in the highest regard of all the three. The Priest was perceived to be the final teacher, as "he who shall teach righteousness at the end of days" (CD VI, 11). He was perceived to have a unique and divine authority to interpret Scripture (1QpHab VII, 3–5). Such beliefs bred in the Essenes what I call a radical charismatic fundamentalism. There was perceived to be neither correct scriptural interpretation nor works toward salvation apart from the Teacher. Even the King Messiah, the Branch of David, was to defer to the Teacher's priestly authority on all legal matters: "As they teach him, so shall he judge; and as they order, [so he will pass sentence]" (4Q161 8–10, 4). With all the authority perceived and vested in him by the Essenes, the Teacher of Righteousness emerged as a very powerful charismatic presence in first-century Palestine, a man who left a definite mark on early Christianity, though surely not the one he intended.

It has been rightly said that Jesus could have arisen only from within Judaism, from its unique teachings and the all-important dialectical process that honed those teachings. Although Jesus and the Teacher were both Essenes, each arising out of the same basic religion and messianic fervor, their respective worldviews were diametrically opposed. Perhaps without the Teacher of Righteousness, Jesus would not have been the man we now know through the Gospels. But the Teacher was not Jesus's gentle midwife. The Teacher was Jesus's purifying fire, who probably opposed him more than any man alive. That is sad, for it was not this way in the beginning. But I am getting ahead of myself. First I must complete the Teacher's identification.

53 ASTROLOGY

My restoration will soon show that the Teacher of Righteousness was believed to be Gabriel incarnate, the angel of annunciation. Gabriel was obviously of great significance for early Christianity, for, with his annunciation of the births of John the Baptist and Jesus, he almost single-handedly began the Christian epoch (Lk 1:8–20, 26–35). Paul wrote, "But when the time had fully come, God sent forth his Son" (Gal 4:4a). It thus fell to the Teacher to know when the fullness of time had come, or more specifically to those who would raise and educate the Teacher, about the role that he was to fulfill. One of the strongest reasons the Essenes believed themselves living at the exact time when the fulfillment of all messianic prophecies was at hand is that they practiced astrology. The expected arrival of the Teacher is found in Cave 4 at Qumran among a collection of horoscopes, which claim a correlation between a person's birth and an accompanying configuration of the stars. For example, in column two of these horoscopes there is this reference: "And his birthday on which he is to be born: in the foot of the Bull . . . his animal is the bull" (4Q186 1 II, 8–9) that refers to the sun in the lower part of the constellation of Taurus at the moment of this person's birth. While some may find it disturbing that the Scrolls make use of astrology, Vermes notes that the Hellenistic Jewish writer Eupolemus credited the invention of astrology to Abraham himself.[22]

Other Jewish writers attribute the invention of astrology to Enoch. The Book of Enoch, numerous copies of which were found at Qumran, gives astrological correlations by which all the traffic of Jacob's ladder is regulated: "I beheld twelve gates open for all the spirits from which they proceed and blow all over the earth" (1 En 76:1; cf. Gen 28:10–17). There is even a reference for the constellation of the Son of Man, the revealed Messiah of the Book of Enoch, whom Jesus understood himself to be, as I covered in chapter 4 (section 39). It says, "The second is called the south, because the Most High there descends, and frequently there descends he who is blessed forever" (1 En 77:2).

Many scholars have sought to make sense of the Star of Bethlehem (Mt 2:1–12). After much study, I have concluded that the three Magi who journeyed to see Jesus were Babylonian astrologers (likely diasporic Jews) following "the bright morning star" that appeared "with the clouds." That is, these astrologers set upon their journey due to the *Great Conjunction,** a triple conjunction of Jupiter and Saturn that, in Jesus's day, appeared in the constellation of Pisces. The verse "We have seen his star in the East [*en te anatole*]" (Mt 2:2b) is surely a faulty transcription. The better wording is: "We have seen his star in the first rays of dawn [*en te anatolai*]," which perfectly describes the heliacal rising of this rare and brilliant astronomical event.[23] These men of Nineveh were relying upon all the magic of the earth and skies to read the sign of the times (cf. Mt 12:38–42 // Lk 11:16, 29–32, see especially "sign of Jonah": three days in the belly of a fish = triple Jupiter/Saturn conjunction in Pisces).

Therefore, in reading these horoscopes in the Scrolls, we should understand that astrology probably held a much more powerful meaning for this ancient sect of Jews than the modern reader would be comfortable with. Vermes cannot bring himself to believe that astrology was actually relied upon to correlate prophetical events.[24] On the contrary, I believe that is precisely how these horoscopes were used. Ancient Jewish astrologers believed the stars to rightly mark the seasons of humankind's walk with God, especially the season of the Messiah. For example, the medieval rabbinic writer Isaac Abarbanel confirmed the reappearance of

---

*See ch. 35, "The Star of Bethlehem," in Werner Keller, *The Bible as History* (New York: Bantam Books, 1988); also ch. 8, "Triple Conjuctions: A Key to Unlocking the Mystery?" in Mark Kidger, *The Star of Bethlehem: An Astronomer's View* (Princeton: Princeton University Press, 1999). Technically the Star of Bethlehem was likely a "Greatest Conjunction," a rarer form of Great Conjunction in which Jupiter and Saturn align three times at or near their opposition to the Sun. Planetariums often re-create the 7 BCE Greatest Conjunction in their annual Star of Bethlehem Christmas shows. According to Keller's thinking, the first conjunction of the Magi's Star of Bethlehem took place on May 29, 7 BCE, at daybreak. But summer is no time to cross the desert, so the Magi likely began their journey on or about the September 29th second conjunction. When the Magi arrived in Jerusalem on or about the December 4th third conjunction, the brilliant ascending aligned planets—or "bright morning star" as many almanacs still refer to it (cf. Rev 22:16)—would have shone directly in front of them as they traveled the Hebron Road to Bethlehem. ". . . and lo, the star which they had seen in the East (perhaps 'in the first rays of dawn' [*en te anatolai*] due to a transcription error) went before them, till it came to rest over the place where the child was" (Mt 2:9b; my substitution).

the bright morning star of the Magi, just as it had arisen more than a thousand years before his time.[25] The use of astrology in this context is perfectly scriptural: "Let there be lights in the firmament of the heavens to separate the day from the night, and let them be for signs and for seasons and for days and for years" (Gen 1:14).

54 THE BIRTH OF NOAH

But let us put aside the astrological meaning the Essenes attached to their horoscopes, particularly the exact times and dates. It is enough for us to know that they wrote horoscopes for their messianic figures because their expected arrival was imminent. One such horoscope reads:

> . . . of his hand: two . . . a birthmark. And the hair will be red. And there will be lentils on . . . and small birthmarks on his thigh. [And after t]wo years he will know (how to distinguish) one thing from another. In his youth, he will be like . . . [like a m]an who knows nothing until the time when he knows the Three Books.

> And then he will acquire wisdom and learn und[erstanding] . . . vision to come to him on his knees. And with his father and his ancestors . . . life and old age. Counsel and prudence will be with him, and he will know the secrets of man. His wisdom will reach all the peoples, and he will know the secrets of all the living. And all their designs against him will come to nothing, and (his) rule over all the living will be great. His designs [will succeed] for he is the Elect of God. His birth and the breath of his spirit . . . and his designs shall be for ever . . . (4Q534 I, 1–11)

This horoscope has been identified by Scrolls scholars as announcing the birth of Noah. But it is also obvious on its face that this passage speaks of one of the Essenes' expected messianic figures, as the official Scrolls team editor, J. Starcky, has recognized.[26] Since the Essenes believed in reincarnation, there is no contradiction between these two interpretations. Noah, "the Elect of God," was expected to be incarnate in the Teacher of Righteousness. He would "reveal Mysteries like the Highest Angels" and be "like a man who knows nothing until the time when he knows the Three Books." Therein lay his perceived unique ability to interpret and reveal Scripture (1QpHab VII, 3–5). Especially because of the above predictions, it makes no sense to think Noah would have been perceived as either of the other two messianic figures, the Prophet or the Messiah of Israel. According to the Essenes, the latter were to defer to the former's authority in all scriptural matters (4Q161 8–10, 24).

So have I emptied the mystery of the Teacher and his role in prophecy? Not quite. The raised Noah who knew all mysteries was like unto a teacher of esoterica in Kabbalist or Gnostic mystery sects. He would have been quite a powerful figure for the Essenes, who set up a hierarchical system for discovering and revealing to one another such matters as the incarnations of angels (*War* 2.142). But what we still lack is a complete picture of the dynamic Righteous Teacher found in the Scrolls, one who held the self-understanding of God's high priest, the chosen Messiah of Aaron. We still lack an understanding of his authority to be God's lawgiver, the holder of the covenant. Recall that in chapter 4, I discussed how ancient Kabbalist writings teach the reincarnation sequence of Moses to be Seth, Noah, and Abraham. I supported this reincarnation sequence with Bible passages so they could now be of aid in grasping the Teacher's self-understanding. As forerunners of the Hasidic and Kabbalist tradition, the Essenes would have interpreted these passages in the same way.

55 THE TEACHER OF RIGHTEOUSNESS PROPHESIED BY MALACHI

The prophet who I believe most clearly foretold the coming of the Teacher of Righteousness is Malachi, the last prophet in the Hebrew canon. At the time of this writing, very little evidence that the Essenes were familiar with Malachi has surfaced. A scroll fragment known as *Apocryphal Malachi* has been found (5QapMal) that indicated they were at least aware of him.* Certainly the Essenes/scribes of the New Testament were familiar with Malachi. Jesus's disciples reported that the scribes quoted Malachi's prophecy stating that Elijah would precede the Messiah (Mk 9:11; cf. Mal 4:5). Other than this, New Testament references to Malachi are rare. In fact, Malachi is directly quoted in the New Testament only once: Gabriel told Zechariah that his son would go before the Lord in the spirit and power of Elijah "to turn the hearts of the fathers to the children" (Lk 1:17, quoting Mal 4:5–6). Nevertheless, the prophet Malachi is essential for understanding early Christianity, and particularly Jesus's interactions with the Righteous Teacher.

Here is why Malachi is so important. Hidden in his prophecy is the annunciation of the arrival of *another* messianic figure in addition to Elijah:

> "Behold, I send my messenger to prepare the way before me, and the Lord you seek will come suddenly upon his Temple; the messenger in the covenant in whom you delight, behold he is coming," says the Lord of hosts. But who can endure the day of his coming, and who can stand when he appears? For he is like a refiner's fire and like a fuller's soap; he will sit as a refiner of and purifier of silver, and he will purify the sons of Levi and refine them like gold and silver, til they present right offerings to the Lord. (Mal 3:1–3)

Practically every commentator I have ever read collapses the prophetical figure above into Elijah. Elijah's coming is indeed foretold by Malachi

---

*Copies of all the books of the Bible were found at Qumran, including Malachi. But scholars have so far gauged the importance the sectarians attached to each book based on how many copies of it were found. I contend my Essene/scribe identification should now be taken into account and the New Testament examined in its own right to recover Essene theology.

too, but not until the next chapter. Elijah is not specifically brought out until verse 4:5, where it says: "Behold, I will send you Elijah the prophet before the great and terrible day of the Lord comes." There are clearly *two* messianic forerunners foretold in the final chapters of Malachi: Elijah in chapter 4, and "the messenger in the covenant in whom you delight" in chapter 3. We must read carefully or we will miss him.

This figure was far more important to the Essenes than Elijah. Note the third verse where it says "He will purify the sons of Levi." The Essenes were a priestly sect. The hierarchy at Qumran was very strict and formal, and the priests of Aaron had all authority over the Levites (CD XIII; 1QS II, 20). It has been rightly pointed out that the Teacher himself was of Levitical descent, and was even the legitimate heir to the high priesthood in the Jerusalem Temple before his exile. The Teacher's self-understanding is identical to that of this figure from Malachi's prophecy. In fact, if all of the Scrolls' directives on purification can be thought of as one body of law, then Malachi's prophecy can be thought of as its founding constitution. We find further into Malachi's prophecy a promise of salvation, the very eschatological hope that drove the Essenes: "They shall be mine says the Lord of Hosts, my special possession on the day when I act, and I will spare them as a man spares his son who served him" (Mal 3:17; cf. 1QM).

We also find there the familiar apocalyptic dualism, the authority to judge between the sons of darkness and the sons of light: "Then once more shall you distinguish between the righteous and the wicked, between one who serves God and one who does not serve him" (Mal 3:18; cf. 1QS III, 15–IV, 1). I could develop text after text correlating Malachi's prophecy and the Scrolls, but I will leave that to the reader's own satisfaction. The Teacher is completely empowered by Malachi's prophecy. It is nothing short of his personal prophetical directive, just as the Davidic messianic prophecies would have been to Jesus.

The valuable key to the Righteous Teacher's self-understanding is found in the very first verse of chapter 3 of Malachi. Note that he is the "messenger of the covenant in whom you delight" (3:1). Since the verb is in the present tense—"in whom you delight (*chaphet*)"—this verse must refer to the messenger of a covenant the Jews already delighted in during the day of Malachi (500–450 BCE). Elijah was never a messenger of a covenant, so we begin by ruling him out. Moses immediately comes to mind, but there are others for us to consider out of thoroughness. For example, there is the covenant between God and David. God gave his word that the lamp of David would never fade from Jerusalem (2 Sam 7).

There is also the covenant that Joshua entered into with the nation of Israel. When they finally settled in the Promised Land, Joshua said, "But as for me and my house, we will serve the Lord," whereby Israel joined him in his personal covenant; they agreed to forsake all other gods and serve the Lord alone forevermore (Jos 24). But the messengers of these covenants would not fulfill Malachi's prophecy. The first covenant ran only to David personally, and the second was merely a reaffirmation of the covenant of Moses and the second commandment of the Torah. Thus he who was to come in fulfillment of Malachi's prophecy was neither David nor Joshua. He was another. Of the covenant holders, covenants to which all Israel would have been party, Scripture shows there can be but three: God's covenant with Noah (Gen 9:8–17), with Abraham (Gen 17:1–14), and with Moses (Ex 19:3–6).

But which of these three was to come in fulfillment of the prophecy of Malachi, "the messenger of the covenant in whom you delight"? The authors of the Scrolls would have understood the "messenger of the covenant" to be each of these and all of these. Noah's reincarnation sequence, which I explored in the last chapter, includes them all. It should now be dawning on the reader why the Teacher of Righteousness had such a powerful charismatic hold on the Essenes, and why the Scrolls witness such a stalwart observance of Mosaic law as had never been seen before or since. *The Teacher of Righteousness was Moses incarnate.*

56 THE MESSIANIC ANTHOLOGY (4Q175) REVISITED

Perhaps the reader will now understand how, at the outset of this chapter, I claimed the Deuteronomy passage found in the Messianic Anthology or Testimonia from Cave 4 (4Q175 I, 7–8) alone identified the self-understanding of the Teacher of Righteousness to me. When Moses's final address to Israel, "The Lord your God will raise up for you a prophet *like me* from among you, from among your brethren—him you shall heed" (Dt 18:18; my emphasis), is read by someone who understands the subtleties of reincarnation in Scripture, this is as personal a reference to Moses as "I will send you Elijah" (Mal 4:5) or "He will go before him in the spirit and power of Elijah" (Lk 1:17) is to Elijah. Taken together with the passages from Scripture I have developed above, and my restoration of the Scrolls as a whole, I doubt the Essenes could have understood their Teacher to have been anyone other than Moses. That is the meaning of the sympathetic association in the pesher term, the "Messiah of Aaron" (1QS IX, 11). There is only one higher than Aaron in the Levitical hierarchy, and that is his brother, the lawgiver (Num 12:1–9).

57 A BRIEF SCROLL EXEGESIS ON THE TEACHER'S SELF-UNDERSTANDING

Josephus wrote of the Essenes, "After God, they hold in awe the name of their lawgiver, any blasphemer of whom is put to death" (*War* 2.145). By "the lawgiver" Josephus meant Moses, for that is how he consistently referred to him.* The Thanksgiving Hymns, which scholars now agree were composed by the Teacher,† show an undeniable self-awareness

---

*Most translators rightly footnote or add *Moses* in parenthesis here. Josephus was writing to a Greek audience about the Jews. "Their lawgiver" is how Josephus referred to Moses in all his writings (*Ant* 3.178–82, 185–89).

†This is due primarily to the content and the use of the first person singular voice. See Charlesworth, *Jesus and the Dead Sea Scrolls,* 145 n. 36.

of being that lawgiver: "All those who are gathered in Thy Covenant inquire of me, and they hearken to me who walk in the ways of Thy heart. . . . [For in] Thy righteousness Thou hast appointed me for Thy Covenant" (1QH XII, 24; XV, 19). If the Teacher did not think himself the lawgiver Moses, these statements would have been capital blasphemy. Furthermore, scholars have rightly noted that the Teacher perceived in himself the authority to increase or amend the law of Moses, for in him was both a preexistent and ongoing lawgiver's self-understanding. One commentator has said that the Temple Scroll—which scholars also generally agree was written by the Teacher—could only have been written by a man "who sought superiority over Moses."[27] Try to imagine, if you can, what it is like to look upon Scripture you know that you yourself wrote eons ago, from the *Aleph* to the *Tav*. Only then will you begin to understand what was in the mind of the Righteous Teacher when he wrote passages like these:

> [A]nd they shall recount Thy glory throughout all dominion For Thou hast shown them that which they had not [seen by removing all] ancient things and creating new ones, by breaking asunder things anciently established, and raising up the things of eternity. For [Thou art from the beginning] and shalt endure for ages without end.
>
> And I, Thy servant, I know by the spirit Thou hast given me [that Thy words are truth] and that Thy works are righteousness, and that Thou wilt not take back Thy word. (1QH V, 17–19; 24–25)

58 THE HISTORICAL NAME OF THE TEACHER REVEALED

For my restoration to be accurate, the Teacher must have been a living person at the time of Jesus's ministry. Specifically, the conflict between the Righteous Teacher and the Wicked Priest described in the Habakkuk Commentary (1QpHab) must describe gospel events. One reason mainstream scholars concluded the Teacher was pre-Christian is that the Damascus Document reports that the covenanters of Qumran originated "three hundred and ninety years" after the fall of Jerusalem, which historians date in the year 586 BCE (CD I, 5–6). The Damascus Document also reports that "twenty years" transpired before God raised "the Teacher of Righteousness" (CD I, 11). If we interpret these dates literally—and so far, there seems to be no compelling reason why we should not—the Damascus Document places the Teacher in the early Hasmonean era, at least 150 years before Jesus was born. This seems to rule out my restoration, for even if we take into account the one hundred-plus-years life spans reported of the Essenes (*War* 2.151), it is unreasonable to stretch a single human life span that far.

Several scholars have speculated, however, that Scrolls references to the Righteous Teacher describe an office held by a series of persons, because they appear to cover such a lengthy period.[28] In fact, James H. Charlesworth notes that scholars have offered various candidates for the Teacher spanning over four hundred years! But Charlesworth also notes that the consensus view is that the Teacher was a distinct personality, because Scrolls references to him are so unique.[29] I think both views are correct. Because the Essenes believed in reincarnation, Scrolls references to the Righteous Teacher could have designated both an office held by a series of persons *and* a unique personality. Sound like a stretch? Not at all. This was exactly the governing system used in Tibet until Tenzin Gyatso, the current Dalai Lama, fled Chinese persecution in 1959. Perhaps just as one finds reference to "His Holiness the Dalai Lama" spanning hundreds of years in Tibetan writings, one likewise finds Scroll references to "The Teacher of Righteousness" spanning hundreds of years because they refer to the same personality through a series of reincarnations. His Holiness is believed to be the fourteenth reincarnation of the first Dalai Lama placed in power by the grandson of Genghis Kahn in the fifteenth century.

When I began this project, I thought it unlikely that the historical identity of the Teacher who opposed Jesus as a Wicked Priest would ever surface. It was enough for me to grasp the prophetical self-understanding of the Teacher; that he had a historical identity I could take on faith. But surprisingly, once I explored the Teacher's prophetical self-understanding, his historical identity also came forth. This is largely due to the work of Barbara Thiering, though she did not realize it at the time. Thiering and I differ on many details, but she and I agree that the Scrolls have been misdated by the consensus of scholars, thereby obscuring their relevance to the life and times of Jesus as presented in the Gospels. Thiering has presented an exegesis identifying Simeon, the high priest of Jerusalem (Lk 2:25–35), as the angel Gabriel, which I will fully develop next chapter. For now, it is enough to show he would have understood himself to be the Teacher of Righteousness.

Note that Malachi's prophecy says, "Behold, I send *my messenger* to prepare the way before me" (3:1a; my emphasis). The speaker Malachi is quoting is "the Lord of Hosts" (3:5b), which is a commonly used term for Michael. Recall in chapter 4 how I brought forth the identification of Jesus by the author of Hebrews as Melchizedek? Vermes noted that Melchizedek is "identical to the archangel Michael,"[30] which is absolutely correct. The Bible gives subtle clues to the angelic personas of the Messiah, which are picked up in Merkabah and Pseudepigrapha literature. Melchizedek, Metatron, Michael: these are all variations on the same theme. How that helps us in identifying Moses as Gabriel is that the words "my messenger" were spoken by Michael, and Gabriel is always Michael's revealing angel (4Q529; Dan 7:13–14; 8:15–16; 10:5–14; 12:5–7; Rev 1:1; 1:12–16; 10; 22:16). See also my discussion of patriarch as angels in chapter 4 (section 37).

Thiering suggests that Simeon the high priest was also Simon the Essene reported by Josephus, who in the reign of Archelaus was famous for his prophecies (*Ant* 17.346–47). I really cannot confirm that for sure, for there were probably a lot of Essene Simons in first-century Palestine, so it is possible they were completely different persons (regardless of the difference in spelling). But Thiering's identification of Simeon as the high priest reported in Luke's Gospel squares up wonderfully with my restoration. Joseph and Mary came to the Temple in Jerusalem so that they could have Jesus circumcised (Lev 12:2–8), and there they met Simeon. Here is what Luke says of him:

> Now there was a man in Jerusalem, whose name was Simeon, and this man was righteous and devout, looking for the consolation of Israel, and the Holy Spirit was upon him. And it had been revealed to him by the Holy Spirit that he should not see death before he had seen the Lord's Christ. And inspired by the Spirit he came into the Temple; and when the parents brought in the child Jesus, to do for him according to the custom of the law, he took him up in his arms and blessed God and said, "Lord, now let thy servant depart in peace, according to thy word; for mine eyes have seen thy salvation which thou hast prepared in the presence of all peoples, a light for revelation to the Gentiles, and for glory to thy people Israel." (Lk 2:25–32)

Simeon knew that he would meet Jesus face to face, for it was uniquely promised him in prophecy: "I will send my messenger before me, *and the Lord you seek will come suddenly upon his Temple*" (Mal 3:1; my emphasis). Simeon did not die after Jesus's circumcision as commonly supposed; "let thy servant depart in peace" (Lk 2: 29) means he went into exile. According to the Gospel of Nicademus, Simeon died shortly before Jesus's trial (Nic 12:16). Having seen the baby Jesus, Simeon retires as high priest to prepare the way, engrossing himself in scriptural study, purifying the Levitical priesthood. However, the Teacher had not fully understood Malachi's prophecy. Simeon and Jesus were due to meet again.

That encounter is the subject of chapter 7. To take in our story, we must remember how, despite their common background, the two men had grown radically apart. There was Jesus, the young man on the hillsides teaching new ways. He broke the old rules steeped in tradition. He flouted the Essenes' purity laws and openly violated their Sabbath.

He unleashed rebukes on the Essenes, for they were his greatest spiritual enemies. Opposing him was the elder Teacher, who grew more fanatical in his fundamentalism, whose hardened heart condemned Jesus as a "Wicked Priest," a "seeker of smooth things." He beheld Jesus as a dangerous schismatic, and that it was his duty to purge Israel of such a man. The stage was now set for a divine tragedy. The Righteous Teacher who had awaited his promised Christ was to have the darkest role of anyone in the upcoming Passion of Christ, his trial, suffering, and crucifixion. I will try to do this tragedy justice. I doubt that any fiction writer could ever weave together as heartrending a tale as the historical role of the Teacher in the Passion of Christ, which I am about to bring forth.

6

The Secret Role of Gabriel in the Virgin Birth

And behold, a young woman shall give birth to a son, and they shall call his name Immanuel.

ISAIAH 7:14, RSV

Every Sunday, Christians recite in our various creeds that Jesus was "born of the Virgin Mary." And in that brief statement of belief, yet another wedge is driven between Jews and Christians. Contemporary Jews have no notion whatsoever that the Messiah would be born of a virgin. Nor does it seem most Jews believed differently throughout history. Early in the third century CE, Hippolytus wrote that Jews still waited in anticipation of the Messiah, but "they say that his generation will be from the stock of David, but not from a virgin and the Holy Spirit, but from a woman and a man, according as it is a rule for all to be procreated from seed" (*Refutation of All Heresies* IX, 25). The idea of the virgin birth is at odds not only with contemporary and historical Judaism, but also with the modern scientific worldview. Yet early in the first century, belief in the divine conception of heroic figures was fairly common, especially in the Gentile world. The philosophers Plato and Pythagoras were believed to have been of divine origin, as were the mythological figures of many lands, such as Hercules (fathered by the Greek god Zeus), or Seth (fathered by the Egyptian god Ra).

Madonna stories are found in cultures the world over, which is why the story of Jesus's virgin birth was so readily accepted in the formative years of Christianity. The Christian apologist C. S. Lewis offered the explanation that in Jesus "myth became fact," but the contemporary Jewish scholar rightly views this statement with skepticism. The story of the virgin birth appears to have come about by outright syncretism, by deliberately adopting a Gentile myth into Jewish thought where it had no place. The Dead Sea Scrolls shed more light on the virgin birth story than was ever thought possible, and far more light than a good many devout Christians will find comfortable.

59 PARTHENOS OR ALMAH?

What is curious, given that Gentile cultures readily accepted the idea of a virgin birth, is that Paul, who specifically tailored his preaching to the Gentiles, never once mentioned the idea in all his letters. Luke, a Gentile physician converted by Paul, wrote about the virgin birth at the outset of his Gospel, as did the author of Matthew. According to Matthew, Mary was found to be with child "of the Holy Spirit" when she was still betrothed to Joseph and "before they came together" (1:18): "All this took place to fulfill what had been spoken by the prophet: 'Behold, a virgin shall conceive and bear a son, and his name shall be called Emmanuel'" (1:22–23). Matthew quoted the prophet Isaiah's messianic predictions, the passage cited at the outset of this chapter, that a "virgin" (*parthenos* in New Testament Greek) was to give birth. But Isaiah himself never claimed a "virgin" would give birth. In the original Hebrew, which comes down to us in the Masoretic texts, the version of the Bible that is in use in Jewish synagogues today, Isaiah said, "an *almah* would give birth to a son . . ." (7:14; my emphasis). *Almah* is the feminine form of *elem,* which is consistently quoted throughout the Bible as a "young man" (1 Sam 17:56; 20:22). *Almah* is elsewhere found in the Bible, meaning "girl," "maid," or "young woman" (Gen 24:43; Ex 2:8; Ps 68:25). For centuries, English Christian Bibles have simply translated *almah* in the Isaiah passage as "virgin" in an attempt to whitewash the glaring doctrinal difference between the texts. Finally, when the 1946 edition of the Revised Standard Version was published, the editors of a widely read English Christian Bible chose to correctly translate *almah* as "young woman" and let the controversy stand.[1]

Martin Luther once wrote an apologetic tract supposedly directed at Jews called *That Jesus Christ Was Born a Jew*. In actuality, it was to defend himself against Catholic claims that he denied the virgin birth. He addressed the almah inconsistency as follows: "Christians can readily answer from St. Matthew and St. Luke, both of whom apply the passage from Isaiah [7:14] to Mary, and translate the word *almah* as 'virgin.' They are more to be believed than the whole world, let alone the Jews. Even though an angel from heaven [Gal 1:8] were to say that *almah* means virgin, we should not believe it. For God and the Holy Spirit speaks through St. Matthew and St. Luke; we can be sure that He understands Hebrew speech and expressions perfectly well."[2] The passage Luther cites from Paul's letter to the Galatians reads in full: "But even if we or an angel from heaven should preach a gospel other than the one we preached to you, let him be eternally condemned!" (1:8). How incredibly ironic! Luther was the one preaching a gospel other than that preached by Paul. If the virgin birth was so central to our salvation that Christianity could not exist without it, Paul would certainly have covered it at length. But he did not.

As I said earlier, there is not one single mention of the virgin birth in all Paul's letters, not one. Furthermore, Luther's dogmatic position that Matthew and Luke were right to have mistranslated Isaiah 7:14 because they had God's blessing to do so was downright arrogant and presumptuous. In fact, Luther grossly misquotes Scripture to make his point; nowhere does Luke specifically quote Isaiah 7:14 in his account of Jesus's birth. Matthew alone does this. Luther's arguments in support of the virgin birth are at best erroneous and at worst anti-Semitic. Sadly, much of the anti-Semitism that still pervades the world is directly attributable to Luther.[3] Paul was never the problem, nor, for that matter, Jesus either. Like Paul, the Gospels record no statement whatsoever by Jesus regarding the virgin birth.

60   THE SEPTUAGINT

So the question remains: In translating Isaiah 7:14, did Matthew directly import the idea of the virgin birth from the Gentiles, or was the idea already present in Jewish thought at the time? This is not an easy question. The idea may have come from the Greeks, but if so it was imported subtly and over a period of centuries. Due to the conquests of Alexander the Great, Greek language and culture had made broad inroads into the Mideast at this time. Although the extent is subject to heated debate, elements of Greek theology came along with the importation of Greek language and culture. There was a Greek translation of the Hebrew Bible in existence perhaps as early as 300 BCE, but certainly by the first century, known as the Septuagint. Many Greek-speaking Jews knew the Septuagint as their only Bible. In fact, it is often debated whether the New Testament authors and perhaps Jesus himself quoted the Septuagint as their Old Testament source.[4] The Septuagint translated Isaiah 7:14's *almah* ("young woman") as *parthenos* ("virgin"), just as did Matthew. More important, when the Hebrew word *almah* is translated elsewhere in the Septuagint—for example, Exodus 2:8 and Psalms 68:25—it is translated *neanis*, meaning "young woman."* Thus, it appears that the word *parthenos* was specifically chosen for use in the Septuagint's Isaiah 7:14 verse for its doctrinal content, subtly importing Greek theology. The idea of the virgin birth was present in Jewish thought earlier than the New Testament, for the Septuagint clearly predates Jesus.

---

*Genesis 24:43 uses *parthenos,* which is usually translated "maiden" or "young woman" in English Bibles. But in this instance, context called for it.

61 HOW FAR BACK DOES THE DOCTRINE GO?

The Isaiah scroll found at Qumran used the Hebrew word *almah* ("young woman") at verse 7:14,[5] not the Hebrew word *bethulah* ("virgin"), which would have been consistent with the Septuagint then in use. This confirms that the Masoretic version now used in the Old Testament is older and more authentic. It also raises a key question: When was the virgin birth doctrine first introduced? Is the Septuagint the only evidence of it in early Judaism? Not at all. Interestingly, there are early Jewish texts in which we find miraculous virgin-birth stories. Some years ago, I came across a work by James H. Charlesworth entitled *The Old Testament Pseudepigrapha and the New Testament: Prolegomena for the Study of Christian Origins.*[6] A prolegomena is an outline and set of queries that encourage other scholars to help with a particular problem. In this case, Charlesworth was seeking help in understanding how Pseudepigrapha may have affected the Christian idea of the virgin birth. He cited two stories in which angels fathered divine offspring by sleeping with human women. The first is the story of Noah's birth; the second, the birth of Melchizedek. "I would like to find someone," said Charlesworth, "who can help me understand this tradition and its importance for the theology of Early Judaism and the earliest Christologies. . . . Does either [of these birth stories] provide a background to the Christian concept of the virginal conception of Jesus by Mary?"[7] With the help of the Dead Sea Scrolls passages I explore in this chapter, I believe I can now answer this question in the affirmative.

Let us look at the passages Charlesworth cited. The following is the story of Noah's birth as found in 1 Enoch. The speaker is Methuselah, who is addressing his father, Enoch, concerning the spectacular birth of his grandson, Noah:

Now, my father, hear me: For unto my son Lamech a son has been born, one whose image and form are not like unto the characteristics of human beings; and his color is whiter than snow and redder than a rose, the hair of his head is whiter than white wool, and his eyes are like the rays of the sun; and (when) he opened his eyes the whole house lighted up. And (when) he rose up in the hands of his midwife, he opened his mouth and blessed the Lord of heaven. Then his father Lamech became afraid and fled, and he did not believe that the child was of him but of the image of angels of heaven. (1 En 106:10–12)

Methuselah suspected his grandson had been fathered not by Lamech but by an angel. Some translators make this clearer by stating the child was "from angels" instead of the more vague "of the image of angels."[8]

We find this same theme in the original ending of 2 Enoch, which contains the birth story of the mysterious biblical figure Melchizedek. According to the Epistle to the Hebrews, Melchizedek's birth, when read literally, is even more difficult to believe than that of Jesus's as popularly perceived. Melchizedek was "without mother or father or genealogy and has no beginning of days or ending of life" (7:3a). Since nothing else appears in the Bible concerning Melchizedek's birth, it now appears that the author of Hebrews must have drawn from 2 Enoch or similar sources reporting the same legend.* Second Enoch explains that Melchizedek was fathered by an angel and born of a corpse mother; hence, it can be said figuratively that he had neither father nor mother:

And Sothonim . . . conceived in her womb, but Nir the priest had not slept with her. . . . Sothonim was ashamed, and she hid herself. . . . And Sothonim came to Nir, her husband; and behold, she was pregnant, and at the time for giving birth. And Nir saw her, and he became very ashamed about her. And he said to her, "What is this

---

*Charlesworth offers this comment: "Neither Josephus nor Philo preserves traditions about Melchizedek that approximate so close to that of Hebrews as the ones in 2 Enoch." *The Old Testament Pseudepigrapha and the New Testament: Prolegomena for the Study of Christian Origins* (New York: Cambridge University Press, 1985), 174n62.

that you have done, O wife?" . . . And it came to pass, when Nir had spoken to his wife, that Sothonim fell down at Nir's feet and died. Nir was extremely distressed. . . . And the archangel Gabriel appeared to Nir, and said to him, ". . . this child which is to be born of her is a righteous fruit. . . ." . . . And Noe (and Nir) . . . placed Sothonim on the bed. . . . And when they had gone out toward the sepulcher, a child came out from the dead Sothonim. And he sat on the bed. . . . And behold, the badge of priesthood was on his chest, and it was glorious in appearance. . . . And Noe and Nir . . . called his name Melchizedek. . . . And the Lord . . . said to him, ". . . don't be anxious, Nir; because, in a short while I shall send my archangel Gabriel. And he will take the child, and put him in the paradise of Edem." (2 En 71:2–28[A])

The Second Book of Enoch dates to about 1000 CE. It does not appear, however, that this portion of 2 Enoch was influenced by Christian theology. Rather, it seems to be taken from an earlier Jewish source or perhaps from oral tradition. So argued Charlesworth.[9] Both texts indicate that there was a Jewish tradition, already in effect by the time of Jesus, in which divine offspring were miraculously fathered by angels.

62 IS THE VIRGIN BIRTH DOCTRINE TRACEABLE TO THE ESSENES?

Portions of 1 Enoch were found among the Dead Sea Scrolls in caves 1, 2, 4, and 6.[10] But 1 Enoch as it has come down to us from other sources appears to be a composite. Parts of it were composed in Hebrew, others in Aramaic, indicating multiple authorship. So, although it is known that the Essenes read or perhaps even wrote portions of 1 Enoch, whether the particular passage concerning Noah's birth was known to them is hard to determine. We do know this: As opposed to the command of God to "be fruitful and multiply" (Gen 1:28) followed by most Jews, the Essenes were ascetic in matters of sex. The philosopher Philo said they "abstained from marriage" (*Apology for the Jews* 11.14).

On the other hand, the ancient historian Josephus writes that not all the Essenes did without marriage—to do so would have quickly led to their extinction. Some Essenes put their wives through a three-year probationary period, after which they had sexual relations with them, but purely for the sake of procreation (*War* 2.161). Here are doctrines at least sympathetic with the virgin birth, for inherent in the idea of the virgin birth is the notion that normal sex between a husband and wife is unholy.

63 THIERING'S VIEW

On Palm Sunday, 1990, I, along with several million other American television viewers, tuned in to ABC to witness Barbara Thiering's documentary, *The Riddle of the Dead Sea Scrolls*. I had read something of Thiering's work during the course of my own research. At this time, I had already identified the Teacher of Righteousness in the Bible and knew that Jesus must, at some point, have led an Essene schism. It was encouraging to find another scholar whose conclusions were similar to my own. But I had no idea, until that evening, what Thiering believed the Scrolls had to say about the virgin birth. Thiering claims the Scrolls support the idea that Jesus was conceived out of wedlock in the normal, biological manner and that Joseph was Jesus's real father. Thiering's argument is that Essene brides-to-be were known as "virgins" because they belonged to an order of nuns and, normally, because they were virgins physically. Joseph and Mary violated Essene purity laws by having sex prior to marriage, hence it can be said, as a play on words, that a "virgin" conceived.[11]

At the end of the broadcast, I reviewed the relevant Gospel passages to examine Thiering's claim. According to Matthew, Mary was discovered to be pregnant when she and Joseph were betrothed, but "before they came together" (1:18b). Joseph determined to quietly divorce Mary instead of having her stoned, which was the usual penalty for adultery (1:19). A few verses later, Matthew records that Joseph took Mary as his wife "but knew her not until she bore a son" (1:24–25). Thiering, in my mind, had gone too far. It makes little sense for Joseph to have nearly divorced Mary at the shock of finding her pregnant if he knew himself to be the father all along. There is no logical way these texts can be construed to say that Joseph fathered Jesus without directly contradicting them. And I have found nothing in my years of Scrolls and Bible research to indicate the need for that.

64 A KNIGHTS TEMPLAR TRADITION AND THIERING'S IDENTIFICATION OF GABRIEL

Recently, I read a book called *The Second Messiah* by Christopher Knight and Robert Lomas. Knight and Lomas trace the legends of the Knights Templar as they believe they pertain to the Shroud of Turin. In the course of their research, they came across a verbal tradition, which had been passed father to son for generations by the descendants of the Knights Templar. According to the tradition, the high priests of Israel would impregnate young virgins to preserve the purity of the priestly bloodlines:

> At the time even before Jesus was born, the priests of the Temple of Jerusalem ran two schools: one for boys and one for girls. The priests were known by titles, which were the names of angels, such as Michael, Mazaldek [*sic*] and Gabriel. This was the way in which they preserved the pure lines of Levi and David. When each of the chosen girls had passed through puberty one of the priests would impregnate her with the seed of the holy bloodline and, once pregnant, she would be married off to a respectable man to bring up the child. . . . Thus, a virgin called Mary was visited by a high priest known as "Angel Gabriel" who had her with child. She was then married off to Joseph who was a much older man.[12]

Traditions of this sort can sometimes be traced to a historical source, and in this case I believe I have done so. This Knights Templar tradition reminded me of a passage in Thiering's work in which she identified the high priest Simeon as the "angel Gabriel." Although I believe Thiering was in error about Mary and Joseph, I believe her views on this subject to be right on. Thiering's identification of Simeon as Gabriel, in fact, was the final breakthrough I needed to name Simeon as the Teacher of Righteousness, as I covered in chapter 5. Incidentally, I had a little help from above that I think the reader will find interesting. It came about by means of what Carl Jung called "synchronicity." I was attending the University of Southern Mississippi in Hattiesburg at the time, working on my master's degree in philosophy. I knew through study of biblical prophecy that the Teacher was the angel Gabriel. If Thiering's identification of Gabriel as Simeon was correct, then I knew Simeon was the Teacher. When the query finally brought itself into focus in my mind, I walked into the campus chapel late at night to pray and meditate upon it. After sitting in silence for nearly an hour, I walked to an open Bible, on a podium to the right of the altar. Someone before me had already opened the Bible to a painting of Gabriel's annunciation to Mary (Lk 1:26–30)!

There were three priestly dynasties under King David: those of Zadok, Abithar, and Levi. According to Thiering, "Under the growing influence of Iranian thought in the intertestamental period, the heads of the dynasties had come to be called by the names of the archangels, in the belief they were the incarnations of heavenly figures."[13] The War Scroll lists the names and order of the dynasties (1QM IX, 15–17). The head of the Zadokite dynasty was called Michael. His "second" (*mishneh*), the head of the Abithar dynasty, was called Gabriel. Luke's Gospel records Gabriel's annunciation of not only Jesus's arrival to Mary, but also John the Baptist's arrival to Elizabeth and Zechariah. Zechariah was then serving as high priest, and "there appeared to him an angel of the Lord standing to the right side of the altar of incense" (Lk 1:11).

Later in the passage, the angel identifies himself to Zechariah: "I am Gabriel who stands in the presence of God" (Lk 1:19a). Thiering interprets the language "on the right side [*ek dexion*] of the altar" as a term of art specifically used to describe the place occupied by the second priest in the order of hierarchy, which at the time of Zechariah was Simeon.[14]

The Knights Templar tradition now finds support in the Gospels reconstructed by the Dead Sea Scrolls, inasmuch as the angel Gabriel can be identified as a historical high priest of Jerusalem. "Mary," literally translated, means Miriam, the name of the sister of Moses, calling to mind one schooled from her birth to serve as a priestess or handmaiden of God. One can easily read beneath the surface of Gabriel's language to Mary: "The Holy Spirit will come upon you and the power of the Most High will overshadow you" (Lk 1:35a), particularly if one believes Thiering's interpretation that the highest Essene priests formed a ruling threefold hierarchy known as "Father, Son and Holy Spirit."[15] Believing himself to be the literal incarnation of the angel Gabriel, and the embodiment of the Holy Spirit, a high priest, it is not hard at all to see, could believe himself to be the instrument of divine seed, in the tradition of the 1 and 2 Enoch stories I covered earlier.

65 JESUS'S FIRST BIRTHDAY HYMN

Now let us get down to specifics. Do the Dead Sea Scrolls contain passages that speak directly to the above arguments that a high priest, namely the Teacher of Righteousness, believing himself to be the incarnation of Gabriel, fathered Jesus? The first question is whether the Teacher of Righteousness lived contemporaneously with the birth of Jesus. It has been generally established among Scrolls scholars that the Teacher wrote most of the Thanksgiving Hymns.[16] In this scroll, we find what can only be interpreted as a hymn celebrating the birth of the eagerly awaited Messiah.

[And] like a woman in travail
with her first born child,
upon whose belly pangs have come
and grievous pains,
filling with anguish her child bearing crucible.

For the children have come to the throes of Death
For amid the throes of death
she shall bring forth a man-child,
there shall spring from her child-bearing-crucible
a Marvelous Mighty Counselor
and a man shall be delivered from out of the throes.
        (1QH XI, 7–9)

This reference to a Marvelous Mighty Counselor is one of the most singular lyrics from another famous hymn about Jesus's birth. Vermes used the translation "Marvelous," but the better-known synonym is "Wonderful." We Christians sing the praises of the "Wonderful Mighty Counselor" every Christmas. This reference is also found in Handel's *Messiah,* which, like the Teacher's hymn above, draws from passages in Isaiah: "For unto us a child is born, to us a son is given; and the government will be upon his shoulder, and his name will be called, *'Wonderful Mighty Counselor,* Mighty God, Everlasting Father, Prince of Peace.' Of the increase of his government and of peace there will be no end, upon the throne of David and over his kingdom (Is 9:6–7; my emphasis).

To my knowledge, I am the first scholar to identify the passage above as a hymn in praise of Jesus's birth. The reason it has been so hard to recognize is that the Teacher's messianic expectations of him were so drastically different from Jesus's life as it actually played out. Notice as the hymn continues how the Teacher perceives the Messiah as one who is to come in anger, to judge the world and deliver the righteous while bringing hellfire and damnation upon the unrighteous:

When he is conceived
all wombs shall quicken,
and the time of their delivery
shall be in grievous pains;
they shall be appalled
who are with child.
And when he is brought forth
every pang shall come upon the child bearing crucible.
. . . .

And the gates [of Hell] shall open
[on all] the works of Vanity
and the doors of the Pit shall close
on the conceivers of wickedness;
and the everlasting bars shall be bolted
on all the spirits of Naught. (1QH XI, 10–12; 17–18)

Simeon likewise said of Jesus at his circumcision: "This child is destined for the falling and rising of many in Israel" (Lk 2:34). Such harsh apocalyptic expectations were eventually why Jesus broke away from the Essenes and the Teacher. Jesus did not perceive his coming to be the end, but the beginning of a new kingdom: "For God sent his Son into the world, not to condemn the world, but that the world might be saved through him" (Jn 3:17).

66 GABRIEL'S REFLECTION ON HIS SECRET TASK

The doctrine that high priests among the Essenes were angels incarnate was, of course, highly esoteric. Hence, we would not expect to find a direct statement in the Scrolls discussing how the Righteous Teacher fathered the Messiah, serving in the role of an angel. If there are any such statements to be found, they would surely be shrouded in allegory. Once we realize this, our eyes are opened to just such a statement found in the Thanksgiving Hymns, 1QH XVI, 4–16.

Charlesworth translated the following hymn,[16] which he interpreted as describing the Teacher's self-understanding:

4 I [praise you, O Lord, because you] placed me
as an overflowing fountain in a desert,
and (as) a spring of water in a land of dryness,

5 and (as) the i[rri]gator of the garden.
You [have plant]ed a planting of cyprus,
and elm,
with cedar together (*yhd*) for your glory;

6 (these are) the trees of life hidden
among all the trees of the water
beside the mysterious water source.
And they caused to sprout the shoot (*nsr*)
for the eternal planting.

7 Before they shall cause (it) to sprout they strike root,
then send forth their roots to the river (*ywbl*).
And its trunk shall be open to the living water;

8 and it shall become the eternal fountain.
But upon the shoot (*nsr*)
every [beast] of the forest shall feed.
And its trunk (shall become) a place of trampling

9 for all those who pass over the way (*drk*).
And its branches (shall be food) for every bird.
And all the tre[es] of the water
shall exalt themselves over it,
because they shall become magnified in their planting.

10 But they shall not send forth a root to the river (*ywbl*).
And he who causes to sprout the hol[y] shoot (*nsr*)
for the planting of truth is concealed

11 with the result that he is not esteemed,
and the sealing of his mystery is not perceived.
    (1QH XVI, 4–11)

This hymn is rich in allegory. But, as Charlesworth himself noted, "Details must not be pushed to create a full allegory. That would distort the subtlety of the story and pull it out of its historical context."[17] In other words, absent a compelling reason otherwise, the text should be read as literally as possible to preserve the author's intended meaning. Charlesworth probed the allegories found in this important hymn, but he was unable to see how it linked up to his work years earlier involving the virgin birth.

The Teacher sees himself as a key figure in bringing about God's eschatological plan, as one elected by God for this purpose: "I praise you, O Lord, for you have placed me as an overflowing fountain in the desert." The Teacher is the "irrigator of the garden" in whom God has placed the "autumn rain" as found in verse 16.

16 And you, O my God, have put in my mouth
as it were an autumn rain (*kywrh gšm*)
for all [the sons of men],
and as a spring of living waters
Which shall not run dry.

Charlesworth perceptively noted that "autumn rain" meant the rain that falls near the end of October and breaks the long drought.[19] The rain indicates God's covenant loyalty and, to this day, causes rejoicing throughout Israel (Dt 11:14; Joel 2:23). The term "autumn rain" also highlights the central theme of this hymn, which is how the Teacher is the instrument of God's fertility, both in terms of charisma, which Charlesworth grasped, and literally, which he did not. Autumn is the time for the planting of a garden. As lines 10 and 11 make clear, the Teacher is he who, through God's power, "causes to sprout the holy shoot." Moreover, the Teacher knows that his procreative role is a secret one. The Teacher is "not esteemed" because his identity is "not perceived." It is an esoteric matter, fit only for those of his immediate group.

The passage also shows that it is the Messiah that is spoken of when the Teacher uses the term "holy shoot." God has planted a planting of "cyprus, and elm, with cedar." These are likely the three messianic figures expected by the Essenes: the Priest, the Prophet, and the King. They are the "trees of life hidden among all the trees of water beside the mysterious water source." The "mysterious water source" is the Holy Spirit, which the Teacher closely identified with himself. The Teacher, as Priest, believed he would serve as a charismatic guide to all the messianic figures. Their "trunk" shall be open to the "living water," which is the Teacher.

This remarkable hymn shows, in language as clear as can be expected under the circumstances, that the Teacher was the father of the Messiah. Lest there be any confusion that this is exactly what we are viewing, let us look at verse 12.

> 12 Thou didst hedge in its fruit, [O God],
> with the mystery of mighty Heroes
> and of spirits of holiness
> and of the whirling flame of fire.[20]

God hedged in the fruit of the "holy shoot" the mystery of mighty Heroes. Namely, just as Noah and Melchizedek were conceived by angelic intervention, as we saw in 1 and 2 Enoch, so conceived was the "holy shoot." Yet, the mystery is "not perceived" so that down to this day the virgin birth story has been popularly believed.

67 COMMENTS IN ANTICIPATION OF MY CRITICS

Let me offer a word or two of comment before I close this chapter. I have herein challenged one of the most sacred beliefs in Christianity. But I did not do it lightly. In anticipation of my critics, let me answer that I have not written this chapter for the sake of sensationalism, but instead to fulfill the sincere desire for truth and to further the understanding and evangelism of the Christian faith; at the same time, I dare to redefine the Christian faith. In that sense, this work is apologetic. Indeed, it falls squarely within the tradition of the early apologetics. I believe the virgin birth doctrine is superfluous to being Christian. Inasmuch as it has been a stumbling block to some, I seek to remove it.

This chapter was years in the making, years of mulling it over and discussing it with fellow Christians. Not all reactions have been favorable. The most vehement reactions have been from Catholics, and understandably so. Most Catholics believe Mary was a perpetual virgin, whereas Protestants who believe in the virgin birth believe that Jesus had half-brothers and -sisters through Mary's natural husband, Joseph (cf. Mt 13:55; Jn 7:3). But if this chapter is true, and I believe it is, it settles a great many inconsistencies. There have always been problems with the Sunday-school notion that Jesus's family knew of his messianic secret. The Gospels show just the opposite. When Jesus began his public ministry, Mary and Jesus's sisters came to take him away as a madman (Lk 8:19–21). Jesus's brothers once challenged him to present himself, for "even his brothers did not believe in him" (Jn 7:5). It is hard to believe that Jesus's family would not have held him in more esteem if he had in fact been conceived without a human father. But if he were conceived according to this chapter, by a high priest coming to a young, naive girl and directing her to do this incredible thing, then it is easy to see how Mary's acceptance of her role waned over the years, especially given that Jesus did not live up to Essene messianic expectations.

In answer to those who believe every word of the King James Version is literally true as written, let me point out that Mary may in fact have been a "virgin" at the time she gave birth; the Teacher may have practiced a primitive form of artificial insemination. The Scrolls mention nothing of the particulars of how the Righteous Teacher had Mary with child, but I personally think artificial insemination is a strong possibility given Essene asceticism. In this context, the debate may not be over *whether* a miracle occurred; the debate is really over *how* it occurred. Those involved certainly thought they were working a miracle in bringing about the birth of the Messiah. In offering up a natural explanation of Jesus's conception, I am not necessarily engaging in textual criticism.

Finally, there are those who will say I have written this chapter because I am a modern who cannot bring himself to believe in miracles. Not true. Actually, my metaphysics are open enough to believe in the resurrection and most of the miracles found in the Bible.* My entire restoration depends on a wholly supernatural miracle, as you will see in chapter 7. But let us not lose sight of the fact that all human births are miraculous. And none are less holy than that of Jesus. The greatest contribution this chapter could make to Christianity is to smash the remnant Christological heresies that separate us from Jesus. Each time the virgin birth is confessed, we place Jesus on a substantially different plane than the rest of humankind, thus placing him beyond our comprehension and ourselves beyond the moral responsibility to follow him. I shy not from calling Jesus "brother," nor should anyone else.

---

*I say I believe in *most* of the miracles in the Bible, for some, I believe, are allegorical, or contemporary scholars have nearly lost the context for understanding them. A good example is when Balaam's jackass started talking to him (Num 22:28–30). I believe primitive religious scholars may offer the best insight into this passage. It likely refers to a trance state in which the jackass served as Balaam's spirit-guide. To question whether the events of such a trance state are "real" or not is to miss the whole point. If it was real to Balaam, it was real. From a primitive religious perspective, "supernatural" means that which transcends mundane reality, not that which is exclusive of it.

7

The Teacher of Righteousness and the Passion of Christ

If I forget you, O Jerusalem, may my right hand wither.

PSALMS 137:5

It is the morning of the eve of the Passover Sabbath, Good Friday of the first Easter, as a weary Jesus is brought before Pontius Pilate, the Roman governor. The night before, a detachment of men sent by the Essenes, Pharisees, and other Jewish elders seized Jesus while he was praying in the garden of Gethsemane.* The Jewish soldiers bound Jesus and led him away for grueling indictment proceedings that ran into the wee hours of the morning. Throughout his ministry, Jesus's inquisitors had tried to trap him into admitting that he was the Messiah, for no man is allowed to proclaim this of himself, only God can so identify him through God's prophets or angels. Finally, Jesus could escape their

---

*Many scholars have concluded through the years that both Roman and Jewish soldiers seized Jesus in Gethsemane. All the Synoptic Gospels, however, state unequivocally that Jesus was apprehended by Jewish soldiers only (Mk 14:43 // Mt 26:47 // Lk 22:52).

query no more: "I adjure you by the name of the living God, tell us if you are the Christ, the Son of God," demanded Caiaphas, the high priest. Although exhausted, Jesus keenly followed Scripture to the very end. He answered, "You have said so" (Mt 26:63–64). Jesus still had not identified himself as the Messiah; Caiaphas did (cf. Jn 18:37). Jesus's subtlety was lost on his audience, for in the next moment Caiaphas ripped his garments, enraged at this apparent blasphemy. For daring to utter such a thing, Jesus was slapped, spat upon, and beaten. Jesus was indicted and bound over to Pilate, for the elders sought a crucifixion, which they were not allowed to perform under Roman law (Jn 18:31; *War* 2.117). Still bound, Jesus now stands before a very confused Gentile who is about to pass judgment upon him.

68 THE TRIAL ACCORDING TO NICODEMUS

We really have no reliable eyewitness testimony of Jesus's trial before Pilate in any of the Gospels, since none of the Gospel writers seem to have been present. There is a book in existence that purports to be an eyewitness account of the trial, although it has long since been rejected from the Christian canon. It is known as the Gospel of Nicodemus. Despite its lack of scriptural authority in the orthodox canon, I am perfectly willing to take it seriously for purely historical reasons.* According to internal reference, the author of the Gospel of Nicodemus

---

*The translation I cite is by Gryæus in the *Orthodoxographa,* vols. 1 and 2. See *The Lost Books of the Bible and Forgotten Books of Eden,* eds. Rutherford Hayes Plat and J. Alden Brett (New York: Penguin, 1994). The Gospel of Nicodemus, sometimes called the Acts of Pontius Pilate, is divided into two sections: the first contains a no-nonsense account of the trial, but the second is a revelatory section filled with heavenly visions. I personally have great difficulty with the second section, parts of which I accept as authentic revelation (Nic 20:1–4; Rev 11), parts of which may have been heavily edited. The book as it has come to us was rightly excluded from the canon. The section dealing with the trial, however, is in complete agreement with the four canonized Gospels and other reliable accounts and seems to be what it purports. One of the many details that convince me that Nicodemus is an authentic historical account is that the author refers to proceedings that take place in and out of the "hall" (Nic 3:1, 6; 4:1; 7:1; Jn 18:28, 33, 38). The trial was

was Nicodemus himself, the Pharisee and member of the council of elders who befriended Jesus (cf. Jn 3:1–21). Nicodemus claims to have been present at all of the proceedings, and even to have given arguments before Pilate that Jesus be released. The Gospels report only those portions of the trial that seem to be taken from oral tradition or, perhaps, from an early draft of the Gospel of Nicodemus itself. The Gospel of Nicodemus contains by far the most detailed account of the trial to be found.

In Nicodemus's account, Pilate emerges as a career politician whose hand was forced against a man whom he felt to be innocent. The prosecutors* had come to Pilate charging Jesus with many violations of the law of Moses that the Gentile had difficulty understanding. Mark's Gospel tells us, "And the chief priests accused him of many things" (15:3). These "many things"—or, as a contemporary jurist would say, "multiple charges of the indictment"—are never fully detailed in our Gospels (cf. Lk 23:1–5; Jn 18:29–30). Fortunately, Nicodemus lists them: "We are assured that Jesus is the son of Joseph, the carpenter, and born of Mary, and that he declares himself the Son of God, and a king; and not only so, but attempts the dissolution of the Sabbath, and the laws of our fathers" (Nic 1:2). While the four Gospels parallel the charge of kingship, little mention is made of disturbing the Sabbath rest. Jesus healed many on the Sabbath, and each time he did he enraged the Jewish elders (Lk 6:1–11; Jn 5:1–18; cf. Ex 31:14).

Jesus is accused of charges other than those listed above as well. For example, Pilate takes some interesting testimony on whether Jesus was

---

constantly interrupted by these back-and-forth treks. The reason is that the Jews refused to enter the inner dwelling of a Gentile, Pilate's praetorium, on Passover. I seriously doubt that a Christian forger would have been this sensitive to Jewish custom. History has shown that, until recent times, Christian awareness of Jewish custom has been way off the mark. For example, Michelangelo's famous statue of the naked David shows him to be uncircumcised.

*According to Nicodemus, the prosecutors were Annas, Caiaphas, Summas, Datam, Gamaliel, Judas, Levi, Nepthalim, Alexander, Cyrus, "and other Jews" (Nic 1:1; Mk 15:1; Jn 18:12–14, 28).

born of fornication (Nic 2:7–15). But the Sabbath charges take up the greater part of Pilate's time. The prosecutors are hard put to get a conviction, for Pilate simply cannot grasp their anger. At one point in the trial, Pilate clears the hall of all but Jesus's supporters and asks them, "Why do the Jews have a mind to kill Jesus?" They answered, "They are angry because he wrought cures on the Sabbath day." Pilate said, "Will they kill him for a good work?" They answered, "Yes, sir" (Nic 2:16–17). Pilate can only shake his head in disbelief.

Pilate finally rules that there is insufficient evidence to crucify Jesus for healing on the Sabbath, a ruling that infuriates the prosecutors: "Then Pilate calling together the elders and scribes, priests and Levites, saith to them privately, 'Do not act thus; I have found nothing in your charges [against him] concerning his curing sick persons, and breaking the Sabbath worthy of death.' And the priests and Levites replied to Pilate, 'By the life of Caesar, if anyone be a blasphemer, he is worthy of death; but this man has blasphemed against the Lord'" (Nic 3:6–7). Note carefully how the elders responded to the dismissal of the Sabbath charges: They were outraged at Pilate because he failed to understand how Jesus had "blasphemed."

This reaction may perplex the reader, as it should, for we have come upon the focal point of this entire Passion story. To understand how Jesus could commit blasphemy by merely disturbing the Sabbath, we must look to John's Gospel. In the following passage, Jesus had just healed a paralytic: "And this was why the Jews persecuted Jesus, because he did this on the Sabbath. But Jesus answered them, 'My Father is working still, and I am working.' *This was why they sought all the more to kill him,* because he not only broke the Sabbath but also called God his own Father, making himself equal with God" (Jn 5:16–18; my emphasis). The elders were infuriated not only that Jesus broke the Sabbath, but that he claimed to have special authority to do so. When Jesus flouted the letter of the Sabbath law, he would often utter, "The Sabbath was made for man, not man for the Sabbath; so the Son of Man is Lord even of the

Sabbath" (Mk 2:27–28). Jesus always worked with purpose. Therefore, we have to look behind his every action, his every word. We must pay particularly close attention to this mysterious epithet "Son of Man" and why it relates to the Sabbath rest.

69 THE SABBATH AND THE "SON OF MAN"

The Sabbath rest is a curious thing. To Jews and Christians alike, the Sabbath is considered a profound mystery whose roots run deep into history.* It had long been the tradition in Judaism to forbid certain forms of work on the Sabbath, particularly the work of a healer or physician.[1] Jesus knew this tradition but openly violated it. Was it merely his distaste for the letter of the law? Not really. We find the Sabbath interpreted loosely in the Mishnah and other rabbinical writings, so Jesus's distaste of legalism for legalism's sake was probably nothing new. To the question of why Jesus kept the Sabbath loosely, Geza Vermes offered:

> The short answer attributed to Jesus in Mark 2:27, "The Sabbath was made for man and not man for the Sabbath," is also firmly rooted in rabbinic thought. [In an excerpt from the Mekhilta], uninfluenced by the New Testament, R. Simeon ben Menasiah, a late second-century CE Tannaitic teacher, voices the same doctrine, in connection with Exodus 31:14, "You shall keep the Sabbath for it is holy *to you*": "The Sabbath is delivered up to you and not you to the Sabbath." The same exegesis is handed down in the name of R. Jonathan ben Joseph, a pupil of R. Ishmael (bYoma 85b). The saying put in Jesus's mouth is surely not the source of the rabbinic dictum:

---

*Exodus 20:8 reads, "*Remember* (my emphasis) the Sabbath day to keep it holy," which indicates that Jews were already honoring the Sabbath in Moses's time. See Nathan A. Barrack, *A History of the Sabbath* (New York: Jonathan David, 1965), ch. 2.

it rather suggests that the idea had been current in Judaism for some time.[2]

Vermes, however, missed a crucial distinction. For sure, the "short answer" in Mark 2:27, "The Sabbath was made for man and not man for the Sabbath," is very similar to rabbinical writings. But the full answer, the full quotation found in Mark and the other Gospels, "The Son of Man is Lord of the Sabbath" (Mk 2:28 // Mt 12:8 // Lk 6:5), has Jesus utter something unique, unlike the pronouncements of any rabbi who lived before or since. The latter can only be read as a claim to divine ordination, a messianic utterance.

What brought Jesus to attach a special Sabbatical authority to this mysterious epithet "Son of Man"? For that matter, why did it ever cross this devout Jew's mind to purposefully work on the Sabbath? For, if we carefully read the Gospels, that is precisely what Jesus did: He went out of his way to preach and heal on Saturday, the seventh weekday, as well as to preach and heal on the more solemn feast days. This practice was as unheard of in first-century Judaism as it is today. As I suspect they have always been, Shabbat services are today held on Friday evening, and are never, unless a Seder or holiday falls thereon, held during the Sabbath daylight hours, which are reserved for rest. Jesus, on the other hand, openly preached during the Sabbath daylight hours. There are no simple answers to these questions.

I feel Jesus purposefully broke the Sabbath rest to try to invoke an understanding that he was the heavenly Son of Man, the Messiah figure described in 1 Enoch, an important text found among the Dead Sea Scrolls. As we have seen in chapter 4, many mysteries involving the Sabbath attend the epithet "Son of Man." For example, Jesus believed himself to be the literal reincarnation of Enoch, the seventh generation from Adam (1 En 71; Jn 3:13; 6:62; Jude v. 14). Also, for what it is worth, the archangel Michael, whom many early Jewish texts identify with Enoch and therefore with Jesus by implication, is sometimes called "Sabbathiel" in Gnostic literature. Sabbathiel translates as Lord, literally "god," of the Sabbath.

There is a definite continuity of the Sabbath mysteries from Judaism to Christianity. But, like most doctrines that separate the two faiths, what distinguishes the mystery of the Christian Sabbath from the Jewish Sabbath is how the Sabbath relates to Jesus as the Messiah. The early Christians, like the Essenes from whom they broke, found great fascination with the mystical number seven and all things Sabbatical, but always centered upon Jesus. For example, great care is taken to show that Jesus descended from King David, Abraham, and Adam in multiples of seven generations (Mt 1:1–17; Lk 3:23–38). Matthew's genealogy records that Jesus, and perhaps though not explicitly stated John the Baptist also (Lk 1:36), were seventh-generation descendants of a Zadokite priest (Mt 1:14), a curious fact given that the Dead Sea Scrolls place such emphasis on the "sons of Zadok the Priest, whom God has chosen to confirm his Covenant forever" (1Q28b III, 22–23).

John's Revelation also makes extensive use of the mystical number, be it the seven letters to the seven churches, the mystery of the seven seals, the seven periods of apocalyptic history, and so on, all relating in some way to Jesus. Unfortunately for Jesus himself, whatever esoteric meaning he meant to attach to the Sabbath was completely lost on the audience of his day. Owing to Ezra and the trials of the diaspora during the Persian exile, first-century Jews had become fundamentalist in their observance of the Sabbath, thus breaking down its subtle mystical meaning into superstition.*

I hope I have impressed on the reader how intimately related Jesus's messianic claims and perceived Sabbath violations were, and why the Sabbath drew so much attention during the trial. Simply put, Jesus deliberately chose to break the Sabbath as a means of revealing

---

*For example, note that Peter, a typical first-century Jew, asked Jesus if he should forgive his neighbor only seven trespasses (Mt 18:21–22; Gen 4:15, 23–24).

himself to be the Messiah. In so doing, his messianic claims were unmistakable, but at the same time shockingly blasphemous to first-century Jews. A parallel to this tactic in comparative religion is the "crazy wisdom" method employed by thirteenth-century Sufi mystic Mullah Nasrudin. But what Jesus did was even more unsettling to the first-century Jewish mind. Even today, imagine trying to convince a Hasidic Jew that his Messiah would purposefully violate the Sabbath rest.

70 THE PROSECUTORS CUT THEIR LOSSES

The trial continued. Jesus was finally convicted on a charge of sedition, for claiming to be a king and therefore opposing Caesar. This was the only charge the prosecutors could make stick. We know Jesus was convicted on this charge alone, and not that of Sabbath violations or of claiming to be the Messiah, by the sign affixed to his cross. The sign affixed to a criminal's cross was intended by the Romans to deter others from committing the same offense. Written in Hebrew, Latin, and Greek, it read only: "Jesus of Nazareth, the King of the Jews" (Jn 19:19). The prosecutors took advantage of Pilate's loyalties to secure a conviction, for they could not obtain a conviction under the laws of Moses.

You can feel Pilate's frustration as you read the Gospels amplified by Nicodemus. Pilate's wife had been having fitful nightmares about Jesus. She sends word to her husband during the trial: "Have nothing to do with that righteous man, for I have suffered much over him today in a dream" (Mt 27:19). Pilate also is uneasy about convicting a righteous man; he tries to exonerate Jesus again and again. Filled with anger, Pilate says, "I call the whole world to witness that I can find no fault in that man!" (Nic 3:1). He even dismisses the fatal charge of sedition at one point in the trial. Jesus had admitted being a king, but one whose kingdom is not of this world, a spiritual kingdom. Pilate refuses to interpret Jesus's mysticism in an earthly way and rules that Jesus is not a Zionist.* Then, however, Pilate succumbs to political pressures. Nicodemus reports that Pilate calls him aside and asks, "What shall I do, seeing there is likely to be a tumult among the people?" (Nic 6:1).

At this point Pilate seeks a political solution to his political dilemma. He searches and finds a loophole in the law by which one prisoner can be released on Passover. It is obvious that Pilate desperately seeks Jesus's release. Of all the Jewish prisoners he has to choose from, he offers only Jesus and Barabbas, a murderous Zealot who lusted after Caesar's very blood, to the crowd, giving them a life-or-death choice between the two. Surely, Pilate thinks, the crowd dare not release Barabbas.† But the crowd, stirred up by the chief priests, daringly defy Caesar by asking for Barabbas's release (Mk 15:1–11). Still not wishing to crucify him, Pilate has Jesus brutally scourged. "Behold the man," said Pilate. He presents the prosecutors with a freshly scourged Jesus, wearing the infamous crown of thorns and his purple robe, no doubt bleeding profusely and trembling in pain. Pilate had hoped the pitiable sight would move the prosecutors to quit their case: "See, I am bringing him out that you may know that I find no crime in him." But it was not to be: "Crucify him! Crucify him!" they scream. Pilate becomes increasingly angry: "Take him yourself and crucify him, for I find no

---

*See Nic 3:6–4:1, especially 3:9; Jn 18:32–38. Pilate dismisses the charge of sedition after the "What is truth?" dialogue—a dialogue that should have impressed upon Pilate that Jesus was a peace-loving philosopher, not a militant. The term Zionist was coined in 1897, but it is quite applicable. A Zionist is essentially an Israeli nationalist. Zionism fits the messianic expectations of First Isaiah but not the universal messianic expectations of second Isaiah, which Jesus followed. In arguing that Jesus was not a Zionist, I am deliberately politicizing his message for contemporary times. In particular, I am denouncing the pro-war Christian Zionist movement. Some may brand me an anti-Semite for this, similar to the criticism that recently befell Jimmy Carter for his book *Palestine: Peace Not Apartheid* (New York: Simon and Schuster, 2006). But hopefully readers will see that I am recovering and teaching the true way of the Cross—nonviolence. Instead of taking up arms, Christians should work toward nonviolent resolution of all the world's conflicts.

†Pilate's logic here is evident; otherwise, he would have offered up either of the two harmless thieves who were crucified alongside Jesus (Mk 15:27).

crime in him!" Then, in their zeal, the prosecutors resort to blackmail: "If you release this man, you are not Caesar's friend; everyone who makes himself a king sets himself against Caesar" (Jn 19:1–12). Nicodemus records an even more vicious threat in this blackmail: "But are you inclined that he should be king, and not Caesar?" (6:8).

There was no mistaking this threat. If he failed to crucify Jesus, Pilate himself could be brought up on the capital charge of treason. "You seditious people!" he exclaims in disgust (Nic 6:9). Pilate now sees a riot beginning. He knows he is beaten. He is coerced into reversing his ruling on the charge of sedition. Taking water, Pilate symbolically washes his hands, saying, "I am innocent of this man's blood, see to it yourselves" (Mt 27:24). He brings Jesus before him and passes sentence. Nicodemus records the order of conviction: "Thy own nation hath charged thee as making thyself a king; wherefore I, Pilate, sentence you to be whipped* according to the laws of the former governors; and that thou first be bound, then hanged upon a cross in that place where thou art now a prisoner; and also two criminals with thee, whose names are Dimas and Gestas" (6:23). Whereupon Jesus is led away in swift execution of his sentence through the streets of Jerusalem, moving among the jeering crowds. Finally he reaches what in Hebrew was called Golgotha, the place of the skull. There, Jesus meets the Cross.

71 THE AFTERMATH

After the spectacular events of the first Easter, it is likely that Pilate sent some form of documentation to Caesar setting forth all that had occurred: the trial, the crucifixion, perhaps even the resurrection. Early Christians claim to have recovered these documents. Whether they are genuine is highly questionable. Most scholars believe them to be apolo-

---

*The Gospels record no additional scourging after the sentence as the order suggests, but this detail is easily explainable. Likely Pilate gave what contemporary jurists call a *nunc pro tunc* order (Latin, meaning "then as now") for the earlier scourging so that he could clean up the record (cf. Mk 15:15).

getic forgeries, but one is never certain; there is an outside chance the documents might be authentic.* The following excerpt would, if genuine, qualify as the official court record:

> To the most potent, August, divine and awful Augustus Caesar, Pilate, the administrator of the Eastern Province:
>
> I have received information, most excellent one, in consequence of which I am filled with fear and trembling. For in this province, which I administer, one of whose cities is called Jerusalem, the whole multitude of Jews delivered unto me a certain man called Jesus, and brought many accusations against him, which they were unable to establish by consistent evidence. *But they charged him with one heresy in particular, namely, that Jesus said the Sabbath was not a rest, nor to be observed by them.* For he performed many cures on that day, and made the blind see, and the lame walk, raised the dead, cleansed lepers, healed the paralytics who were wholly unable to move their body or brace their nerves, but could only speak and discourse, and he gave them power to walk and to run, removing their infirmity by his word alone.
>
> But Herod and Archelaus and Phillip, Annas and Caiaphas, with all the people, delivered him to me, making a great tumult against me in order that I might try him. Therefore, I commanded him to be crucified, when I had first scourged him, though I found no cause in him for evil accusations or dealings. [my emphasis]

Now let me explain why I have cited this document of highly questionable authenticity. By the same reasoning I cited the Gospel of

---

*I am quoting from the Report of Pontius Pilate. A copy of this letter is found in a Syriac manuscript, ca. 600 CE, in the British Museum. While some scholars are hesitant to accept the validity of these documents, I personally believe them to be authentic, primarily for their agreement with the Gospels and this Passion story on details such as the Sabbath charges that would be very hard to explain otherwise. Second-century lawyer, Justin Martyr recorded that Pilate's letter to Caesar existed and was the authentic trial record. See *The Lost Books of the Bible and Forgotten Books of Eden*.

Nicodemus earlier, I submit that whether Pilate was the real author of the document or whether it is an early Christian forgery, as some scholars suppose, is irrelevant to the point I am making about the Sabbath. The letter proves on its face that some ancient author or authors, with nothing whatsoever to gain from the restoration I am now putting forth, once believed the Sabbath more important than any other element in Jesus's trial. Note the importance the author attaches to the Sabbath even now that the trial is over. The overwhelming portion of the trial had been taken up in addressing the Sabbath, and the record reflects this. Not once does Pilate even mention evidence taken on a messianic charge. Neither does he address evidence on sedition, the charge under which Jesus was finally convicted. Unheard of for a trial judge, Pilate candidly admits to his reviewer that he can offer no supporting evidence whatsoever for his order of conviction. He reports to Caesar only that he was politically coerced into crucifying an innocent man.

72 PILATE PASSES FROM THE SCENE

Little is known of Pilate's fate after the Passion. Some scholars say he died soon after he left his post at Jerusalem, but no one really knows. Pilate passes into the pages of history, like most of us, with an unsung death. Whatever Pilate's actual fate, Christians would come to see him as a keen instrument of prophecy. Through him was Jesus crucified, and not beheaded or stoned under Jewish law (Jn 18:32; 12:32–33; 8:59). Through him was Jesus, the Suffering Servant foretold in Isaiah, "pierced for our transgressions" (Is 53:5 cf. Jn 19:34). Through him were the Psalmist's messianic prophecies fulfilled: "Yea, dogs are all around me; a company of evildoers encircle me; they have pierced my hands and feet" (Ps 22:16). From the Cross, Jesus called out, "My God, my God, why to Psalms 22, 23, and 24, which speak mysteriously of Jesus's crucifixion, point of death, and ascension into heaven, in that order. These Psalms are among the most stirring messianic prophecies that Christians believe were fulfilled in Jesus.

Even Pilate's soldiers at the foot of the Cross-fulfilled prophecy. When they cast lots for Jesus's garments, it was again to fulfill the Psalmist's words: "They parted my garments among them, and for my clothing they cast lots" (Ps 22:18; cf. Jn 19:23f). Jesus knew prophecy was fulfilled at the circumstance of Pilate and forgives him at the trial: "You would have no power over me had it not been given you from above" (Jn 19:11a). Without relieving responsibility, God's Logos, his world-ordering reason, works through circumstance. In the Nicodemus account, Jesus's fatalism is even more pronounced: "Pilate asked of Jesus, 'What shall I do with thee?' Jesus answered him, 'Do as it is written.' Pilate asked, 'How is it written?' Jesus replied to him, 'Moses and the prophets have prophesied concerning my suffering and resurrection'" (Nic 3:8–11).

So be it. We Christians have beaten up Pilate long enough. We are all Pontius Pilate to some degree; we all wash our hands of Christ. I hope I have exonerated Pilate to the reader's satisfaction, for this story is not about him. Pilate did not send for Jesus; he did not bring him to his court. It was another. Jesus spoke of him briefly during the trial: "He who delivered me to you has the greater sin" (Jn 19:11b).

73 ASSESSING THE REAL RESPONSIBILITY FOR THE CRUCIFIXION

Who was this one who delivered Jesus up for death? Many will think of Judas Iscariot, another of the Passion's most popular villains. Even the Gospel writers speak scathingly of him, despite Jesus's command not to judge one another. Yet, in the overall scheme of things, Judas had a minor villainous role, did he not? Consider this: To whom did Judas deliver Jesus? Were not Jesus's enemies already screaming for his blood long before Judas played his role? Of course they were. When the elders finally wanted Jesus badly enough, they would simply have seized him on the street. It was only a matter of time. We must dig deeper than Judas. We must seek the one who first whipped the elders into their murderous frenzy. In him was once the greater sin. I say "was once" because the crucifixion was Jesus's personal wrong to forgive, not ours. He forgave from the Cross, and that was the end of it: "Father forgive them, for they know not what they do" (Lk 23:34a).

In the document mentioned in the last section, the trial record, Pilate speaks of a Sabbath healing Jesus wrought that escaped the attention of Nicodemus's account,* but was apparently thought important enough (by whatever author) to be included in the record: "And again there was another who had a withered hand, and not only the hand but rather half of the body of the man was like a stone, and he had neither the shape of a man nor the symmetry of a body: even he healed him with a word and made him whole." This healing was the turning point of world history.

Of the infamous murders in the annals of history, most can be remembered to a date certain. We can recall with great precision, even to the moment, when Martin Luther King Jr., the Kennedys, and Lincoln were shot (Lincoln, for example, was shot on Good Friday, 1863, 7:22 PM, EST). It is rare that we can know the exact moment the murder was planned, the very instant the thought formed in the mind of the evildoer. But of the murder of Jesus, the most infamous of them all, we indeed have this knowledge. Jesus knew the very same healing recorded by Pilate above had sealed his fate. He makes this known to us in the Gospel of John: "[Jesus said], *'Why do you seek to kill me?'* The people answered, 'You have a demon! Who is seeking to kill you?' Jesus answered them, *'I did one deed and you all marvel at it. . . .* If on the Sabbath a man receives circumcision, so that the law of Moses may not be broken, *are you angry with me because on the Sabbath I made a man's whole body well?'"* (7:19c–23; my emphasis).

I now take the reader to a time not too distantly removed from the

---

*According to Nicodemus, no testimony was given by this man, either by the defense or by the prosecution. Nicodemus seems to record in detail all the testimony given, so this man was apparently not present. The reader may wish to note this fact again toward the end of this chapter.

trial and the fury of the Passion, when Jesus first begins his public ministry. Miracles and rumors of miracles are starting to trickle through Palestine. Jesus is just beginning to gather his disciples and seems as yet unwilling to take on the awesome burden of his ministry when circumstances force him to heal a leper. Jesus warns the healed leper not to make known what has happened and specifically not to identify him to anyone. But fate has a different plan: "But he went out and began to talk freely about it, and to spread the news, so that Jesus could no longer openly enter a town, but was out in the country; and people came from every quarter" (Mk 1:45). Word of Jesus spreads like a wildfire, of his miracle cures, of his strange and wonderful new teachings.

And almost from the very beginning, Jesus gets himself in trouble over the Sabbath. Now unable to travel about openly and scrounging for food, Jesus and his starving disciples are gleaning grain from the fields. Unfortunately, their hunger has made them outlaws, for they have broken the Sabbath rest. They are discovered and reproached by the Pharisees. Jesus counters the Pharisees with an absolutely startling claim: "The Sabbath was made for man, and not man for the Sabbath; so the Son of Man is Lord even of the Sabbath" (Mk 2:27). Word instantly spreads among the Pharisees and Essenes, among the priests and all the elders of Israel, about this lawless young man, a blasphemer and sorcerer whom they suspect heals by the devil.

Then it happens.

Jesus walks into a synagogue at Capernaum. He finds there the man with the withered hand:

> Again he entered the synagogue, and a man was there who had a withered hand. And they watched him, to see whether he would heal him on the Sabbath, so that they might accuse him. And he said to the man with the withered hand, "Come here." And he said to them, "Is it lawful on the Sabbath to do good or to do harm, to save life or to kill?" But they were silent. And he looked around at them with anger, grieved at the hardness of their heart, and said to the man,

"Stretch out your hand." And he stretched it out, and his hand was restored. *The Pharisees went out and immediately held counsel with the Herodians against him, how to destroy him.* (Mk 3:1–6; my emphasis; cf. Mt 12:9–15 // Lk 6:6–11)

"Jesus, aware of this, withdrew from there" (Mt 12:15a). Jesus was marked for death, and he knew it. All the events of the upcoming Passion turned on this fateful encounter with the man in the synagogue. It is the very instant of history in which the crucifixion of Jesus was conspired.

Note that Jesus had come upon a synagogue whose congregation was a mixture of Pharisees and *Herodians,* the latter being the Essenes whom scholars have rightly shown to be followers of the Teacher of Righteousness. How do we know this? In addition to correlating the Herodians and Essenes as I did in chapter 2, the historian Josephus records that the Essenes were more rigid in their observance of the Sabbath than any other Jewish sect (*War* 2.147–49). Essene reverence for the Sabbath was well known to this Greek-educated historian, but all the more so to Jesus, who was raised an Essene. That is why, when we read the parallel citation to the synagogue incident in Matthew's Gospel, Jesus makes a very telling reference: "[Jesus] said to them, 'What man of you if he has one sheep and it falls into a pit on the Sabbath, will not lay hold of it and lift it out? Of how much more value is a man than a sheep! So it is lawful to do good on the Sabbath'" (Mt 12:11–12). The Essene halakhah (purity laws) specifically prohibited rescuing an animal fallen into a pit on the Sabbath (CD XI, 12–14). When Jesus asked, "What man of you—?" he was doubtless addressing the Pharisees among the assembly, openly ridiculing the Essenes who were present. He was definitely not addressing the latter, who faced a seven-year imprisonment for the slightest Sabbath infraction (CD XII, 4–5). Of one thing we may be certain: If an Essene's sheep fell into a pit on the Sabbath, there the wretched beast remained. The Essenes were radical Sabbatarians in comparison with the Pharisees,[3] and the Pharisees probably thought Jesus was amusing.* So strict were the Essenes, it was forbidden on the Sabbath *even to speak* of labor to be done the next day (CD X, 19).

Now let me evoke, if I can, the emotion of this incident, bringing life to the lifeless words upon the page. When Jesus healed the man, it was not a calm affair. Jesus "looked around at them with anger, grieved at the hardness of their heart" (Mk 3:5). The frustrated young man lost his temper, quite like the time he overthrew the tables of the money-changers in Jerusalem (Mk 11:15). He took it upon himself to heal the man against even the man's own wishes. The Essenes were shocked that he would do such a thing, and filled with anger. In their minds, Jesus had violently broken the Sabbath rest and profaned their worship. The synagogue was cleared in an instant, like a covey of quail stumbled upon in the field. Jesus was probably left standing there completely alone. Perhaps a few Pharisees lingered behind, their mouths wide open, gaping. (Jesus had, after all, just performed a wondrous miracle!) So enraged were the Essenes that they completely abandoned, as we are about to see, the most important religious festival of the year. They immediately rushed out and plotted Jesus's death with the Pharisees.

Befitting the Essenes' reaction and obsession with scriptural study, the Scrolls are teeming with pesharim over this incident. One pesher in particular, an interpretation on Habakkuk, gives a telling reference to the healing of the man with the withered hand:

> *Woe to him who causes his neighbors to drink; who pours out his venom to make them drunk that he may gaze on their feasts!* (Hab 2:15)
> Interpreted, this concerns the Wicked Priest who pursued the Teacher of Righteousness to the house of his exile that he might

---

*To get a feel for what Jesus was doing, imagine a mixed assembly of Pentecostals, whose men wear their hair very short in contrast with the very long hair of their women in a literalist interpretation of 1 Corinthians 11:14–15, and either Catholics or Protestants of the more liberal persuasion. Now imagine some outrageous preacher ridiculing the hairstyles of the Pentecostals to the other members of the congregation.

confuse him with his venomous fury. And at the time appointed for rest, for the Day of Atonement, he appeared before them to confuse him and to cause them to stumble on the day of fasting, their Sabbath day of rest. (1QpHab XI, 2–8)

Many scholars have sought to understand how the Wicked Priest apparently wronged the Teacher in the above passage. Some have even thought it speaks of a murder, but these interpretations are in error.[4] What emerges from the Scrolls and Gospels instead is an absolutely startling revelation: *The man with the withered hand whom Jesus healed was the Teacher of Righteousness himself.* Jesus, the Wicked Priest in the above pesher, had come upon him in his synagogue, his "house of his exile," not just on any Sabbath, but on the Day of Atonement, or, as it is better known by its Hebrew name, Yom Kippur.

How do we know the two recorded events are the same? We may infer generally that events that were significant enough to show up in the Gospels would likely show up also in the Scrolls. It is clear enough that Jesus could have been referred to as the Wicked Priest in the above pesher from the arguments given in chapter 2, where I identified the Essene Scrolls authors as traveling under the names "Herodians" and "scribes" in the Gospels. The scribes were the spiritual archenemies of Jesus, enemies whom he verbally blasted for all to hear (Mt 23:1–36). The above and many other pesharim references to the Wicked Priest reflect the Essene response to Jesus's animosity toward them and their ways. It will soon emerge quite clearly that the Righteous Teacher and Jesus were contemporaries, and that the Essenes had Jesus put to death. If my restoration is correct, we would expect to find the synagogue incident described in the Scrolls with specificity, for the Gospels then say that Jesus flouted an important Sabbath (as evidenced by the mixed assembly in a synagogue) among an Essene/Herodian congregation, and that the Essenes were so infuriated they immediately rushed out and planned Jesus's death. If the

Gospel synagogue incident is not found in the Scrolls, I would suspect that my entire restoration is in error, for it is unreasonable that such an important detail would be missing.

74 RECOVERING THE TEACHER OF RIGHTEOUSNESS'S "HOUSE OF EXILE"

The threshold question in determining whether the Gospels and Scrolls describe the same event is whether the Essenes could have had a settlement at or near Capernaum. It is now generally recognized that the Essenes were not confined to Qumran but scattered throughout all of Israel. The classical sources told us this all along. But we must now ask whether the Teacher of Righteousness himself could have chosen a Capernaum synagogue as his "house of exile," which is mentioned numerous times in the Scrolls. Is it possible that the Teacher did not live at Qumran at all, despite the many Qumran scrolls that mention him and despite the present scholarly consensus? Could the many scrolls believed written by the Teacher simply have been transported to Qumran? Or could they have been copies? If so, could the Essenes have once held a major settlement at Capernaum, as the presence of the Teacher there would imply, a settlement that rivaled or surpassed Qumran in importance, if not in size?

We need only look to the Scrolls for the answers. In a series of hymns that scholars have attributed to the Teacher of Righteousness, we find a passage in which the Teacher says of God: "Thou hast caused me to dwell with the many fishers who spread a net among the face of the waters" (1QH XIII, 7–8). This passage could not possibly refer to the Qumran settlement on the shore of the Dead Sea. The Dead Sea is aptly named: At greater than 30 percent salinity by volume plus a high concentration of other heavy elements, it is presently the most lifeless body of water on the planet. No significant marine life is found there, let alone enough fish to support a fishing industry. Nor were fish found there in gospel times. According to Josephus, the Dead Sea, or as he called it, the Asphaltitis or "Bituminous" lake, has been barren since at least the time of Moses (*War* 4.456, 476–77; *Ant* 1.174, 203; 4.85). Ezekiel confirms this by recording an apocalyptic vision in which God transforms the Dead Sea's salty waters into fresh (47:1–12). Thus, as early as Ezekiel, we know that the Dead Sea was just that, *dead*. If the Teacher lived "among the fishermen," reason suggests that he lived near the Sea of Galilee, which, in contrast to the Dead Sea, was loaded with fish. Sure enough, several hymns after the fishermen passage, we find what appear to be additional descriptions of the Teacher's surroundings: "I [thank Thee, O Lord, for] Thou hast placed me beside a fountain of streams in an arid land, and close to a spring of waters in a dry land, and beside a watered garden [in a wilderness]" (1QH XIV, 4–5). Unlike the shore of the Dead Sea, which supports plant life today only by irrigation and could not possibly be called a garden, the above description perfectly describes the breathtaking oasis that was ancient Capernaum.

Fertile Capernaum lay at the edge of the Sea of Galilee amid beautiful flowing streams. Like the Teacher, Josephus spoke of the Capernaum region, which he called the "plain of Gennesaret" near the "lake of Gennessar," with great admiration: "Skirting the lake of Gennesar, and also bearing that name, lies a region whose natural properties and beauty are very remarkable. There is not a plant which its fertile soil refuses to produce, and its cultivators, in fact, grow every species" (*War* 3.516). Critical scholars unwilling to give up their old conclusions without a fight will surely counter that the Teacher's descriptions should not to be taken literally, that they are merely the vivid imaginings of a mystic-poet. But this quibble argument and many others will fall away once we focus more closely upon the texts.

75 RECOVERING THE "NAHUM" OF THE NAHUM PESHARIM

From chapter 3, we know the Nahum pesharim describes an age following the struggle between the Teacher and the Wicked Priest. It speaks of the enemies of the Essenes as "Manesseh" and "Ephraim," code names that I believe I have correctly identified as the followers of Jesus and his half-brother James, respectively. Ephraim, then, likely referred to Jamesian Christians. But could the code name Ephraim also have referred to a place? It seems so. Note the following pesher.

> *Woe to the city of blood; it is full of lies and rapine.* (Nah 3:1a–b)
> Interpreted, this is the city of Ephraim, those who seek smooth things during the last days, who walk in lies and falsehood. (4Q169 3–4 II, 1–2)

We know from the groundbreaking work done by Robert Eisenman that here the Scrolls speak of the region near Jericho, where James fled during his persecution by the Essenes. The city of Ephraim was located about ten miles north of there. Given the complex associative psychology of the pesher method, it is reasonable that code names could have referred to both persons and places, especially if there was some underlying connection to be made. In this case, it seems the Essenes drew an association not only between James and the person Ephraim found in Genesis, but also between the region in which James's followers flourished and the city named for Ephraim. Again, I point out that pesher associations may make no sense at all to the modern westerner. But this highly imaginative way of associating Scripture and contemporaneous events was exactly how the Essene thought when he did his pesharim. And it is how we must think if we are to understand these curious people who lived so long ago.

76 WHY WRITE PESHARIM ON THE BOOK OF NAHUM?

A question that popped into my mind when I first read the Nahum pesharim was, exactly why would the Essenes have chosen to comment on the Book of Nahum in the first place? Nahum prophesied the fall of Nineveh in the seventh century BCE, an event which, causally speaking, has no connection whatsoever with the first century CE. Most scholars have misdated these key scrolls and thereby missed the enmity between the Essenes and the early Christians altogether. I dissent from the consensus for the same reason as did the late scholar Yigael Yadin. Yadin held that the Essenes chose to write pesharim on Nahum because it speaks not of the persecution of the Essenes, but of Essene persecution of *their* enemies, the "seekers of smooth things." In other words, instead of speaking of the annihilation of the Assyrians, as did Nahum seven hundred years earlier, it speaks figuratively of the annihilation of early Christians. If you are seeking scriptural inspiration for a holy war against the enemies of Israel, no more appropriate prophet is to be found; just how appropriate, we are about to see.

Capernaum, or *Kephar-Nahum,* as it would have been in the Semitic, means "village of Nahum."[5] Capernaum was, according to the historian Josephus, located on a "highly fertilizing spring" that skirted the Sea of Galilee (*War* 3.519). Villages change names quickly in this part of the world and often for no apparent reason, but apparently the "village of Nahum" was so named because it once was the home of the prophet Nahum. According to the prophet himself, he claims to have lived in a village once known as Elkosh (Nah 1:1), a village that Jerome later placed in Galilee, calling it Elkesi.[6] In all likelihood, Capernaum was literally the home of the prophet Nahum, or at least it was popularly believed to be in the first century. If so, then the Essenes would have had all the more reason to associate Capernaum with the prophet's writings.

77 CAPERNAUM: THE BIRTHPLACE OF CHRISTIANITY

There can be no doubt that the early Christians were active in Capernaum. Galilee, not Jerusalem, was the real birthplace of Christianity. Jesus was by and large rejected in Nazareth, his hometown (Mk 6:1–6; Mt 13:53–58). Thus Jesus spent most of his time in and around Capernaum (Lk 4:16–31). Matthew interpreted the move prophetically (4:13–16; cf. Is 9:1–2). For whatever reason God saw fit to place Jesus at Capernaum, we know it was there that Jesus gathered most of his disciples, including the twelve apostles. It was there that Jesus preached the Sermon on the Mount. And it was there that he performed many miracles (Mk 1:28, 33; 1:29–34; etc.). Capernaum was the center of Jesus's wandering ministry, so much so that Mark called it Jesus's "home" (2:1).

Now that we know how the Essenes were prone to make sympathetic associations between persons and places in Scripture, tying them together to interpret contemporary events, what do you suppose an Essene would make of the fact that Capernaum, the "village of Nahum," was the center of that emerging heretical religion we now call Christianity? I suggest that the Essenes wrote the Nahum pesharim not only because the prophet brought to mind a holy war against God's perceived enemies, but because Christianity sprang out of the prophet's very hometown. These compound associations are complex, to be sure, but there is an underlying rationality to them when seen from the Essenes' point of view.

78 CAPERNAUM: THE CENTER OF AN ESSENE SCHISM

Is my unraveling of Essene pesharim sufficient to show that the Essenes once had a synagogue there, and that said synagogue was the site of a fateful meeting between the Teacher and Jesus? Probably not, in and of itself. It is sufficient to establish the general mood of the times. If the Essenes had a settlement at Capernaum, clearly Jesus would have stepped all over them. Jesus was storming the countryside, picking up disciples right and left from the Essenes' very ranks. Given what we know about the radical differences between Essene and Christian theologies, it appears that Jesus was leading a major schism right in the Essenes' backyard. Could this really have happened? Could Jesus have really taken the fight so close to the enemy, preaching right in the Teacher's face? Yes, the Gospels and Scrolls suggest that this is exactly what happened.

If you remember the discussion in chapter 2 of the Sermon on the Mount, namely that tradition placed the sermon just south of Capernaum, the sermon had a distinctively anti-Essene message. Jesus expressly aimed his "love your enemies" message at the Essenes, the only Jewish sect ever to have preached it godly to "love all [God] has chosen and hate all that He has rejected" (1QS I, 3–4; cf. Mt 5:43–45). When Jesus delivered the Sermon on the Mount just south of Capernaum, he was, as Yigael Yadin rightly held, addressing none other than Essenes soon to be converts: "[I]t is my opinion that the people [Jesus] were addressing were . . . close to the Essene sect and believed in its doctrines, but who had now converted or were about to convert to the views of Jesus and follow him."[7] There were definitely Essenes to be found at Capernaum when Jesus preached there. I wish archaeological evidence were available to confirm this fact at the time of writing, perhaps evidence of an Essene settlement similar to that we have been able to gather from Qumran, or evidence such as the rediscovered Essene quarter at Jerusalem.[8] Perhaps we will be lucky, and such evidence will be forthcoming. Nevertheless, establishing that the Essenes were found at Capernaum archaeologically is not enough. I must place the Teacher of Righteousness and Jesus together in a Capernaum synagogue, and I must do so precisely on Yom Kippur sometime around the year 23 CE.* Archaeology could never be this precise. I must rely instead on

---

*We know that the synagogue incident could have occurred no earlier than this date by a few simple deductions. Jesus was "about thirty years of age" when he began his ministry

textual evidence, evidence that, fortunately, I need go no further than the Gospels and Scrolls to find.

79 CORRELATING THE SCROLL AND GOSPEL DESCRIPTIONS

The Scrolls state that the synagogue incident occurred on Yom Kippur. Have we any evidence in the Gospels to confirm this date? Absolutely. The Synoptic Gospels all record that the Pharisees discovered Jesus and his disciples gleaning grain on the Sabbath; the synagogue incident is recorded immediately afterward (Mk 2:18–3:6 // Mt 12:1–15 // Lk 6:1–11). I can therefore reconstruct the chronology.

Luke fixes the date for the grain-field incident as "the second Sabbath after the first" (*Sabbato deutero-proto*) (6:1, KJV).* One might hastily conclude that Luke fixed this date as the second Sabbath after the beginning of Jewish months. The second Sabbath in the first month of Nisan, however, falls during the week of Passover, a detail that would hardly have escaped the attention of all the Gospel writers.

Another Sabbath or series of Sabbaths come to mind, namely the Festival of Weeks, otherwise known as Pentecost: "You shall count seven weeks; begin to count the seven weeks from the time you first put the sickle to the standing grain" (Dt 16:9). Luke could have been referring to the second Sabbath of Pentecost. This date makes more sense than Passover, for Pentecost was a time of grain harvest. Passover

---

(Lk 3:23). Some historians place his birth not at 0 CE but at approximately 7 BCE due to errors in formulating the Julian and Gregorian calendars. See Werner Keller, *The Bible as History* (New York: Bantam Books, 1988), chs. 35, 36.

*The RSV relegates this verse to a footnote, an editorial decision I find puzzling. This fragment is found only in the Byzantine text, but we have no good reason to doubt its authenticity. The renowned form critic John Creed urged its omission, but his reason was merely that this difficult text (*Sabbato deutero-proto*) "has never been satisfactorily explained"; see *The Gospel According to St. Luke* (London: Macmillan, 1953), 84. I believe I am in the process of offering up a satisfactory explanation right now. Very few scholars have tried to explain this text. See George Wesley Buchanan and Charles Wolfe, "The 'Second-First Sabbath' (Lk 6:1)," *Journal of Biblical Literature* 97, no. 2 (June 1978): 259–62.

ran then as it runs now, in the spring, whereas Pentecost ran in the summer. We should at least infer from the Gospels that Jesus and his disciples were gathering grain that was ripe enough to eat, therefore the second week of Pentecost is a better answer than Passover. I say that Pentecost is a "better" answer, but it is still not the *best* answer.

Luke was a Gentile writing for Gentiles. And even if we posit the existence of Q* or some similar source document, which he may have drawn from, it is not likely that Luke alone would have fixed the date of the grain-field incident on an obscure Jewish festival when the Jewish Gospel writers failed to do so. It is far more likely that, when Luke spoke of "the second Sabbath after the first," he was referring to the second Sabbath after Rosh Hashanah, the more widely known agricultural New Year celebrated by the Festival of Trumpets, which fell, according to the ecclesiastical calendar, at the beginning of Tishri, the seventh Jewish month (Lev 23:24; Ex 12:2). Now we are getting somewhere. Yom Kippur always falls on the tenth day of Tishri!

Yom Kippur falls just five days before the Jewish Thanksgiving holiday known as the Feast of Tabernacles.† It is important to note that during this time frame Jesus and his disciples would still have had ripe grain to eat, very ripe grain, in fact. Summer grain, the grain of Pentecost, was harvested green and needed cooking before it was edible; not so autumn grain, which was edible right off the stalk. So where did the grain come from if the fields should have been harvested? To commemorate the years spent wandering in the wilderness during the Exodus, God commanded Israel long ago not to harvest the land to its borders and to leave the stalks

---

*Q, or *Quelle* from the German for "source," is a theoretical document from which some of the Gospel narratives might have been drawn. See Burton L. Mack, *The Lost Gospel of Q* (San Francisco: HarperCollins, 1993).

†The Feast of Tabernacles is also known as the Ingathering; it is a gathering of the harvest at the end of the year, such as fruit, grapes, and olives. The Feast of Tabernacles is a time of new wine and merriment; it is also, together with the Day of Atonement, one of two other major ancient Jewish festivals that are not celebrated in Christianity, as are Passover and Pentecost. Passover is celebrated as Easter, while the day of Pentecost is celebrated as the outpouring of God's Holy Spirit (Acts 2; Jl 2:28–32). Christians await the Ingathering at the return of Christ.

standing so as to leave enough food for sojourners (Lev 23:22). Jesus and his disciples were engaging in common practice for sojourners; they were "gleaning among the sheaves" (Ru 1:22–2:17).*

I must now synchronize the grain-field and synagogue incidents based on geography. Mark's Gospel places the grain-field incident in Capernaum, the same town where we find our fateful synagogue (2:1; cf. 1:21; 3:1). So does Matthew's version. The most likely spot for the grain-field incident would have been either Capernaum itself or, if the Gospel writers were a bit sloppy, the nearby suburb of Chorazin (Mt 11:21; Lk 10:13).† But even if the grain field was found somewhere in Chorazin, and not Capernaum itself, we are still only talking about a distance of a couple of miles or so, well within a leisurely afternoon's walk. Matthew's chronology is that Jesus left straightaway from the Capernaum grain field "and entered their synagogue" (Mt 12:9). It is not only likely but probable, according to Matthew, that the interval was merely that between daytime and nightfall, when the Jewish celebration of this particular Sabbath began. According to the Mishnah, the preparation for the day began at midnight (Yoma 1:8). Given this time frame, it seems very likely to me that Jesus interrupted a Kol Nidre service.

The Essenes used a slightly different liturgical calendar than the rest of first-century Judaism,[9] but that is of no real concern to us here. No other Sabbath squares with both the seasons and the geography of the Gospels, and I do mean *all* the Gospels. In this instance, even John is a helpful historian. Earlier, I pointed out that John records why Jesus knew himself to be marked for death in verse 7:1:

[Jesus said], "Why do you seek to kill me?" The people answered, "You have a demon! Who is seeking to kill you?" Jesus answered, "I

---

*Creed noted that in the grain-plucking text Luke added *psao* to the Greek cognitive *psoko,* meaning "to rub" or "glean." *The Gospel According to St. Luke,* 84. Incidentally, it was not unlawful to glean grain by hand, so long as no sickle was used. The reproach of the Pharisees was for the Sabbath violation alone (Dt 5:14, 23:25).

†The Talmud praises Chorazin and its surroundings as an area famous for its early grain harvest (bMenahot 85a). This is due to its rich volcanic soil.

did one deed and you all marvel at it. Moses gave you circumcision (not that it is from Moses, but from the fathers), and you circumcise a man upon the Sabbath. If on the Sabbath a man received circumcision, so that the law of Moses may not be broken, are you angry with me because I made a man's whole body well?" (Jn 7.19c–23)

This passage is absolutely filled with correlations now that we know what to look for. First, Simeon circumcised Jesus according to Luke 2:21–35, and with Barbara Thiering's help I believe I have correctly identified Simeon as the Righteous Teacher. If Jesus's own circumcision were performed on a Sabbath day or if Simeon ever performed circumcisions on the Sabbath in general, Jesus may very well have been pointing out the Teacher's hypocrisy. Second, John records that these words were spoken by Jesus shortly after he had traveled from Galilee to Jerusalem.* The reason his listeners were surprised at Jesus's announcement that their fellow travelers were trying to kill him was likely because Jesus had outdistanced other news carriers. Finally and most definitively, John has Jesus utter these words when the "feast of Tabernacles was at hand" (7:2)! The Feast of Tabernacles falls on the fifteenth day of Tishri. The synagogue incident had occurred just five days earlier on Yom Kippur, and Jesus was mindful of it.

At every level of this investigation, no other Sabbath squares as solidly with the texts. Geza Vermes found it unbelievable that the early Jews would have marked Jesus for death merely for healing on the Sabbath.[10] On the other hand, Jesus's flagrant disrespect for Yom Kippur would have invoked *precisely* the reaction from the Essenes as the Gospels and Scrolls together record. It is difficult to impress

---

*See Jn 7:1–23 in full context and compare it against the other Gospels for Jesus's itenerary. When the Herodians/Essenes rushed out of the Capernaum synagogue and planned with the Pharisees how to destroy him (Mk 3:6), "Jesus, aware of this, withdrew from there" (Mt 12:15a). Likely Jesus withdrew to his hometown Nazareth, where he hid with his family a day or so because he knew "the Jews sought to kill him" (Jn 7:1b). Then he journeyed to Jerusalem where John 17:19–23 took place.

upon the Gentile reader how significant it was that Jesus was perceived to have violated not just another weekday Sabbath, but the solemn Sabbath of the Yom Kippur. Visit your local rabbi and ask him or her what this ancient festival means to Judaism. Yom Kippur is to Judaism something akin to Christianity's Easter and Christmas rolled into one. It is the holiest of all the High Holy days. Now recognize that the solemnity of this holy day only increases as we regress in history, particularly back to Temple times.[11] And never, I suspect, were the festivals honored as rigidly as they were by the Essenes, especially by the Teacher of Righteousness himself.

I am in agreement with other Scrolls scholars that the Teacher was once the high priest of Jerusalem, a renegade priest who may have made off with the holy garments when he exiled himself for greater purity. This was one of the reasons I concluded that the Teacher was Simeon the Essene mentioned in the Gospel of Luke (Lk 2:21–35; *Ant* 17.346–47; *War* 2.113). It is possible, then, that Jesus came upon a Simeon after he had bathed and was untouchably purified, clad in the holy garments as was the prescribed ritual (Yoma 1–8). He may even have come upon Simeon just as he prepared to go beyond the veil into a substitute Holy of Holies to atone for the sins of the "elect," the true Israel, Essenes now living in exile. The high priest was to enter the Holy of Holies only once a year, and that was on Yom Kippur.* In short, Yom Kippur was the most solemn Sabbath rest God ever directed Moses to follow:

> [And the Lord said to Moses], On the tenth day of this seventh month is the day of atonement; it shall be for you a time of holy assembly, and you shall afflict yourselves and present an offering by fire to the Lord. And you shall do no work on this same day;

---

*See the description of the rituals of the Day of Atonement in Leviticus 16:1–34. Of particular interest to me is the scapegoat ritual: Two goats were to be gathered in atonement for sin; one was to be offered as a sacrifice to God, the other was to be sent into the wilderness of Azazel (16:7–10). The scapegoat ritual seems to me related to Jesus and the Teacher in a way that is haunting. See next footnote.

for it is a day of atonement, to make atonement for you before the Lord, your God. For whosoever is not afflicted on this same day shall be cut off from his people. *And whosoever does work on this same day, that person I will destroy from among his people. You shall do no work; it is a statute forever throughout your generations in all your dwellings.* It shall be to you a Sabbath of solemn rest, and you shall afflict yourselves; on the ninth day of the month beginning at evening, from evening to evening shall you keep your Sabbath. (Lev 23:26–32; my emphasis)

Not only were Jews to do no work, which the Essenes interpreted rigidly on any normal weekly Sabbath, but Yom Kippur was set aside particularly as a time for soulful mourning and reflection. To "afflict oneself," as God commanded, meant to purposefully bring upon oneself great mental and physical suffering, to grievously agonize over one's sins. It did *not* mean, to the Teacher, a time to joyfully have one's afflictions healed.

Just imagine how confused our lawgiver would have been. He is suddenly healed of a lifelong affliction, yet on Yom Kippur when he is commanded to be utterly somber. Jesus drove the poor man right out of his mind! To make matters worse, it is highly likely this healing was interpreted as a sin, not just upon Jesus, but a sin also upon the Teacher. Note the following pesher:

The wicked watches out for the righteous and seeks [to slay him. The Lord will not abandon him into his hand or] let him be condemned when he is tried. (Ps 32:33)
Interpreted, this concerns the Wicked [Priest] who [watched the Teacher of Righteousness] that he might put him to death [because of the ordinance and the law which he sent to him]. (4Q171 IV, 6–9)

This pesher suggests that the Teacher stood trial and, if so, was likely acquitted. Tried for what? Knowing the Essenes, perhaps it was for merely raising his withered hand as Jesus directed.* The lawgiver was tricked into breaking his own law, and not just any law but a capital offense at that. It is not surprising that the Teacher's fear and confusion turned into rage at Jesus. Jesus's actions were perceived as cruel and wicked. This pesher says that the Wicked Priest confused the Teacher by way of his "venomous fury" (1QpHab XI, 4–6), which is confirmed in the Gospels, for Jesus "looked around at them with anger" (Mk 3:5a).

Another point raised by Scrolls scholars is that the Teacher would not have been a respecter of miracle cures. He no doubt believed them to be sorcery.† In the Teacher's own prophecy, the foretelling of his life's mission found in Malachi, we find: "Then I will draw near to you for judgment; I will be a swift witness against the sorcerers" (Mal 3:5). Perhaps he reread this verse after this life-shaking event. To the Teacher's hardened heart, this Scripture now seemed a prophetical directive against Jesus. There can be no doubt whatsoever of the course of action he now pursued.

---

*Of the many rituals for the Day of Atonement, one in particular catches my eye, though I can offer little more than speculation. Luke's Gospel records that Jesus healed the unidentified man by asking him to stretch out his right hand (6:1, 10). According to the Mishnah, the high priest was attended by a prefect on his right and "the chief of his father's house" on his left (Yoma 3:9). The high priest shook a box with two lots in it and drew one out with each hand. One was marked "For the Lord," the other "For Azazel." If the lot bearing the Lord's name came up in his right hand, the prefect would say, "My lord High Priest, raise up thy right hand" (Yoma 4:1). Mere coincidence? Perhaps not. If Jesus's break from the Essenes was not complete at this point, then I think it very likely that he would have served as the Teacher's prefect. Thiering alludes to this view (although she has misidentified the Teacher) in her *Jesus and the Riddle of the Dead Sea Scrolls*, 94–96, 340–41. An added note: If the lot came up in the high priest's right hand, it was considered a good omen. Schauss, *The Jewish Festivals, supra*, 136.

†See Charlesworth, *Jesus and the Dead Sea Scrolls*, 28, and notes therein that suggest the Essenes may have seen Jesus as a sorcerer: M. Smith, *Jesus the Magician* (New York: Harper and Row, 1978), 4Q268, 4Q272, discussed by J. M. Baumgarten, "The 4Q Fragments on Skin Disease," *Journal of Jewish Studies* 41 (1990): 153–65.

80 AMASSING FURTHER EVIDENCE

From chapter 2, we know that the Gospels speak of Essene participation in the Passion, where they are called "scribes" (Mk 11:18; Lk 19:47, etc.). Let us now look at the events leading up to the Passion from the Essene point of view:

> *O traitors, why do you stare and stay silent when the wicked swallows up one more righteous than he?* (Hab 1:13)
> Interpreted, this concerns the House of Absalom and the members of its council, who were silent at the time of chastisement of the Teacher of Righteousness and gave him no help against the Liar who flouted the Law in the midst of the whole [congregation]. (1QpHab V, 8–12)

The House of Absalom is the Pharisees, who from this point forward are in league with the Essenes to destroy Jesus, as we know from the many Gospel appearances of the Pharisees and scribes traveling together as Jesus's inquisitors. The "time of the chastisement of the Teacher" was his healing in the Capernaum synagogue. A more coherent restoration of the Pharisees' relationship to the Essenes now emerges. As Vermes notes, but dismisses, the name Absalom is symbolic of how Absalom shamed his father, David (2 Sam 13).[12] As I have argued, consistently with older historians, the Pharisees were a splinter group of Essenes. The Teacher would have been an authority figure to both. The pesher rationale for invoking the symbolic name of Absalom is that the Pharisees failed to come to the aid of the Teacher during the synagogue incident. This newly uncovered relationship of the Pharisees and Essenes also strengthens my identification of the Essenes as the scribes of the New Testament. Vermes notes that Jesus's opponents in the synagogue incident are described as Pharisees and Herodians in Mark (3:6), just Pharisees in Matthew (12:14), and scribes and Pharisees in Luke (6:7). Vermes then asks,

"Were all these the same?"[13] In a sense they were. The Essenes/scribes were the Herodians, and the Pharisees were a splinter group of Essenes.

> *Because of the blood of the city and the violence done to the land . . .*
> (Hab 2:17)
> Interpreted, *the city* is Jerusalem where the Wicked Priest committed abominable deeds and defiled the Temple of God. (1QpHab XII, 6–9)

This is undoubtedly a reference to Jesus driving the money changers out of the Jerusalem Temple (Mk 11:15–18, 27–28). The fact that Jesus unleashed his righteous fury during the week of Passover completely sealed his fate. By now, all the elders, not just the Essenes, saw Jesus as a "Wicked Priest."

The following horrific series of pesharim refer to Jesus's suffering under Pontius Pilate.

> And God will pay [the Wicked Priest]* his reward by delivering him into the hand of the violent of the nations, that they may execute upon him [judgment]. (4Q171 IV, 9–10)

> *Shall not your oppressors suddenly arise and your torturers awaken; and shall you not become their prey? Because you have plundered many nations, all the remnant of the peoples shall plunder you.* (Hab 2:7–8a)
> Interpreted, [this concerns the] Priest who rebelled [and violated] the precepts of [God . . . to command] his chastisement by means of the judgments of wickedness. And they inflicted horrors of evil maladies and took vengeance upon his body of flesh. (1QpHab VIII, 13–IX, 2)

---

*Vermes' translation uses the pronoun "him" here, which raises a slight problem of identifying the referent, but most scholars agree that "him" refers to the previously mentioned Wicked Priest.

Because of the blood of men and the violence done to the land, to the
city and to all its inhabitants. (Hab 2:8b)
Interpreted, this concerns the Wicked Priest whom God delivered
into the hands of his enemies because of the iniquity committed
against the Teacher of Righteousness and the men of his Council,
that he might be humbled by means of a destroying scourge, in
bitterness of soul, because he had done wickedly to his elect.
(1QpHab IX, 8–12)

81 THE CRUCIFIXION MENTIONED

Jesus's crucifixion is not specifically mentioned in the above pesharim,
but keep in mind that crucifixion was an everyday occurrence under
Greek and Roman occupation. Jesus's scourging would have left more
of an impression on first-century Jews, just as Mel Gibson's controversial film *The Passion of the Christ* depicts.

Jesus's crucifixion is described in the Nahum Commentary after the
fact, when the Jewish persecution of the early Christians described in the
Book of Acts was under way.

[*And chokes prey for its lioness; and it fills*] *its caves* [*with prey*] *and*
its dens with victims. (Nah 2:12 a–b)
Interpreted, this concerns the Furious Young Lion [who executes
revenge] upon those who seek smooth things and hangs men alive,
. . . formerly in Israel. Because of a man hanged alive on [the] tree,
He proclaims, "Behold I am against you," says the Lord of Hosts.
(4Q169 3–4 I, 4–9)

From chapter 3, it appears the "Furious Young Lion" may very well
have been Saul/Paul, who was persecuting early Christians before his
conversion. The above pesher shows that the Furious Young Lion persecuted the "seekers after smooth things" by "hang[ing them] alive."
"Seekers after smooth things" is how the Essenes consistently referred

to the non-ascetic Christians who were flouting Essene halakhah. "[H]angs men alive" seems an obvious enough reference to crucifixion. This pesher also mentions that the Christians followed a *single* "man hanged upon a tree," who must have been Jesus. The Essenes' anger at Jesus only increased as their numbers dwindled, feeding the growing new religion.

Paul, and all first-century Jews before conversion, once believed that following a crucified Messiah was blasphemy. Paul quoted the Torah in his letter to the Galatians, "Cursed be anyone who hangs on a tree" (Gal 3:13, quoting Dt 21:22–23), to show why he believed as he once did. Early Jews believed that a man hanged on a tree was particularly accursed by God. This belief goes all the way back to when Moses first handed down the Torah. It is important to note this belief in retrospect, for perhaps it still stands in the way of common dialogue today. Fundamentally, what separates Jews and Christians is the belief that Jesus was the Messiah. Thus, for any Jewish reader to grasp why we Christians believe Jesus to be the Messiah, he or she must first work through the difficult question of the Cross, try to grasp how this extreme act of sacrifice on behalf of the Good Shepherd could possibly break into human history and bring salvation for all (Jn 10:1–42, especially v. 6; Heb 12:24–25). However, apologetics aside for the moment, we have also come upon an important historical detail for a greater understanding of the Teacher's role in the Passion. As I noted above, it "appears" obvious that when the pesher speaks of being "hanged upon a tree" it meant crucifixion. However, the ancient Torah of Moses, the Torah we know from both the Septuagint and Masoretic texts, did not proscribe crucifixion. Rather, the accursed of God was ignominiously hanged upon a tree *after* being put to death by another means, such as stoning or beheading. According to the Torah as originally written, the hanging upon a tree was purely symbolic. This issue needs careful examination.

In gospel times, Israel was occupied by the Romans. Thus, the laws of Israel were enforced by a form of federalism, a system of shared and diversified jurisdiction very similar to the way state and federal laws are currently enforced in the United States. Mentally substitute Israel for the individual state and Rome for the U.S. federal government, and you pretty much capture the concept of federalism in this or any other first-century Roman occupied territory (which should come as no great surprise, since the founding fathers purposefully modeled U.S. federalism after ancient Rome). We find evidence of this federalism in John's Gospel, where he records a comment by one of Jesus's prosecutors to Pilate: "We have a law, and by that law [Jesus] ought to die" (Jn 19:7). Most scholars believe this verse means that the death penalty fell strictly under Pilate's jurisdiction, even a death penalty demanded by Jewish law. This interpretation is contradicted by several facts.

First, we have the fact that Herod beheaded John the Baptist with no apparent intervention or censure by Pilate (Mk 6:14–29 // Mt 14:1–12 // Lk 9:7–9). Second, we know that the Jews attempted to stone both Jesus and an adulteress (Jn 8:59; 10:31–39); and that they actually did stone Stephen, a hellenized Jew and early Christian (Acts 7:58). These acts seem to have passed right by the Romans without censure. We know also that Saul/Paul put many Christians to death on the sole authority of the high priest (Acts 9:1–2). At this point, early Jewish Zealots may have crossed the limit of what the Romans were willing to tolerate in the name of home rule. But there is no reliable verse in the New Testament* or any other historical source that suggests that Israel had less than autonomous sovereignty over Israelis during gospel times— prior to Jesus's death, burial, and resurrection. Israeli autonomy is shown convincingly in the final and most compelling piece of evidence: Pilate tried repeatedly to foist the responsibility of dealing with Jesus on the Jewish elders themselves. Luke even records a brief interruption† during

---

*I reject John 18:31–32 on the basis of form criticism. These verses are obviously an attempt on behalf of the author of the Fourth Gospel to validate Jesus's predictions of how he would die. But they have no basis in historical fact. The Gospels and Acts overwhelmingly demonstrate the Jews had sovereignty to execute their own criminals according to Jewish law.

†I say a "brief" interruption, for it had to be brief. At one time I suspected that this detail of Luke's was in error, a conclusion that I was prepared to accept for form-critical reasons.

the trial in which Pilate tried unsuccessfully to extradite Jesus over to Herod (Lk 23:6–11). The Jewish elders were perfectly free to execute Jesus as a criminal under their own laws, with absolutely no assistance from Pilate.

The correct exegesis of the prosecutor's statement is that the elders were forced to come before Pilate because they purposefully sought death by the Roman manner of crucifixion. The Machiavellian Romans jealously wanted to keep their terrifying manner of execution to themselves, so they prohibited the Jews from crucifying anyone, including their own criminals (*War* 2.117). The odd fact that now emerges from a fuller understanding of John's Gospel is that the prosecutors were apparently asking Pilate to enforce a death penalty in a manner prescribed by Jewish law but enforceable only by the Romans. This highly unusual jurisdictional quirk tells us that Jesus must have been prosecuted under the laws of none other than the Essenes. How do we know this? Under my restoration, there are several reasons.

If Pilate recognized any sovereignty of the Jews, it would surely have been the law according to Herod, the puppet king installed by the Romans. The Herodian dynasty was largely left over from the Greek occupation. Pompey wisely split the kingship and high priesthood by allowing the Hasmonean priesthood to continue for three decades (*Ant* 13.288). Rome appointed Herod the Great to the throne in 37 BCE. The entire Herodian dynasty, including Antipas, who took

---

It seemed to me that the time frame was too short to allow Jesus to have been hauled all about Jerusalem and still have him tried before Pilate and nailed to the Cross within the hours between daybreak and "the third hour" (Mk 15:25), meaning about 9:00 a.m. I satisfied myself that this detail was accurate only after carefully noting that Luke makes a point of recording that Herod just happened to be visiting Jerusalem for Passover and was probably a guest of Pilate (23:7, 12). The detail that Herod had Jesus dressed in a royal robe may explain the presence of the robe in the other synoptic Gospels (Mk 15:17–20 // Lk 23:11; also the *Lost Gospel of Peter*, v. 3). Nicodemus fails to mention any proceedings before Herod, apparently concerning himself only with Pilate. It is of note that, according to Pilate's report to Caesar, which we covered earlier, Herod was listed among the Jews who delivered Jesus to him.

part in the Passion, were Edomites, not true Jews according to blood (the Edomites were a Semitic-speaking people who lived in the region that is now southern Israel and Jordan). We saw in chapter 2 that the Gospel writers occasionally gave the Essenes the derogatory title of "Herodians," which literally means "little Herods." Politically speaking, the Essenes and Herod were bedfellows; they used each other for their own purposes. Thus if Herod honored the legal opinion of any Jewish sect, it would have been that of the Essenes. It follows that Essene law would have been the only Jewish law honored by Pilate. Moreover, my Essene/scribe restoration confirms this, for the Gospels implicitly state that the Essenes were Jesus's accusers before both Herod and Pilate. Luke records that "the chief priests and *scribes* stood by, vehemently accusing [Jesus]" (Lk 23:10 my emphasis; cf. Mk 14:53; 15:1).

A more comprehensive aspect of my restoration is that I deal head-on with Jewish politics during the turbulent years of Greek and Roman occupation. Whatever the shifting makeup of the Sanhedrin happened to be at any given time (the Sanhedrin was the legislative council of Israel, which, like the Gospel writers, I have been loosely calling "the elders"), it seems clear that the Essenes were the steadfast "keepers of the Torah." That is, they were the law-interpreting and, when necessary, law-making body of Judaism long before and well through gospel times. This is one reason for their title "scribes" in the New Testament. The Essenes/scribes were primarily a sect of Levite priests who had been the keepers of the Torah since the time of Ezra. My guess is that they continued to serve in this capacity right up until the Jewish defeat by the Romans at Masada. The Essenes/scribes were the oldest Jewish sect, from which all other sects eventually splintered. The Pharisees and Sadducees were relative newcomers on the Jewish political scene. These newcomers did not yet have the pull to take over legal authority from the Essenes, especially during the Herodian dynasty. As Jesus put it, the scribes sat "on the seat of Moses" (Mt 23:2). If I have interpreted what Jesus said correctly, the puzzling fact remains that the elders came to Pilate seeking a crucifixion, which, according to John's Gospel, was demanded by Jewish law. The only possible solution seems to be that the Essenes, if they were indeed the keepers of the Torah, should have amended the Torah to prescribe crucifixion as a means of execution. My reasoning is confirmed, for the Essenes did this very thing.

82 THE FATAL LAW

Crucifixion is the most wretched form of execution ever conceived by humankind. The practice became all too well known to the Jews during the Greek and Roman occupation. The Jews saw this hideous manner of execution inflicted on many of their number who opposed the conquerors. The Essenes wished to take advantage of crucifixion for their own purposes, as a humiliating punishment for those whom they deemed to be God's greatest enemies. We find that the Essenes adopted the penalty of crucifixion in the Temple Scroll. The following is, without any doubt on my part, the very law under which Jesus was prosecuted. It differs from the original Torah in that it lists with greater specificity the crimes punishable by death, and instead of reading "[When] he is put to death . . . you shall hang him on a tree" (Dt 21:22), it reads, "You shall hang him upon a tree and he shall die." The latter is a subtle difference, to be sure, but a difference that meant Jesus's crucifixion would not be a symbolic gesture after his death. Jesus would die by crucifixion and not by stoning or beheading, as had previously been Jewish law:

> If a man [a] slanders his people, and [b] delivers his people up to a foreign nation, and [c] does evil to his people, you shall hang him on a tree and he shall die. On the testimony of two witnesses and on the evidence of three witnesses he shall be put to death and they shall hang him on a tree. If a man [d] is guilty of a capital crime, and [e] flees (abroad) to the nations, and [f] has cursed his people, the children of Israel, you shall hang him also on the tree and he shall die. But his body shall not stay overnight on the tree [Mk

15:42–43; Mt 27:57–58]. Indeed you shall bury him on the same day. For he who is hanged on the tree is accursed by God and men. (11Q19 LIV, 6–12)[14]

To aid the eyes of the present-day jurist, I have inserted letters to show the multiple counts of this law that Jesus would have faced. Jesus was probably indicted on a combination of the above counts, any one of which was fatal. His perceived Sabbath violations and messianic claims likely came under the catchall counts [c] or [d], since these were crimes worthy of crucifixion in the minds of the prosecutors. The remarkable thing about this law as amended is that death by crucifixion was a Jewish law for only a narrow window of history. We find crucifixion neither in the original Torah nor in the Mishnah, the oral law as passed down and recorded by rabbinical Judaism. The Mishnah prescribed death by four means: burning, stoning, strangling, and beheading (Sanhedrin 7:1). Crucifixion is not among them.

Another haunting fact emerges: It is very possible that this passage from Deuteronomy was amended by none other than the Teacher. To amend the Torah went far beyond prescribing mere halakhah. No other Essene would have dared taken this authority on himself. Thus, not only did the Passion turn on the healing of the lawgiver; Jesus was likely put to death under the lawgiver's very own ex-post-facto law.

83 THE TEACHER PASSES FROM THE SCENE

Following the synagogue incident, we know nothing of what happened to the Teacher. His writings cease. None of the Scrolls pesharim that mention the synagogue incident are written in the first person, characteristic of scrolls written by the Teacher, but instead refer to him in the third person. This suggests that he had already slipped the mortal coil. Father Milik, a Jesuit and renowned Scrolls scholar, wrote the best eulogy: "To sum up, in no place do the texts speak of, nor presuppose, a violent death of the Teacher of Righteousness; they rather favor the hypothesis that he died naturally. Moreover, whatever the historical truth may have been, the fact and manner of the Teacher's death had for the Essenes no theological nor soteriological significance analogous to that seen by the early Church in the death of Jesus of Nazareth."[15]

The Teacher's death seems to have been undramatic compared to the beheading of John the Baptist and the crucifixion of Jesus. No resurrection was expected or given; no glorious kingdom was to be brought about by his passing. Little lasting meaning attaches to this life at all, aside from being remembered as the man who planned Jesus's crucifixion. Of when and how he died we have no mention. The Gospels make no mention of Simeon after Jesus's purification (Lk 2:21–35). Also, it seems reasonable that if Simeon had been living, he would have personally testified against Jesus. The Gospel of Nicodemus does not record the presence of Simeon at trial. In fact, Nicodemus speaks of Simeon's recent funeral (12:16). I believe that once his purpose on earth had been fulfilled, the grave quickly took him. By faith, I know that to have been his fate. We read of his appearance once more in the Gospels. The Teacher appears in the scene known as the Transfiguration, where, from heaven, he meets with Jesus to discuss the then-upcoming crucifixion: "And behold there appeared two men with [Jesus], Moses and Elijah, who appeared in glory and spoke of his departure, which he was to accomplish at Jerusalem" (Lk 9:30–31; my emphasis). Simeon's recent death, as Nicodemus records, would correlate perfectly. The Transfiguration occurred before Jesus's crucifixion and after the Capernaum synagogue incident (Mk 3:1–6 // Mt 12:9–15 // Lk 6:6–11 all chronologically precede Mk 9:2–13 // Mt 17:1–13 // Lk 9:28–36).

After all the scholarly analysis, the powerful theological content of this whole book now comes plainly into focus. Recall from chapter 5 how I maintain that the Teacher was the Priest figure mentioned in the Dead Sea Scrolls. The Priest and the other two Scrolls figures, the Prophet and the King, were identical to the three "elect" of Merkabah literature, the three biblical figures removed and placed at God's side to prepare them to serve humankind. Enoch and Elijah were taken up to heaven while living (Gen 5:24; 2 Kg 2:11), and God took Moses to heaven immediately upon his death (Dt 34:5–6). All three were present in the above passage in the guise of their various incarnations: Jesus (Enoch), John the Baptist (Elijah), and the Teacher (Moses).* Although the role of the Teacher in Christianity has been hidden to this day, it was the lawgiver himself, not John the Baptist, who was the "messenger of the covenant" Malachi prophesied (3:1b), a second messianic forerunner. As I showed in chapters 4 and 5, the Teacher was believed to be the reincarnation of Seth, Noah, and Abraham as well.

84 THE AKEDAH

If the Teacher's previous incarnation as Abraham is accepted; this chapter may answer one of the deepest theological questions of all time. There was once a day when the Teacher/Abraham was called to offer up his beloved Isaac on Mount Moriah, the site later to be named Jerusalem, the very site where Jesus was crucified (Gen 22; 2 Chr 3:1). At God's instruction, Abraham readied his knife to murder his son, but an angel stayed his hand at the last moment. A ram was substituted for the sacrifice instead.

Many scholars have tried to make sense of the *akedah,* Abraham's binding and attempted sacrifice of Isaac. Kierkegaard once termed the *akedah* "a teleological suspension of the ethical." Perhaps Kierkegaard hit the nail on the head. Human beings have always been capable of suspending the immediate good for a perceived, future greater good, such as disciplining a child, or the ultimate example, sending a son or daughter off to war against an evil oppressor. Yet what future event could possibly warrant God asking Abraham to sacrifice his own son?

It is basic reincarnation thinking that each life builds on the last. As Genesis records, the akedah was a "test," a profound preparation for a profound sacrifice that Abraham would one day be called to make.

---

*Since John the Baptist and the Teacher had died, only they appeared as their previous incarnations. Jesus, the incarnation of Enoch, still lived.

It was a preparation for what Kierkegaard aptly called "the leap into the absurd." I believe that, in Jesus's day, God required the absurd of Abraham again, yet this time no angel would interfere: "On the mount of the Lord it shall be provided" (Gen 22:14). God knew that he would once more ask Abraham/the Teacher to sacrifice his very own offspring.

Who can possibly empty the awesome mystery between a man and his God? Who can understand him in whom there is no darkness (Jas 1:13–17), yet says, "I make peace and create evil: I the Lord do all these things" (Is 45:7)? Is it human beings left to their own dreadful devices who habitually do evil, or the omnipresent mind of God that hardens their hearts? That is the mystery of the prophetic verse: "Awake, O sword, against my shepherd, against the man who stands next to me," says the Lord, "Smite the shepherd, that the sheep will be scattered" (Zech 13:7). The sword of God indeed smote the Good Shepherd, for the Teacher's healing, the death-nail in the Cross of Jesus, was foretold in Scripture. Like the rooster crowing twice at Peter's denial (Mk 14:29–30, 66–72), the Teacher's healing was a sudden and spontaneous event that fulfilled prophecy, a "meaningful coincidence," as Jung would say. Either Jesus was led unconsciously to the Teacher's temple, or he knowingly walked in, lusting after the Cross. Either way, Jesus always moved with divine appointment. And he had an appointment: "I will send my messenger to prepare the way before me, and the Lord whom you seek *will come suddenly upon his Temple*" (Mal 3:1a; my emphasis). Malachi's prophecy spoke not only of the sacrificial offering-up of the infant Jesus by Simeon, the high priest, in Jerusalem (Lk 2:21–35), which I covered in chapter 5, it spoke of another time, another place. It spoke also of that fateful Yom Kippur. What human mind could ever devise a tale such as this, an epic stretching over lifetimes, over eons?

A haunting fact: As is still the tradition, Simeon's symbolic offering up of the first born was done in remembrance of the akedah, Abraham's travail with Isaac (cf. Lk 2:21–35; Gen 22; Ex 13:1–16).

85 "RIGHTEOUSNESS IS NOT IN
A HAND OF FLESH"

Perhaps the reader still doubts this restoration. How do we know that the sudden turn of events in the Teacher's synagogue was the same as spoken of in prophecy? More directly, how do we know that Simeon, the Teacher, bore a withered hand for Jesus to heal? Some may argue that this presents a real problem for my restoration. Under Mosaic law, priests had to be whole and without blemish. But with this particular priest, I believe an exception was made. The Teacher was believed to be Moses incarnate. Due to lineage, signs of various kinds, and certainly astrology, his identity was unmistakable to those who awaited him. The Essenes well knew who this child was supposed to be. Once he was born, the messianic era had begun. There was no turning back, even if the child were born with a withered hand. Whatever the actual explanation, too many details of this restoration fit into place for the story to be otherwise. The final clue, the keys to the Kingdom, so to speak, are found in the Thanksgiving Hymns, which most scholars agree were written by the Teacher. There, the Teacher makes personal references to himself and to his Maker that are too distinctive to be given any other interpretation. There, the Teacher refers to his being born with a withered hand:

> I know through the understanding which comes from Thee that *righteousness is not in a hand of flesh,* that man is not the master of his way and that it is not in mortals to direct their step. . . . Thou alone didst establish [all] in its [ways] before ever creating it, and how can any man change Thy words? Thou alone didst [create] the just and establish him from the womb for the time of Thy good-will that he might harken to Thy Covenant. (1QH VII, 15–18; my emphasis)

Benediction

After fourteen years of researching and writing this book, I would like to take a moment to share my reflections with the reader. When I fully understood the implications of the preceding Scrolls passage, it was the most powerful personal revelation I ever received. Jesus taught that love is the fulfillment of the law, whereas the Teacher could not see past the law. Not only did the law crucify Jesus, but also the lawgiver. In one fateful moment of history, the old covenant collided with the new. Yet beholding his fate, as he surely must have, Jesus saw not an enemy before him that day, only an old man in need. Thinking nothing of himself, he healed him. Why would Jesus do such a thing? What I have learned after years of searching my heart for the answer is this: *Love has no why*. It was enough for Jesus to know that a withered hand cannot hold on to anything. It cannot hold on to him. Someone had a withered hand, and he made it whole.

Notes

————•————

CHAPTER 1. A NEW DAY DAWNS IN
DEAD SEA SCROLLS RESEARCH

1. See a recent reprint: Ernest Renan, *The Life of Jesus* (New York: Prometheus, 1991), originally published in French as *La Vie de Jésus,* 1863.

2. Albert Schweitzer, *The Quest of the Historical Jesus* (New York: Macmillan, 1968), originally published in German as *Von Reimarus zu Wrede: Eine Geschichte der Leben-Jesu-Forschung,* 1906.

3. Robert Bultmann, *Jesus and the Word* (New York: Scribner's, 1934), 14.

4. Martin Buber, *Two Types of Faith* (New York: Macmillan, 1951).

5. For an overview, see Robert Eisenman and Michael Wise, *The Dead Sea Scrolls Uncovered* (Rockport, ME: Element, 1992); Hershel Shanks, *Understanding the Dead Sea Scrolls* (New York: Random, 1992); also Biblical Archeology Review 33 no. 6 (May/June 2007): 30–33, 44–47, 51–53.

6. Geza Vermes, *The Religion of Jesus the Jew* (Minneapolis: Fortress, 1993).

7. James H. Charlesworth, *Jesus and the Dead Sea Scrolls* (New York: Anchor-Doubleday, 1995).

8. See Timothy Jull, et al., "Radiocarbon Dating of Scrolls and Linen Fragments from the Judean Desert," *Radiocarbon* 37 (1995): 11–19.

9. Geza Vermes, *The Complete Dead Sea Scrolls in English* (New York: Penguin Books, 1997), 13.

10. See William Meacham, "The Authentication of the Turin Shroud: An Issue in Archaeological Epistemology," *Current Anthropology* 24, no. 3 (June 1983), 283–311; see also ongoing debates between Meacham and others at the website www.shroud.com.

11. The most infamous of these is Lindow Man. See J. A. J. Gowlett, R. E. M. Hedges, and I. A. Law, "Radiocarbon Accelerator (AMS) Dating of Lindow Man," *Antiquity* 63 (1989), 71–79.

12. R. Gillespie, J. A. J. Gowlett, E.T. Hall, R. E. M. Hedges, and C. Perry, "Radiocarbon Dates from the Oxford AMS System: Datelist 2," *Archaeometry* 27, no. 2 (1985): 245.

13. Appendix to n. 5. above, citing F. M. Cross Jr., Introduction. In J. C. Trevor, ed., *Scrolls from Qumran Cave 1* (Jerusalem: Albright Institute of Archaeology 4, 1972).

14. James H. Charlesworth, *The Pesharim and Qumran History: Chaos or Consensus?* (Grand Rapids, MI: Eerdmans, 2002), 21.

15. See Shanks, *Understanding the Dead Sea Scrolls,* chs. 20, 21.

16. "O Spirit of the Living God," words Henry H. Tweedy, 1935 (from Acts 2).

17. James Carroll, *Constantine's Sword: The Church and the Jews* (New York: Mariner Books, 2002), 32–36, 373.

CHAPTER 2. IDENTIFYING THE ESSENES
IN THE NEW TESTAMENT

1. See F. M. Cross's chapter in Shanks, *Understanding the Dead Sea Scrolls,* 20.

2. Yigael Yadin, *The Temple Scroll* (New York: Random, 1985), 230.

3. See Charlesworth, *Jesus and the Dead Sea Scrolls,* 132f.

4. A book that does a good job exploring the religion of Jesus by both using the Dead Sea Scrolls and projecting later rabbinical literature back into first-century Judaism is Vermes's *Religion of Jesus the Jew;* see also James H. Charlesworth, *Jesus Within Judaism* (New York: Anchor-Doubleday, 1988).

5. See J. N. D. Kelly, *Early Christian Doctrines* (San Francisco: Harper, 1960), chs. 6, 11, 12; also *Christology of the Later Fathers,* ed. E. R. Hardy (Philadelphia: Westminster, 1954).

6. Buber, *Two Types of Faith,* 112.

7. C. F. Potter, *The Lost Years of Jesus Revealed* (New York: Fawcett, 1958), 10.

8. Buber, *Two Types of Faith,* 32.

9. See Charlesworth, *Jesus and the Dead Sea Scrolls,* 8–40, 123–35.

10. We are owing to K. Schubert for uncovering these prooftexts. See his "The Sermon on the Mount and the Qumran Texts," in *The Scrolls and the New Testament,* ed. K. Stendahl (New York: Harper & Brothers, 1957), 120.

11. Yadin, *The Temple Scroll,* 241–42.

12. Vermes, *Religion of Jesus the Jew,* 46, 70f.

13. M. Simon, *Jewish Sects at the Time of Jesus,* trans. J. H. Farley (Philadelphia: Fortress, 1967), 148.

14. See Benedict T. Viviano, "Beatitudes Found Among Dead Sea Scrolls," *Biblical Archaeology Review* 18, no. 6 (November/December 1992): 53–66; also Yadin, *The Temple Scroll,* 240–41.

15. Yadin, *The Temple Scroll,* 241.

16. Charlesworth, *Jesus and the Dead Sea Scrolls,* 24.

17. Magen Broshi, "Beware the Wiles of the Wanton Woman," *Biblical Archaeological Review* 9, no. 4 (July/August 1983): 56.

18. See the classic essay by Leonard Swidler, "Jesus Was a Feminist," *The Catholic World* (January 1971): 177–83.

19. C. Daniel, "Les Herodians du Nouveau Testament, sont-ils Esséniens?" *Revue de Qumran* 6 (1967): 31–53; 7 (1979): 397–402.

20. Betz devoted an entire section to the Herodian/Essene correlation in Charlesworth's *Jesus and the Dead Sea Scrolls,* 76–78.

21. Yadin, *The Temple Scroll,* 80–83. This exegesis is repeated or cited in several popular sources. In addition to the preceding, see Charlesworth, *Jesus and the Dead Sea Scrolls,* 76–78; and Shanks, *Understanding the Dead Sea Scrolls,* 105–7.

22. Charlesworth, *Jesus and the Dead Sea Scrolls,* 76–78.

23. See Anthony J. Saldarini's article "Scribes" in *The Anchor Bible Dictionary,* ed. David Noel Freedman (New York: Anchor-Doubleday, 1992) vol. 5, 1014f.

24. See Martin Buber, *Two Types of Faith,* 59, 61, 77; also his *Origin and Meaning of Hasidism* (New York: Horizon, 1960).

25. See Heinrich Gräetz, *History of the Jews* 2 (Philadelphia: Jewish Publication Society of America, 1944), 26; also Geza Vermes, "The Etymology of Essenes," *Revue de Qumran* 7, no. 2 (June 1960): 439.

26. C. D. Ginsburg, *The Essenes* (Grand Rapids, MI: Eerdmans, 1956) (originally published 1864).

27. *The New Oxford Annotated Bible with the Apocrypha: Revised Standard Version,* edited by Herbert G. May and Bruce M. Metzger (New York: Oxford University Press, 1977), The Apocrypha, 238.

28. Geza Vermes, *The Dead Sea Scrolls in English* (4th ed., New York: Penguin, 1995), 28, 20–21.

29. Shanks, *Understanding the Dead Sea Scrolls,* 238.

30. Robert Eisenman, *Maccabees, Zaddokites, Christians and Qumran* (Leiden: Brill, 1983), 6.

31. Ibid.

32. James H. Charlesworth, ed., *The Messiah.* Charlesworth mentions this and many other works that concentrate on Essene messianic expectations in his *Jesus and the Dead Sea Scrolls,* 14. nn. 108–17; see also Gräetz, *The History of the Jews,* vol. 2, 143–45.

33. See a translation and commentary in "The Messiah at Qumran" by M. Wise and J. Tabor, *Biblical Archaeology Review* 18, no. 2 (November/December 1992): 60; also Eisenman and Wise, *Dead Sea Scrolls Uncovered,* ch. 1.

34. See S. Talmon's contribution "Waiting for the Messiah at Qumran" in *Judaism and Their Messiah at the Turn of the Christian Era,* ed. by J. Neusner et al. (London: Cambridge University Press, 1987), 111–37.

35. See Vermes, *Dead Sea Scrolls in English,* 4th ed., 60–61.

36. Vermes, *Religion of Jesus the Jew,* 34–35.

37. *Anchor Bible Dictionary,* vol. 5, 1012.

38. Norman Golb, *Who Wrote the Dead Sea Scrolls?* (New York: Scribner, 1995), 151–52, 97–98.

39. Charlesworth, *Jesus and the Dead Sea Scrolls,* 29, 68 n. 281.

CHAPTER 3. UNDERSTANDING
THE ESSENE PESHER METHOD

1. Charlesworth, *Pesharim and Qumran History,* 4–5.

2. Michael Baigent and Richard Leigh, *Dead Sea Scrolls Deception* (New York: Touchstone, 1991), 166f.

3. Eisenman and Wise, *Dead Sea Scrolls Uncovered,* 76.

4. See Vermes, *Complete Dead Sea Scrolls in English,* 62.

5. Ibid., 64.

6. Yadin, *Temple Scroll,* 216.

7. Barbara Thiering, *Jesus and the Riddle of the Dead Sea Scrolls* (San Francisco: HarperSanFrancisco, 1992), 20.

8. James Frazer, *The Golden Bough* (New York: Macmillan, 1950), 13–14.

9. Ibid., 16–22.

10. See Dan Merkur, *Gnosis: An Esoteric Tradition of Mystical Visions and Unions* (New York: State University of New York Press, 1994), 37f.

11. See Charlesworth, *Jesus and the Dead Sea Scrolls,* 10–11, nn. 71–76.

12. Vermes, *Complete Dead Sea Scrolls in English,* 62.

13. Ibid.

14. See Baigent and Leigh, who summarize Eisenman's work on this subject, now out of print, in *Dead Sea Scrolls Deception,* 188–98.

15. See Vermes, *Dead Sea Scrolls in English,* 4th ed., 32.

16. See Robert Eisenman, *James the Just and the Habakkuk Pesher* (Leiden: Brill, 1986).

17. Otto Betz and Rainer Riesner, *Jesus, Qumran and the Vatican* (New York: Crossroads, 1994), 112–13. Isolde Betz, the widow of Otto Betz, asked me to correct the sentence "Both complained to have cracked the Qumran code" as it appeared in the original English edition. In German, the verb is *beanspruchenten,* which translates into English as "claimed."

18. Charlesworth, *Jesus and the Dead Sea Scrolls,* 76.

CHAPTER 4. THE LOST CHRISTIAN DOCTRINE
OF REINCARNATION

1. Clayton Sullivan, *Rescuing Jesus from the Christians* (Harrisburg, PA: Trinity Press International, 2002), 114–19.

2. There are many excellent works on this subject. I recommend the following: Morey Bernstein, *The Search for Bridey Murphy* (New York: Doubleday, 1956); Carol Bowman, *Children's Past Lives* (New York: Bantam Books, 1998); R. Yonassan Gershom, *Beyond the Ashes: Cases of Reincarnation from the Holocaust* (Virginia Beach, VA: A.R.E. Press, 1992); Dalai Lama, *Sleeping, Dreaming and Dying* (Somerville, MA: Wisdom Publications, 1997); Karl Schlotterbeck, *Living Your Past Lives: The Psychology of Past Life Regression* (New York: Ballantine, 1987); Elie Kaplanm Spitz, *Does the Soul Survive?* (Woodstock, VT: Jewish Lights, 2001); Ian Stevenson, *Children Who Remember Past Lives* (Charlottesville: University Press of Virginia, 1987); Brian Weis, *Many Mansions* (New York: Simon and Schuster, 1988).

3. See Vermes, *Complete Dead Sea Scrolls in English,* 357–58, 521–22. Although Vermes categorized the horoscope of the birth of Noah differently in his latest edition, earlier editions and other scholars group the Noah horoscope with the rest of the horoscope fragments found in Cave 4.

4. See John Mansley Robinson, *An Introduction to Early Greek Philosophy* (Boston: Houghton Mifflin, 1968), 57–62.

5. Ibid., 61.

6. Many scholars are now noting the Essene/Pythagorean connection. For example, see Eibert J. C. Tigchelaar, "The White Dress of the Essenes and the Pythagoreans in Jerusalem, Alexandria, Rome," *Studies in Ancient Cultural Interaction in Honour of A. Hilhorst,* edited by Florentino García Martínez and Gerard P. Luttikhuizen (Leiden, Boston: Brill, 2003), 301–21.

7. James Hasting, ed., *Encyclopedia of Religion and Ethics* (New York: Scribner's, 1951), vol. 12, 437.

8. See J. Head and S. L. Cranston, eds., *Reincarnation* (New York: Causeway, 1967), 104.

9. These translations are taken from Jay Green, ed., *Interlinear Greek–English New Testament* (Grand Rapids, MI: Regency, 1996).

10. See Alan F. Segal's chapter in Charlesworth, *Jesus and the Dead Sea Scrolls,* 302.

11. See James H. Charlesworth, ed., *The Old Testament Pseudepigrapha,* vols. 1 and 2 (New York: Anchor-Doubleday, 1983 and 1985).

12. Both texts are found in Charlesworth's *Old Testament Pseudepigrapha.* See vol. 1 for the Testament of Abraham and vol. 2 for the Prayer of Joseph.

13. Vermes, *Complete Dead Sea Scrolls in English,* 500.

14. See J. T. Milik and M. Black, *The Books of Enoch: Aramaic Fragment of Qumran Cave 4* (Oxford: Clarendon Press, 1976); also Charlesworth, *Old Testament Pseudepigrapha,* vol. 1, 6f.

15. See Claude Tresmontant's classic *Study of Hebrew Thought* (New York: Desclee, 1960), 87–106.

16. *The New Oxford Annotated Bible with the Apocrypha: Revised Standard Version,* Apocrypha, 111.

17. For an in-depth explanation of the anatta doctrine, see David J. Kalupahana, *A History of Buddhist Philosophy* (Honolulu: University of Hawaii Press, 1992), ch. 6.

18. See Paul Tillich's chapter "Being and Love" in *Four Existentialist Theologians,* ed. by Will Herberg (New York: Doubleday-Anchor, 1958), 345.

19. See Martin Buber, *I–Thou* (New York: Scribner's, 1958), or see relevant excerpts in *Philosophers Speak of God,* edited by Charles Hartshorne and William L. Reese (Chicago: University of Chicago Press, 1953), 302–6; while there, see also the views of Nicolas Berdayev, especially no. 397 at 288–89.

20. Buber, *Two Types of Faith,* 158.

CHAPTER 5. THE TEACHER OF RIGHTEOUSNESS REVEALED

1. Vermes, *Complete Dead Sea Scrolls in English,* 86.

2. See Thiering, *Jesus and the Riddle of the Dead Sea Scrolls,* 333f.

3. Ibid., 338f.

4. See Otto Betz's discussion "Was John the Baptist an Essene?" in Shanks, *Understanding the Dead Sea Scrolls,* 205. Betz was more committed to John's Essene background than most consensus scholars.

5. It is possible that the exact location of John's ministry has now been found. See Shimon Gibson, *The Cave of John the Baptist* (New York: Doubleday, 2004).

6. Gräetz, *History of the Jews,* vol. 2, 146.

7. Charlesworth, *Jesus and the Dead Sea Scrolls,* 55, n. 146. See the contrasting opinion by M. Black, *The Scrolls and Christian Origins: Studies in the Jewish Background of the New Testament* (New York, 1961; repr. *Brown Judaic Studies* 48; Chico, CA, 1983), 95–97.

8. See E. S. Drower, *The Mandaeans of Iraq and Iran* (Oxford: Clarendon, 1937, reprinted 1962); G. Widengren, *Mani and Manichaeism* (London: Weidenfeld and Nicolson, 1961); Barbara Thiering, "The Mandaeans and the Dead Sea Scrolls," *Mandaean Thinker* 4 (July/August 1995).

9. Shanks, *Understanding the Dead Sea Scrolls,* 212.

10. Eisenman and Wise, *Dead Sea Scrolls Uncovered,* 11.

11. A color photograph of this impressive scroll taken by John C. Trevor is found opposite the title page in *Scrolls from Qumran Cave I* (Jerusalem: The Albright Institute, 1972).

12. Betz and Riesner, *Jesus, Qumran and the Vatican,* 112.

13. For a good discussion of Zoroastrianism in general, and its influence on the Dead Sea Scrolls, see *The Concise Encyclopedia of Living Faiths,* edited by R. C. Zaehner (New York: Beacon, 1967), 209–22, especially 212–13.

14. Eisenman and Wise, *Dead Sea Scrolls Uncovered,* 12.

15. Elaine Pagels, *The Gnostic Gospels* (New York: Vintage Books, 1989), xxix–xxxiii.

16. Ibid., 12.

17. See Stephen D. O'Leary, *Arguing the Apocalypse: A Theory of Millennial Rhetoric* (New York: Oxford University Press, 1994); also Rosemary Radford Reuther, *Gaia and God: An Ecofeminist Theology of Earth Healing* (San Francisco: HarperSanFrancisco, 1994), 81.

18. For a good collection of essays on the Book of Job and the problem of evil in general, see Leo G. Perdue and W. Clark Gilpin, eds., *The Voice from the Whirlwind: Interpreting the Book of Job* (Nashville: Abingdon Press, 1992).

19. This is a central theme of Matthew Fox's *Creation Spirituality*. See his latest book, *Creativity: Where the Divine and the Human Meet* (New York: Jeremy P. Tarcher, 2004).

20. See the full poem "On Good and Evil" in Kahlil Gibran, *The Prophet* (New York: Knopf, 1923), 64.

21. *Biblical Archaeology Review* (July/August 1992), 81.

22. Geza Vermes, *Scripture and Tradition in Judaism* (Leiden: Brill, 1973), 80–82.

23. See ch. 35, "The Star of Bethlehem," in Werner Keller, *The Bible as History* (New York: Bantam Books, 1988); also ch. 8, "Triple Conjunctions: A Key to Unlocking the Mystery?" in Mark Kidger, *The Star of Bethlehem: An Astronomer's View* (Princeton: Princeton University Press, 1999).

24. "Whether the sectaries forecast the future by means of astrology, or merely used horoscope like compositions as literary devices, it is impossible to decide at present, though I am inclined towards the latter alternative." Vermes, *Complete Dead Sea Scrolls in English,* 305. I respectfully disagree.

25. Keller, *Bible as History,* 361.

26. See J. Starcky, "Un texte messianique araméen de la grotte 4 de Qumran" in *Memorial du Cinquantenaire 1914–1964 de l'Ecole des Langues Orientales Anciennes de l'Institut Catholique de Paris* (Paris, 1964). See also Vermes, *Complete Dead Sea Scrolls in English,* 521.

27. B. Z. Wacholder, *The Dawn of Qumran: The Sectarian Torah and the Teacher of Righteousness* (Cincinnati: Hebrew Union College Press, 1983), 203.

28. One of the first scholars to hold this view was Theodore H. Gaster. See his *Dead Sea Scriptures* (New York: Bantam Books, 1976), 30.

29. Charlesworth, *Pesharim and Qumran History,* 32.

30. Vermes, *Complete Dead Sea Scrolls in English,* 34, n. 83.

CHAPTER 6. THE SECRET ROLE OF GABRIEL IN THE VIRGIN BIRTH

1. Perhaps the very first English Bible to correctly translate *almah* as "young woman" was a 1912 version by the American Baptist Publication Society. Harry M. Orlinsky and Robert G. Bratcher's *History of Bible Translation and the North American*

Contribution (Atlanta: Scholars Press, 1991), 73, notes the following: "One of its most notable passages is Isa 7:14: 'Therefore the Lord himself will give you a sign; behold a young woman will conceive, and bear a son, and will call his name Immanuel." The following note appears at the bottom of the page: Ver. 14. Behold a young woman. The Hebrew word means 'a young woman of marriageable age.' The ordinary rendering, 'Behold a virgin,' is supported by many scholars. The word in question is used only in six other passages, namely, Gen. 23:43; Exod. 2:8; Ps. 68:25; Prov. 30:19; Song of Solomon 1:3; 6:8. In these cases the translator regards the rendering 'a young woman' as more nearly than any other expressing the exact meaning of the original. [Ed.]"

2. *Faith and Freedom: An Invitation to the Writings of Martin Luther,* edited by John F. Thornton and Susan B. Varenne (Vintage, 2002), 258.
3. See James Carroll, *Constantine's Sword: The Church and the Jews, A History* (New York: Mariner Books, 2002), 367–68, 426, 427–28, 554.
4. See D. M. Smith, *The Use of the Old Testament in the New and Other Essays,* edited by J. M. Efird (Durham, NC: Duke University Press, 1972). The ongoing debate over usage of the Septuagint in the New Testament can be followed at the website www.LXX.org.
5. Paulson Pulikottil, *Transmission of Biblical Texts at Qumran* (Sheffield, U.K.: Sheffield Academic Press, 2000), 86–87.
6. James H. Charlesworth, *The Old Testament Pseudepigrapha and the New Testament: Prolegomena for the Study of Christian Origins* (New York: Cambridge University Press, 1985).
7. Ibid., 24.
8. See the Greek papyrus edited by C. Bonner, reprinted in Charlesworth, *The Old Testament Pseudepigrapha,* 10–12, 87.
9. See Charlesworth, *The Old Testament Pseudepigrapha,* 6–7, 94–95.
10. See J. T. Milik and M. Black, *The Books of Enoch;* also Vermes, *Complete Dead Sea Scrolls in English,* 601f.
11. See Thiering, *Jesus and the Riddle of the Dead Sea Scrolls,* 8.
12. Christopher Knight and Robert Lomas, *The Second Messiah* (Boston: Element, 1997), 77. This story will also be written up in a book that the conveyer of the tradition is cowriting, T. Murphy and M. Hopkins, *Concurrence of the Oracles.*
13. Thiering, *Jesus and the Riddle of the Dead Sea Scrolls,* 335.
14. Ibid., 340.
15. Ibid., 339.
16. See Charlesworth, *Jesus and the Dead Sea Scrolls,* 145–46; also Vermes, *Complete Dead Sea Scrolls in English,* 244.
17. Charlesworth, *Jesus and the Dead Sea Scrolls,* 146.
18. Ibid., 168, n. 58.
19. Ibid., 168, n. 60.
20. The translation I use here is from Vermes.

CHAPTER 7. THE TEACHER OF RIGHTEOUSNESS
AND THE PASSION OF CHRIST

1. See Hayyim Schauss, *The Jewish Festivals: From Their Beginnings to Our Own Day* (Cincinnati: Union of American Hebrew Congregations, 1938), ch. 1.

2. Vermes, *Religion of Jesus the Jew,* 24, cf. 12–13, 22–23, 24.

3. See L. H. Schiffman, *The Halakah of Qumran* (Leiden: Brill, 1975), 77–133. This work and others are cited, and great exposition of the synagogue incident given, by Betz in Charlesworth's *Jesus and the Dead Sea Scrolls,* 77–78. Betz's work here eventually led to this entire book.

4. For various accounts, see Charlesworth, *Jesus and the Dead Sea Scrolls,* 144, 273–77; see also a very imaginative, but I think overreaching, explanation by Thiering in her *Jesus and the Riddle of the Dead Sea Scrolls,* 94f.

5. A very good etymology on Capernaum consistent with this restoration is found in *The Illustrated Bible Dictionary,* edited by J. D. Douglas, et al. (Wheaton, IL: Tyndale House, 1980), vol. 1, 245–46.

6. *Anchor Bible Dictionary,* vol. 2, 476.

7. Yadin, *Temple Scroll,* 241–42.

8. See Charlesworth, *Jesus and the Dead Sea Scrolls,* ch. 7.

9. I have run into a difficult problem I do not wish to belabor in the main body of the text. Unlike the rest of first-century Judaism, which used a lunar calendar, the Essenes adopted a solar calendar consisting of 364 days (11Q5 XXVII, 5–7). Since 364 is divisible by 7, the remarkable quality of this calendar is that the festival days fell on the same day of the week year after year. There is, however, no source that indicates the Essenes honored different days of the week from the rest of the world (Jew and Gentile alike). Thus when the Gospels show that Jesus angered the Pharisees for gleaning grain on a Sabbath, a regular weekly Sabbath suggested by the fact that neither party was in a synagogue or visiting Jerusalem, the Essenes surely honored that same Sabbath. Yet due to their unique solar calendar, the Essene festivals fell slightly out of sync with the rest of Judaism, similar to the way Greek Orthodox Christians presently honor a different calendar day for Easter. There is some possible "play" between the Essene Day of Atonement and the Day of Atonement for the rest of Judaism, perhaps including the Gospel writers, which makes an exact restoration tedious, to say the least. Personally, I am satisfied that the Essenes' own records fix a synagogue incident on what they considered to be the Day of Atonement and that the Gospels also record a synagogue incident, both coinciding within a few days' critical certainty. It stretches the imagination to suppose that two separate and unrelated synagogue incidents occurred, both in the same place, both within days of each other, both important enough to record, yet both escaping the attention of the other party involved. If a hypercritical scholar seeks more certainty than this, please be my guest. Many fine scholars claim to have reconstructed both calendars already, and you need only follow up their

work. See Joseph A. Fitmyer, *The Dead Sea Scrolls: Major Publications and Tools for Study* (Atlanta: Scholars Press, 1990), 180f.

10. Geza Vermes, *The Changing Faces of Jesus* (New York: Penguin Compass, 2002), 20.

11. See Schauss, *Jewish Festivals,* 125f.

12. Vermes, *Dead Sea Scrolls in English,* 37.

13. Vermes, *Changing Faces of Jesus,* 179.

14. See Yadin, *Temple Scroll,* 288–91; also Zias and Charlesworth's contribution to the latter's *Jesus and the Dead Sea Scrolls,* 273f.

15. My translation is from Charlesworth. Milik's work was originally written in French in 1957. See J. T. Milik, *Ten Years of Discovery in the Wilderness of Judea* (London: SCM Press, 1959).

Selected Bibliography

Baigent, Michael, and Richard Leigh. *The Dead Sea Scrolls Deception*. New York: Touchstone, 1991.

Barrack, Nathan A. *A History of the Sabbath*. New York: Jonathan David, 1965.

Betz, Otto. "Was John the Baptist an Essene?" reprinted in Shanks, Hershel. *Understanding the Dead Sea Scrolls*. New York: Random House, 1992.

Betz, Otto, and Rainer Riesner. *Jesus, Qumran and the Vatican*. New York: Crossroads, 1994.

Black, M. *The Scrolls and Christian Origins: Studies in the Jewish Background of the New Testament*. New York, 1961.

Broshi, Magen. "Beware the Wiles of the Wanton Woman." *Biblical Archaeological Review* 9, no. 4 (July/August 1983).

Buber, Martin. *The Origin and Meaning of Hasidism*. New York: Horizon, 1960.

———. *Two Types of Faith*. New York: Macmillan, 1951.

Bultmann, Robert. *Jesus and the Word*. New York: Scribner's, 1934.

Carroll, James. *Constantine's Sword: The Church and the Jews*. New York: Mariner, 2002.

Charlesworth, James H. *Jesus and the Dead Sea Scrolls*. New York: Anchor-Doubleday, 1995.

———. *Jesus Within Judaism*. New York: Anchor-Doubleday, 1988.

———. *The Old Testament Pseudepigrapha*. New York: Doubleday, 1983, 1985.

———. *The Old Testament Pseudepigrapha and the New Testament: Prolegomena for the Study of Christian Origins*. New York: Cambridge University Press, 1985.

———. *The Pesharim and Qumran History: Chaos or Consensus?* Grand Rapids, Mich.: Eerdmans, 2002.

Creed, John. *The Gospel According to St. Luke*. London: Macmillan, 1953.

Dalai Lama. *Sleeping, Dreaming and Dying.* Somerville, Mass.: Wisdom Publications, 1997.

Daniel, C. "Les Herodians du Nouveau Testament, sont-ils Esséniens?" *Revue de Qumran* 6 (1967): 31–53; 7 (1979): 397–402.

Davidson, Gustav. *A Dictionary of Angels.* New York: Free Press, 1971.

Drower, E. S. *The Mandaeans of Iraq and Iran.* Oxford: Clarendon Press, 1937, reprinted 1962.

Eisenman, Robert. *James the Just and the Habakkuk Pesher.* Leiden: Brill, 1986.

———. *Maccabees, Zaddokites, Christians and Qumran.* Leiden: Brill, 1983.

Eisenman, Robert, and Michael Wise. *The Dead Sea Scrolls Uncovered.* Rockport, Md.: Element, 1992.

Eliade, Mircea. *The Myth of the Eternal Return.* Princeton, N.J.: Princeton University Press, 1971.

Fitmyer, Joseph A. *The Dead Sea Scrolls: Major Publications and Tools for Study.* Atlanta: Scholars Press, 1990.

Frazer, James. *The Golden Bough.* New York: Macmillan, 1950.

Freedman, David Noel, ed. *The Anchor Bible Dictionary.* New York: Anchor-Doubleday, 1992.

Gaster, Theodore H. *The Dead Sea Scriptures.* New York: Bantam Books, 1976.

Gershom, R. Yonassan. *Beyond the Ashes: Cases of Reincarnation from the Holocaust.* Virginia Beach: A.R.E. Press, 1992.

Gillespie, R., J. A. J. Gowlett, E. T. Hall, R. E. M. Hedges, and C. Perry. "Radiocarbon Dates from the Oxford AMS System: Datelist 2." *Archaeometry* 27, no. 2 (1985): 237–46.

Ginsburg, C. D. *The Essenes.* Grand Rapids, Mich.: Eerdmans, 1956.

Golb, Norman. *Who Wrote the Dead Sea Scrolls?* New York: Scribner, 1995.

Gowlett, J. A. J., R. E. M. Hedges, and I. A. Law. "Radiocarbon Accelerator (AMS) Dating of Lindow Man." *Antiquity* 63 (1989): 71–79.

Gräetz, Heinrich. *History of the Jews.* Philadelphia: Jewish Publication of Society, 1944.

Hardy, E. R. *Christology of the Later Fathers.* Philadelphia: Westminster, 1954.

Hartshorne, Charles, and William L. Reese, eds. *Philosophers Speak of God.* Chicago: University of Chicago Press, 1953.

Hasting, James, ed. *Encyclopedia of Religion and Ethics.* New York: Scribner's, 1951.

Head, J., and S. L. Cranston, eds. *Reincarnation.* New York: Causeway, 1967.

Jull, Timothy, et al. "Radiocarbon Dating of Scrolls and Linen Fragments from the Judean Desert." *Radiocarbon* 37 (1995): 11–19.

Kalupahana, David J. *A History of Buddhist Philosophy.* Honolulu: University of Hawaii Press, 1992.

Keller, Werner. *The Bible as History.* New York: Bantam Books, 1981.

Kelly, J. N. D. *Early Christian Doctrines.* San Francisco: Harper, 1960.

Knight, Christopher, and Robert Lomas. *The Second Messiah.* Boston: Element, 1997.

Martínez, Florentino García, and Gerard P. Luttikhuizen, eds. *Studies in Ancient Cultural Interaction in Honour of A. Hilhorst.* Leiden, Boston: Brill, 2003.

May, Herbert G., and Bruce M. Metzger, eds. *The New Oxford Annotated Bible with the Apocrypha.* New York: Oxford University Press, 1977.

Meacham, William. "The Authentication of the Turin Shroud: An Issue in Archaeological Epistemology." *Current Anthropology* 24, no. 3 (June 1983): 283–311.

Merkur, Dan. *Gnosis: An Esoteric Tradition of Mystical Visions and Unions.* New York: State University of New York Press, 1994.

Milik, J. T. *The Aramaic Books of Enoch of Qumran Cave 4.* London: Oxford University Press, 1976.

———. *Ten Years of Discovery in the Wilderness of Judea.* London: SCM, 1959.

Neusner, J., W. S. Green, and E. S. Freichs, eds. *Judaism and Their Messiah at the Turn of the Christian Era.* London: Cambridge University Press, 1987.

O'Leary, Stephen D. *Arguing the Apocalypse: A Theory of Millennial Rhetoric.* New York: Oxford University Press, 1994.

Otto, Rudolf. *The Kingdom of God and the Son of Man.* Boston: Star King, 1957.

Page, Charles, II. *Jesus and the Land.* Nashville: Abingdon, 1995.

Pagels, Elaine. *The Gnostic Gospels.* New York: Vintage Books, 1989.

Perdue, Leo G., and W. Clark Gilpin, eds. *The Voice from the Whirlwind: Interpreting the Book of Job.* Nashville: Abingdon Press, 1992.

Plat, Rutherford Hayes, and J. Alden Brett, eds. *The Lost Books of the Bible and Forgotten Books of Eden.* New York: Penguin, 1994.

Potter, C. F. *The Lost Years of Jesus Revealed.* New York: Fawcett, 1958.

Pulikottil, Paulson. *Transmission of Biblical Texts at Qumran.* Sheffield, UK: Sheffield Academic, 2000.

Renan, Ernest. *The Life of Jesus.* New York: Prometheus, 1991.

Reuther, Rosemary Radford. *Gaia and God: An Ecofeminist Theology of Earth Healing.* San Francisco: HarperSanFransisco, 1994.

Robinson, John Mansley. *An Introduction to Early Greek Philosophy.* Boston: Houghton Mifflin, 1968.

Schauss, Hayyim. *The Jewish Festivals: From their Beginnings to Our Own Day.* Cincinnati: Union of American Hebrew Congregations, 1938.

Schiffman, L. H. *The Halakah of Qumran.* Leiden: Brill, 1975.

Schürer, Emil. *A History of the Jewish People in the Time of Jesus.* New York: Schocken Books, 1961.

Schweitzer, Albert. *The Quest for the Historical Jesus.* New York: Macmillan, 1968.

Shanks, Hershel. *The Mystery and Meaning of the Dead Sea Scrolls.* New York: Random, 1998.

———. *Understanding the Dead Sea Scrolls.* New York: Random, 1992.

Simon, M. *Jewish Sects at the Time of Jesus.* Philadelphia: Fortress, 1967.

Smith, D. M. *The Use of the Old Testament in the New and Other Essays.* Durham, N.C.: Duke University Press, 1972.

Smith, M. "The Description of the Essenes in Josephus and the *Philosophoumena*." *Hebrew Union College Annual* 29 (1958): 273–323.

Starcky, J. "Un texte messianique araméen de la grotte 4 de Qumran" in *Memorial du Cinquantenaire 1914–1964 de l'Ecole des Langues Orientales Anciennes de l'Institut Catholique de Paris* (Paris, 1964): 51–66.

Stendahl, K. *The Scrolls and the New Testament.* New York: Harper and Brothers, 1957.

Sullivan, Clayton. *Rescuing Jesus from the Christians.* Harrisburg: Trinity Press International, 2002.

Swidler, Leonard. "Jesus Was a Feminist." *Catholic World* (January 1971): 177–83.

Thiering, Barbara. *Jesus and the Riddle of the Dead Sea Scrolls.* San Francisco: HarperSanFrancisco, 1992.

———. "The Mandaeans and the Dead Sea Scrolls." *Mandaean Thinker* 4 (July–August 1995).

Thornton, John F., and Susan B. Varenne, eds. *Faith and Freedom: An Invitation to the Writings of Martin Luther.* Vintage, 2002.

Tillich, Paul. "Being and Love," reprinted in Will Herberg, ed., *Four Existentialist Theologians.* New York: Doubleday-Anchor, 1958.

Tresmontant, Claude. *A Study of Hebrew Thought.* New York: Desclee, 1960.

Trevor, J. C., F. M. Cross, D. N. Freedman, and J. A. Sanders. *Scrolls from Qumran Cave I.* Jerusalem: The Albright Institute, 1972.

Vermes, Geza. *The Changing Faces of Jesus.* New York: Penguin Compass, 2002.

———. *The Complete Dead Sea Scrolls in English.* New York: Penguin Books, 1997.

———. *The Dead Sea Scrolls in English,* 4th ed. New York: Penguin, 1995.

———. "The Etymology of Essenes." *Revue de Qumran* 7, no. 2 (June 1960): 427–43.

———. *The Religion of Jesus the Jew.* Minneapolis: Fortress, 1993.

———. *Scripture and Tradition in Judaism.* Leiden: Brill, 1973.

Viviano, Benedict T. "Beatitudes Found Among Dead Sea Scrolls." *Biblical Archaeology Review* 18, no. 6 (November/December 1992): 53–55, 66.

Wacholder, B. Z. *The Dawn of Qumran: The Sectarian Torah and the Teacher of Righteousness.* Cincinnati: Hebrew Union College Press, 1983.

Widengren, G. *Mani and Manichaeism.* London: Weidenfeld and Nicolson, 1961.

Wise, M., and J. Tabor. "The Messiah at Qumran." *Biblical Archaeology Review* 18, no. 6 (November/December 1992): 60–65.

Wright, G. Ernest, *The Bible and the Ancient Near East.* London: Routledge & Kegan Paul, 1961.

Yadin, Yigael. *The Temple Scroll.* New York: Random, 1985.

Zaehner, R. C., ed. *The Concise Encyclopedia of Living Faiths.* New York: Beacon, 1967.

Index of Ancient Writings

APOCRYPHA

NEW TESTAMENT

DEAD SEA SCROLLS

ANCIENT HISTORIANS AND PATRISTICS

PSEUDIPIGRAPHA AND OTHER JEWISH LITERATURE

EXTRACANONICAL CHRISTIAN LITERATURE

Index of Modern Authors

Index of Subjects

BOOKS OF RELATED INTEREST

The Mystery of the Copper Scroll of Qumran
The Essene Record of the Treasure of Akhenaten
by Robert Feather

The Secret Initiation of Jesus at Qumran
The Essene Mysteries of John the Baptist
by Robert Feather

The Brother of Jesus and the Lost Teachings of Christianity
by Jeffrey J. Bütz

The Way of the Essenes
Christ's Hidden Life Remembered
by Anne and Daniel Meurois-Givaudan

The Discovery of the Nag Hammadi Texts
A Firsthand Account of the Expedition That Shook the
Foundations of Christianity
by Jean Doresse

Gnostic Secrets of the Naassenes
The Initiatory Teachings of the Last Supper
by Mark H. Gaffney

The Sacred Embrace of Jesus and Mary
The Sexual Mystery at the Heart of the Christian Tradition
by Jean-Yves Leloup

Jesus in the House of the Pharaohs
The Essene Revelations on the Historical Jesus
by Ahmed Osman

Inner Traditions • Bear & Company
P.O. Box 388
Rochester, VT 05767
1-800-246-8648
www.InnerTraditions.com

Or contact your local bookseller